CW00661323

MY LIFE IN MUSIC

SIR
ANTONIO
PAPPANO

My Life in Music

Sir Antonio Pappano

My Life in Music

faber

First published in 2024
by Faber & Faber Ltd
The Bindery, 51 Hatton Garden
London EC1N 8HN
First published in the USA in 2024

Typeset by Agnesi Text, Hadleigh, Suffolk IP7 5LX
Printed in the UK by CPI Group (UK) Ltd, Croydon CR0 4YY

'Mozartian Intermezzo' (Chapter 15) first appeared in Kate Bailey (ed.), *Opera: Passion, Power and Politics* (Victoria and Albert Museum, London, 2017).

The right of Sir Antonio Pappano to be identified as author of this work
has been asserted in accordance with Section 77 of the Copyright,
Designs and Patents Act 1988

A CIP record for this book
is available from the British Library

ISBN 978–0–571–37173–0

MIX
Paper | Supporting
responsible forestry
FSC
www.fsc.org   FSC® C171272

Printed and bound in the UK on FSC® certified paper in line with our continuing
commitment to ethical business practices, sustainability and the environment.
For further information see faber.co.uk/environmental-policy

2 4 6 8 10 9 7 5 3

This book is dedicated to my wife Pamela and
to my parents, Carmela Maria and Pasquale.
They have believed in me and guided me through this life.

CONTENTS

TIMELINE

1959   Born in Epping, Essex, England, on 30 December.

1965   Lives with grandparents in Castelfranco, Italy, for a year.

1970   Begins accompanying his father's singing students on the piano.

1973   Moves with his parents and brother to Bridgeport, Connecticut, USA.

1979   Répétiteur and rehearsal pianist with Connecticut Grand Opera.

1981   Répétiteur and rehearsal pianist with New York City Opera.

1982   Conducts part of a concert with the Kankakee Valley Symphony Orchestra, Illinois.

1982   Conducts first full concert, with the South Jutland Symphony Orchestra, Denmark.

1984   Rehearsal pianist and musical assistant, Gran Teatre del Liceu, Barcelona.

1985   Rehearsal pianist and musical assistant, Frankfurt Opera and Lyric Opera of Chicago.

1985   Makes first recording, with Helsingborg Symphony Orchestra, Sweden.

1986   Assistant to Daniel Barenboim at Israel and Bayreuth festivals.

1987   Conducts first opera: Puccini's *La bohème*, with Den Norske Opera, Oslo.

1990   Appointed Music Director, Den Norske Opera.

1990   Conducts Puccini's *La bohème* at the Royal Opera House, Covent Garden, London.

1992   Appointed Music Director, Théâtre Royal de la Monnaie, Brussels.

1993   Conducts Wagner's *Siegfried* at the Vienna State Opera.

1995   Marries Pamela Bullock.

1995   Begins continuing recording contract with EMI Classics, now Warner Classics.

1996   Conducts Verdi's *Don Carlos* at the Théâtre du Châtelet, Paris.

1996   Conducts the London Symphony Orchestra in a recording of Puccini's *La rondine*.

1997   Conducts Tchaikovsky's *Eugene Onegin* at the Metropolitan Opera, New York.

1999   Appointed Music Director of the Royal Opera House, Covent Garden.

2002   Conducts the Orchestra dell'Accademia Nazionale di Santa Cecilia, Rome.

2002   Begins tenure at the Royal Opera House, Covent Garden.

2005   Appointed Music Director of the Orchestra dell'Accademia Nazionale di Santa Cecilia.

2008   Conducts the world premiere of Harrison Birtwistle's *The Minotaur*.

2010   Presents *Opera Italia* for BBC Television.

2011   Conducts the world premiere of Mark-Anthony Turnage's *Anna Nicole*.

2012   Receives knighthood in the New Year Honours List.

2014   Conducts the world premiere of Sir Peter Maxwell Davies's Symphony No. 10.

2015	Presents *Pappano's Classical Voices* for BBC Television.
2021	Appointed Chief Conductor of the London Symphony Orchestra.
2023	Conducts for the Coronation of King Charles III, Westminster Abbey, London.
	Named International Opera Awards Conductor of the Year.
	Named Musical America Conductor of the Year.
2024	Receives Commander of the Royal Victorian Order.
	Begins tenure with the London Symphony Orchestra.

LIST OF ILLUSTRATIONS

Unless otherwise stated, photos are courtesy of the author.

My parents in 1956, engaged but not yet married.

With my paternal grandfather, also Antonio Pappano.

Castelfranco in Miscano.
Ra Boe Wikipedia

My father, the tenor.

Celebrating my brother Patrick's birthday at the *asilo*, Castelfranco.

Inga Nielsen as Violetta (*La traviata*) in Oslo.
Photo Erik Berg © Norwegian Opera & Ballet

The inimitable Romano Gandolfi.
Lelli e Masotti © Teatro alla Scala, Milan

With my wife, Pamela, at the premiere of *Carmen*, 2006.
© Rob Moore, the Royal Opera House

Susan Chilcott as Ellen Orford in *Peter Grimes* in 1994.
© Théâtre Royal de la Monnaie, Brussels

La Monnaie on tour with *Peter Grimes* in Madrid.
© Théâtre Royal de la Monnaie, Brussels

Discussing *Lohengrin* with Daniel Barenboim, Bayreuth, 1999.
Photo Anne Kirchbach © Bayreuther Festspiele GmbH Foto

In strategic conversation with Keith Warner while rehearsing Wagner's *Ring* in 2012.
© Neil Gillespie, the Royal Opera House

Richard Jones, with me and his then assistant Elaine Kidd, rehearsing *Lady Macbeth of Mtsensk* in 2004.
© Rob Moore, the Royal Opera House

Christof Loy on the set of *Elektra*, 2024.
© Tristram Kenton, the Royal Opera House

John Tomlinson as the Minotaur in Harrison Birtwistle's opera.
Corbis Entertainment/Getty Images

With Eva-Maria Westbroek at the Royal Opera House.
© Neil Gillespie, the Royal Opera House

With Harrison Birtwistle in 2008 at the Royal Opera House.
© Neil Gillespie, the Royal Opera House

Conducting the Orchestra and Chorus dell'Accademia Nazionale di Santa Cecilia in 2019.
© Riccardo Musacchio/MUSA

Taking a bow with the London Symphony Orchestra in 2023, after a performance of *Ein Heldenleben* by Richard Strauss.
© Liam Hennebry, London Symphony Orchestra

1

BEGINNINGS

I've not been one for looking backwards so much, nor for explorative contemplation. I'm more the locomotive type, but I'm in my mid-sixties now and it's perhaps inevitable to gaze back at my life and its achievements, successes, disappointments, friendships, opportunities taken and those missed, and try to piece together the puzzle that helps me figure out how I got to this point. It feels as if I have been living in a whirlwind these last thirty years. So I am thankful that the enforced stop that Covid-19 imposed on us (certainly those of us in the music business) gave me the rare opportunity to think about things calmly: the past, the future, and of course the fraught present.

I've thought a lot about my unusual childhood. I was born to Italian immigrant parents on 30 December 1959 at the Epping Forest Hospital in Essex. My parents, having made their way to London, were working as domestics for a well-to-do family in the area. They had been childhood sweethearts and were engaged for ten years before marrying in London at the age of twenty-four. They came from a tiny farming village called Castelfranco in Miscano in the province of Benevento in the Campania region, a relatively remote community surrounded by astounding natural beauty – not the Tuscan kind of perfectly manicured beauty, but something rougher, more primitive, burned yellows and browns rather than lush green. The village is 760 metres above sea level, the air fresh and invigorating, the views heart-stopping. Today the population hovers around 800, way down from the 3,000 or so in the past.

My mother, Carmela Maria Scinto, was born on 5 January 1934 to Fedele Scinto and Incoronata Pomarico, two of the strongest characters I have ever met. They were carved out of stone. Impossibly hard-working; she quite stern in demeanour, suffering ill health for much of her life; he a chain-smoker with very strong opinions and a mischievous look in his eyes. They lived only a few metres from Antonio and Antonietta Pappano, both families owning and working pitifully small plots of land. Antonio was an intelligent and gentle man. He could read and write and often helped the villagers when they needed to fill out documents, especially when asking for disaster relief following the earthquakes that would occur every so often. Interestingly enough, he never submitted an application for himself. Antonietta was a force of nature, proud, ferocious even, in the way she was protective of her two sons. To this day, the memory of her scares the living daylights out of me, yet I admired her greatly. She worked herself to the bone to nurture her family as best she could in a very poor environment. Antonio and Antonietta made for an incongruous but fiercely united couple.

Antonietta had made it quite plain that Carmela Maria was not good enough for her handsome older son Pasqualino, her golden boy with the gorgeous tenor voice, especially after my mother had to have surgery for a stomach ailment, rendering her damaged goods in Antonietta's eyes. My mother, though desperately in love with him, felt compelled to escape the heartache and torment while Pasqualino was away doing the compulsory military duty that was the norm back then. Her enterprising younger sister, Luisa, had already decided she wanted more from life than the village had to offer. Through the sponsorship of friends, some distantly related, she made her way to England, taking trains and finally a boat across the Channel. London in the late 1950s was one of many immigrant destinations, but the place most favoured by many of the young people from Castelfranco making their inevitable escape from the hardships of cruel winters, poverty and a crushing feeling of stasis. My mother followed – escaped – not long after and received the welcoming embrace of the Castelfranco contingent already established in London.

You will have worked out that my father, after finishing his military service, rushed to London to try to salvage the relationship, which now seemed doomed. He was dumbfounded to find a newly independent young Carmela Maria. At their first encounter, he found her smoking – a cardinal sin in his eyes. It took a while but love finally won out and they were married at St Anne's Swiss Church on Old Pye Street in Westminster on 3 August 1958.

My late arrival caused another familial car crash. After a few months of marriage my father received a letter from his father asking where the fruits of matrimony were. (Those were the words used; many years later I saw this letter.) Naturally the letter was instigated by his mother. Carmela Maria was understandably devastated and became worryingly insecure. I did finally arrive, and my parents decided that they needed to move back to London from Epping, fortuitously having been informed there was a chance of a council flat being available for us. In this they were aided by my future godparents, Paul and Anne Schembri, a Maltese couple who with their son Joey befriended my parents early on and who were determined to help them in any way they could. This gesture will never be forgotten by my family. May future immigrants find such compassionate people as we did to aid them in their quest to survive. My father was restless to be in the big city and both my parents missed their Italian friends, so this opportunity was a godsend. We moved into what would be the first of three different flats in the Peabody Estate Buildings on Old Pye Street, just off Victoria Street in Westminster, but not before I had mastoid surgery in Epping for a chronic ear infection – another shock for my mother.

The concept of work was something sacred to people like my parents: the grit they possessed was somehow from the earth itself. Castelfranco is situated in a region called the Sannio, its people the Sanniti. Very different in character from the vivacious Neapolitans, these people are austere, proud, and will break their backs to scrape a living. I knew nothing of this until about fifteen years ago, when Paolo Baratta, the then *capo* of the Venice Biennale, instructed me on my people's history, telling me that they even fought back against the Roman onslaught on two different occasions before finally succumbing. Everyone I have known from that village has been imprinted with the idea that through blood, sweat and tears anything can be achieved, or at least a dignified existence. It is written on their faces. This life weapon was most definitely passed on to my younger brother Patrick and to me. He was due to be born around St Patrick's Day, so he was baptised Patrizio, but that handle didn't last long in London town.

By the time I was eight years old and my brother six, both of us were working with my mother from six in the morning, helping her clean offices. She held down several of these jobs, and on the side moonlighted as a receptionist for a homeopathic doctor specialising in the treatment of rheumatoid arthritis. My mother had only a third-grade education and very little

English. However, with her winning personality, she quickly learned how to deal with people and make herself invaluable. My brother and I accepted that we had to be little work horses and follow her example. Of course, we didn't love it, but we got on with it and then went to school. Front and centre was our mother's determination to fight for a better life, no matter the hardships, and in this the united front of Pasqualino and Carmela Maria was awesome to behold.

St Vincent's Primary School in Victoria, next door to Westminster Cathedral, was run by the Sisters of Charity of St Vincent de Paul. I remember being very happy there. I liked all subjects, but football and music appealed to me the most. Ann Walsh, one of the teachers, played the piano beautifully, and she would occasionally put together a small choir of children's voices to sing in the cathedral next door. I would sing my heart out for her, even going off piste one time, singing the wrong verse of the hymn, more loudly and more emotionally than everyone else, ruining everything. At least music was in the air at school; the rudiments of notation were taught, a little keyboard work was expected from each of us, and we sang!

Let's go back to Castelfranco . . .

When I was five years old, Patrick and I spent an entire year in Castelfranco. I lived with our paternal grandparents, my brother with our maternal grandparents, who had moved to another part of the village, still only a stone's throw away. At the time my parents were simply overwhelmed with so much work that they couldn't take care of us properly. One might ask why they didn't take life a little more easily. I've been asked that question myself hundreds of times over the years, but one must take into consideration that they came from nothing, and something like that marks you for life. This attitude was certainly genetically and psychologically transmitted to my brother and me, becoming close to an obsession: the need not only to survive but also, for my parents in particular, the need to acquire material possessions, the smallest luxury a sense of achievement.

I have memories of running around the village with my school chums (yes, my brother and I had to enrol in something called an *asilo*), getting into all kinds of scrapes – one time leading to a bad fall that left a serious dent in my forehead. As there was no doctor in the village, I was carried, bleeding profusely, to the barber, who filled the cut with wax, stopping the horror show. I have the strange crevice to prove it, front and centre.

During our first years in London my father's ambition to become a professional singer became more pronounced. He would travel back and forth to Italy to study with the illustrious vocal coach Ettore Campogalliani, but he needed to work in a restaurant at night as a cook to earn survival money. My mother meanwhile kept up the punishing routine of holding down several jobs at once, helping to support him, my brother and me.

After some time, my father finally settled down with his family, friends and the many cousins who had also immigrated. He brought with him a newly discovered talent for the teaching of singing. It fascinated him to observe Campogalliani working with other singers, and he must have picked up much crucial information about the mysterious workings of the human voice. His own voice was of the *lirico spinto* variety of tenor, suited to the core Italian repertoire, predominantly Verdi and Puccini, a masculine, robust but plangent sound that I still have in my ear to this day.

I've often asked myself why my father didn't have the solo career he had dreamed of. I remember his getting quite nervous before performing, but I've also learned in the last forty or so years, surrounded by professional singers, what a complex mixture of elements in one's voice and personality it takes to succeed fully in this endeavour. Teaching was my father's true calling. He loved imparting his passion for melody and for singing freely and unencumbered, but of course his dream of becoming an opera singer was not fulfilled.

My parents bought an upright piano for the council flat; all I remember about it was that it was brown. From the age of about six I was made to take piano lessons. My debut as a performer was at school playing Beethoven's Romance in G in front of the class. Not earth-shattering stuff, but I got through it.

My father owned a collection of LPs of the great tenors, living and deceased. Names that I was exposed to as a youngster included Caruso (of course), Gigli, Pertile, Lauri-Volpi, Corelli, Bergonzi and Del Monaco. Even then, I realised how different they were from each other. Caruso made the biggest impression: the recording was made in the last years of his life and the voice was as if made of bronze. The dark hue and the penetrating high notes shot through me. Later I would get to know the sounds of each of these tenors intimately.

My piano playing improved steadily. I was no prodigy, probably due to a practising regime that was at best inconsistent. I was, however, fortunate to receive the kind of life-changing signal that can define one's path in life. It doesn't happen to everyone, but it happened to me. In the UK, the Associated Board of the Royal Schools of Music offers national examinations from Grade 1 (rudimentary) to Grade 8 (advanced). It is a useful way to plot your progress and so, urged by my teachers, I took Grades 1–4 in Performance and Music Theory and Ear Training, and did well. The 'moment' came when I passed Grade 5 with distinction. I remember opening the envelope with nervous anticipation, reading the marks and feeling something powerful come over me. I said to myself then and there, 'Music is what I have to follow.' With Grade 5, one is not playing very difficult material, no Chopin études, so I look back with bemusement that I would make such an enormous life decision solely on this result.

My life has always somehow been driven by those early memories and the wish – the need! – to match my parents' courage, passion and grit. To come to London from their tiny Italian village with just a few pounds in their pockets took real guts. That kind of daring I have never had. I have had another kind of courage, such as jumping in with a couple of days' notice to conduct a new production of Wagner's *Siegfried* in Vienna almost thirty years ago. But pulling up stakes and going all in, risking everything, throwing oneself into the unknown with almost nothing in your pocket – that takes real bravery. I feel, therefore, that this book is being written from the perspective of someone wanting to emulate my parents, maintaining through perseverance, curiosity and plain hard work their vision of what progress and achievement could be, no matter how humble the beginnings.

When I reached the age of ten, my father decided that I should become part of the family business and accompany his students on the piano. He himself was proficient enough to play the notes on the piano with one hand, but he couldn't provide a full accompaniment with chords and pedal. Having a pianist was obviously a boon for his students, but I was benefiting from being exposed to a very wide range of vocal music: Italian art songs, opera, German lieder, pop songs of the day, songs from American musicals. Most importantly, I was having contact with people, grown-up people. I wasn't shut in a room on my own practising for six hours each day; rather, I was collaborating from the start, and as time went on and I started to become familiar with these new musical surroundings, I was given the opportunity to communicate my knowledge and feelings about the music, transmitting at the same time what I had absorbed from my father about vocal technique.

At the end of my time at St Vincent's, I remember having a rather tetchy conversation with the formidable Sister Claire. She wanted to know what I had in mind in terms of schools for the next stage in my education. She was adamant that Brompton Oratory was the right place for me. I had other ideas. A new comprehensive school had opened in Pimlico, and after an interview there, I was quite taken with the idea of being in this flashy new glass building as part of an educational experiment. Besides, it was much closer to home. Though I was there only a short time and not really involved with things musical, I realise now, looking back, just how advanced the place was with regard to the arts. The school had a symphony orchestra, no less. Wow!

A routine was established. After classes finished, I would get on the 88 bus that took me to Dinely Studios in Blandford Street and I would work with my father and his singing students there for several hours – an obligation that continued when our family made an unexpected move to the United States.

One of the most powerful experiences of my young life was seeing my father sing the role of Canio in Leoncavallo's *Pagliacci*. It was with a small company that had no orchestra, so although the production was performed in full costume, the orchestral part was played on the piano. A small glimpse of my future! The pianist was the inimitable Robert Keys, for many years a senior opera coach and the assistant head of music staff at the Royal Opera House, Covent Garden. Later I was lucky enough to study with him and his wife, Elaine Korman.

9

In the opera Canio kills his unfaithful wife Nedda in a fit of jealousy, and my father became so violent that the plastic prop knife that we had gone out to buy together was totally crushed at the end of the performance. That frightening amount of intensity and passion, the sense of danger I witnessed that day, has never left my memory and I have ever since felt the necessity to be in the midst of that kind of theatrical hysteria. An intensity that is almost narcotic in its power. That bloody dagger and the incredible music that accompanies that intensely emotional situation made an indelible impression on me.

Something else that was passed onto me by my parents was a not too well-hidden restlessness. With my parents, it manifested itself in their insatiable need to achieve, to move on. People have described it in me as boundless energy; sometimes I don't know where the energy ends and the restlessness begins. Focusing can be a lifelong preoccupation. It is so easy to waste time and energy. Ask any performer.

I recall, when I was young, watching my father struggle with his singing. I've described his beautiful voice, full of sunshine and depth, but I realise that, despite being a good teacher, his own vocal technique was somehow not completely in order. How strange. Actually, not so strange, as I believe that a person who has struggled with technique, nerves perhaps, asking so many questions along the way, seeking solutions, is probably better suited to helping others find ways to conquer whatever their individual problems may be. My father was extremely emotional and this made him wonderfully expressive, but I realise now that it was very difficult for him to focus his mental energy, to pinpoint in himself the faults he may have had.

Only after several years of distance did I learn to accept that as a teenager I couldn't possibly have had the necessary expertise or wisdom to help my father work through these vocal issues. It is something that I have done successfully again and again for so many singers, but that skill came quite a bit later. I am not a voice teacher and will never be one, but I have ears for the correct vocal production, the Italian bel canto school. I have to admit that when I hear a singer who doesn't abide by these sacred vocal precepts, I almost can't listen.

The tremendous gift that I received from my father was our regular routine of going through the key works of the Italian repertoire together, with him singing the tenor roles and me playing the piano and, crucially, singing all the other parts. Yes, as a soprano, mezzo-soprano and baritone! The in-depth knowledge that I gained playing and singing, in operas including *La bohème*, *Madama Butterfly*, *Tosca*, *Turandot*, *Un ballo in maschera*, *Otello*, *Aida*, *Il trovatore*, *La forza del destino*, *Rigoletto*, *La traviata*, *Lucia di Lammermoor*, *Norma* and *L'elisir d'amore*, has proved invaluable over the years and I thank my lucky stars that I gained such familiarity with many pieces that would become important to me later on.

When I play the piano now in my alone time, I'm always brought back to my early lessons, the Romance in G, the myriad songs I played, the *Match of the Day* theme, which I learned by ear, and the never-ending list of tenor arias.

In 1972, when I was twelve and Patrick was ten, my mother gave birth to a baby girl, Incoronata. She was named after my grandmother and we called her Tina. Tragically, she died at the age of eight months, and it was shattering for my mother and the rest of the family. After having two boys, she and my father had so hoped for a girl – and now this awful shock. Following a very difficult year, my parents somehow came out from under a considerable dark cloud with a plan for an adventure, a change. My mother's sister Luisa, followed later by their parents, had emigrated from England to America, and now my mother and father said, 'Let's give that a go ourselves for six months.'

2

MOVING TO THE USA

London was not the easiest place to live during the late 1960s and early 1970s. A general bleakness pervaded the city, and the weather and pollution was such that my father always seemed to have a cold. Though my parents were somehow making ends meet, albeit working themselves to death (at least that's how it seemed to my brother and me), there was still a thought in those days that the streets of America, the land of infinite possibilities, were paved with gold. So, in 1973, on 30 June, we boarded a flight and moved to the United States. I was thirteen and my brother was eleven. It was supposed to be a try-out, but astonishingly quickly my parents made the decision that we would settle there.

This complete change came a year after they had bought their very first house in London. It was on Abbeville Road, in Clapham, and they had paid £7,500 for it. A huge and surprising step after so many years of council-flat living. I wonder what that house is worth now. We left behind my father's brother Mario, his wife Maria, their two children, and many cousins and close friends with whom my parents had grown up in the old country. Though I also left behind several schoolfriends, the fact that I hadn't been interacting with them outside school hours meant that the relationships were not cemented to the point that when I left London it was in a state of total devastation. Quite the opposite really. There was, rather, a feeling of restless curiosity.

Silly though it might be, my first indelible image of the United States to this day remains the colour of the Cadillac (ice blue, gorgeous) that picked us up at the airport to take us to Bridgeport, Connecticut, where my mother's family lived. The car belonged to a neighbour who generously drove to John F. Kennedy Airport in New York to fetch us. The look on his face when he saw the monstrous amount of luggage still makes me chuckle. Riding in that car made me think I'd died and gone to heaven. I still remember the revelation that was air-conditioning.

Six months later my parents took a flight back to London and sold the house. They returned, with the money sewn into their clothes, to park themselves, my brother and me permanently in the USA. After a summer spent mainly being invited for meals by a whole slew of relatives I didn't even know we had (barbecue became the new staple), I was enrolled into Central High School. My brother went into seventh grade in a different school, and our own new adventure began. Yes, everyone made fun of my British accent, which I never completely lost. As a journalist called Anna Picard commented in the *Independent* in 2006, 'One lasting effect of his childhood is an accent Rory Bremner might have difficulty reproducing. Pappano's voice combines the clipped consonants of the Eastern Seaboard with the tangy vowels of working-class Westminster and the shadow of a Southern Italian drawl.' My brother lost his accent in what seemed like two days.

The big question mark that hung over the family was what to do about my musical studies. The only place my aunt Luisa knew that had anything to do with music was a piano-and-organ store run by an Italian family, a hundred metres down the road from her house, where we were then staying. (Full-on family living, two households plus the maternal grandparents. The Italian din was deafening.) Verrilli's Piano and Organ Showroom was for me a momentous entry into a world of discovery. After I had first played for Mrs Anna Verrilli, the matriarch, she told me and my parents to wait for her daughter Norma, who was to arrive shortly. Was this a good sign, or was I being turned down? Aside from selling pianos and organs, mother and daughter both taught piano.

Norma made a huge impression on me. So confident, so tall. After she had listened to me play Liszt's *Consolation* No. 3 in D flat, a lovely dreamy piece, which I probably exaggerated to the limit of indulgence, she frostily uttered the words, 'Have you played any Bach?' I began a programme of study with her over several years with an intense diet of Bach (inventions, sinfonias, preludes and fugues, the Italian Concerto, later the partitas, the French and English suites, and much later the Chromatic Fantasia and Fugue), practising every day on a huge ancient upright piano in her basement. The heat in the summer I will never forget; no air-conditioning there. I must have stunk out the place! I made rapid progress. Hours of Hanon finger exercises, Cramer études, Mozart, Haydn and Beethoven sonatas, Chopin pieces of all descriptions, Brahms's Scherzo in E flat minor, rhapsodies, and Sonata No. 3 in F minor, as well as, curiously enough, pieces by Paul Hindemith – his Second Piano Sonata and excerpts from *Ludus Tonalis* – and Bartók's *Mikrokosmos*. It was all Greek to me at the time but I dug in.

Sight-reading was a must: playing the four-hand and two-piano repertoire together with Norma, I was experiencing instrumental chamber music for the first time, rather than collaboration with singers – a very important distinction. The glories of Schubert were revealed to me, and we played transcriptions of every sort and, yes, more Bach, in particular *The Art of Fugue*, but also the Mozart, Beethoven and Brahms symphonies. Soon my fingers were flying across the keyboard and, more importantly, I was slowly becoming a musician, and not just a piano player.

This process was probably quite normal for any talented piano student in his teens, but I was in for several surprises. Norma was part of a duo with her then husband, Joseph Iadone. He, for many years a double-bass player, was urged by none other than Paul Hindemith to turn his attention to early music, and so, incredibly, he ditched the bass and became a lutenist. Norma played the clavichord, and together they performed music written before Bach. I heard the music of Monteverdi, Gesualdo, Senfl, Isaac, Josquin, Sweelinck, Dowland, Campion, Gibbons and Byrd for the first time, and it opened my ears and my heart. Often the shortest of pieces said so much through dazzling harmonies, unexpected turns of phrase, and genuine pathos or playfulness. This music to this day stops me in my tracks.

Norma, whose father was also from Castelfranco, grew up at a time when most of the jewels of the American songbook were written and she fervently believed that I needed to know more about this repertoire. She had a fantastic ear and could play most of the great tunes by heart in an elegant and stylish way, replete with juicy chords. I didn't know what had hit me, but it hit me hard. As with the early music, a two-minute song could say everything there was to say. How ironic that I spend most of my life now conducting extremely long operas and symphonies.

After years of this kind of exposure, Norma introduced me to her former composition and harmony teacher, Arnold

Franchetti. In his early seventies when I met him, he had been a student of Richard Strauss in Munich and had sat on Puccini's lap as a boy when the illustrious composer was visiting Alberto Franchetti (Arnold's father), an opera composer himself and a bigwig at the La Scala opera house. I would drive early in the morning once a week to Lyme, Connecticut, for Arnold to peruse my meagre attempts at composition. Just being in his presence, I felt as if I were somehow connected to those masters of the past. His knowledge of harmony was prodigious and he shared with me the same modulation exercises he had worked on with Strauss. I got to know his own music and came to adore it. Difficult to pinpoint stylistically, it had an Italian lyricism, using folksong with often advanced modern harmonies and timbres. I premiered his Tenth Piano Sonata for his class at the Hartt College of Music. He dedicated his Eleventh Sonata to me, and composed a two-piano sonata for Norma and myself.

I was not the best student. I had so much going on, and composing needs opportunities for peace and quiet that were in woefully short supply in my everyday life. I hugely regret this and it must have been disappointing for Franchetti, though he obviously appreciated my performing his works. He asked me to accompany him on a visit to Aaron Copland. I played Franchetti's works for Mr Copland, and he was very generous with his praise. I have to say that he was in and out of lucidity as the dementia with which he was plagued was quite in evidence. I do remember him bringing up the names of certain important American composers to Arnold, but Arnold wasn't at all in agreement as to their worth. He was impossibly opinionated and not at all politically savvy in certain situations. This greatly damaged him professionally.

Meanwhile I was encouraged by Norma and my parents to take whatever work came my way that would fit in with the family business. So that's exactly what I did through my teens and early twenties. Most definitely there were pluses and minuses. From the very start, I had effectively a 'seat-of-the-pants' life as a real working musician – playing for my father's teaching, playing the organ in church, playing for choirs, many instrumentalists and singers, playing in a cocktail lounge, and so on. I was running around like a maniac, borderline chaotic but very energised, and I was making a little money, which was important to the family at the time. Growing up like that, I certainly missed out on many opportunities to develop relationships with my classmates and do the normal things a teenager does. I made a choice and it governed my life.

It's strange that someone with the career that I have today had no conservatory education or university training. I did study English and music for eighteen months at Housatonic Community College, which allowed me to stay at home with my father and keep the family business going. I didn't have the experience of hearing the symphonic repertoire live in the concert hall or of playing copious amounts of chamber music in a music conservatory – and although I had such a strong foundation for what I would eventually do in my life through working with singers, in later years I unquestionably felt a void, in particular concerning the non-vocal and non-pianistic repertoire. In a way, I have been playing catch-up all these years. At the time, Norma, my parents and indeed I myself felt that with all the practical experience I was getting in the real world, a conservatory setting was not necessary. I am often asked these days if this is a good way for a musician to build a career, forgoing music college. It worked for me in the end, but I have lingering questions.

During this period I made the acquaintance of Gustav Meier, a Swiss-born conductor who was the music director of the Bridgeport Symphony Orchestra, a conducting professor at the University of Michigan and a professor at the Tanglewood Festival, the summer residence of the Boston Symphony Orchestra. Norma admired him a lot and she encouraged me to talk to him. When I finally met him, he shared his ethos of the art of conducting, which I remind myself of very frequently these days. For him the paramount issue was being close to your centre; the arms always returning to the area around your diaphragm, bringing about or maintaining an undeniable focus and grounding. The orchestra was to come to you, not the reverse. I so wish I could have had some lessons with him in front of an actual orchestra. His sense of rhythm was flawless and there was joy in his music-making. Later, as I took on more opera, his ideas, which I truly espoused, became irritatingly more difficult to achieve as I found my arms wanting to reach out for the stage all the time. An occupational hazard.

He encouraged me to sit in on the conducting class at Tanglewood as an observer, and there I not only got to see the young conductors being put through their paces by Gustav, but also visiting teachers such as Leonard Bernstein and André Previn. I remember Bernstein spending forty-five minutes with a student on the first bars of Beethoven's Second Symphony, which was being played on two pianos. He insisted on getting the about-turn from the initial call to attention in the first bar to the totally contrasting woodwind answer just right. He was like a dog with a bone, but not once was he speaking technically. What he wanted to see and hear was the seismic shift of expression in the body language and the face of the undeniably talented young conductor, all to produce that particular kind of unexpected lyricism. He got it in the end.

Watching Bernstein rehearse Copland's Third Symphony with the Festival Youth Orchestra was the climax of this short visit. He was in his element, explaining, coaxing, inspiring, driving music he was born to conduct. One of the key things I took away from this rehearsal was his guidance on how to achieve the loose-limbed rhythm that is a feature of most American music. He pointed out that the notes in between the accented ones had to be considerably lighter, creating an immediately recognisable seductive nonchalance. Not a detail escaped him and to observe his teaching skills left one in awe.

I managed to get Gustav to come and watch me rehearse a couple of times when I was starting to conduct in the United States. At the time I was back and forth: baton, no baton. He didn't think it was such an important issue, as long as I stayed centred. By the way, most orchestral musicians don't seem to care. I've asked them.

As I gained more and more experience working with my father's students, I realised I could communicate with authority. It took several years for me to acquire an in-depth knowledge of vocal technique (a famously elusive and controversial subject), but I was teaching rhythm, intonation and interpretation – all that I do now. I tried to pass on my conviction that music is the most natural vehicle for conveying the scope, the power, of words. I dedicated the first half of my career almost exclusively to this union of words and music.

I tried desperately to keep up with studying the standard piano repertoire, though it was becoming more and more difficult with my peripatetic life. The time I did have, however, helped me observe close up the brilliant storytelling of the great composers. It was all under my fingers, but I sensed that I needed to have the structures more clearly in my head.

———————

In the opening chapter, I mentioned the effect conflict in music had on me. My observations led me to realise just how important the inherent need of music to find resolution actually is, as with any worthwhile story. Let me explain. The predominant structure for most sonatas and symphonies is sonata form. I believe this framework to be naturally theatrical. A theme having certain characteristics is introduced, followed by a second theme, usually contrasting. This is where things get interesting. As these two themes start to converse, their innate differences will lead to conflict. However, the differences of their characters and the individual ways in which they behave (they can be quite extreme, and this section is not necessarily limited to just two themes) are worked out extensively in what we call the development, usually a tumultuous period of creativity on the composer's part, in which they have to resolve the 'issues' by the time of the recapitulation. Ah, but the recapitulation will have gone through a transformation, because a conflict, a discussion of such intensity forces a change in the way the themes behave from now on, and the way in which they are heard by the listener, creating a new reality – a beautiful definition of what I think music drama is all about. Sonatas are in truth mini-operas; the themes are the different characters onstage. Listen to what Mozart does with this form, miracles of theatrical storytelling.

Now, in an opera rehearsal room over a period of weeks, I slowly build up the intensity of the experience to come. If you are a good opera conductor, you find yourself actually becoming the production, embodying through the music exactly what is going on onstage.

Although I can occasionally be operatic in temperament myself, I certainly am no character from an opera – not even close – but I am endlessly fascinated by the need to express something that is on another level of theatricality over and above speech, and that of course has to be singing. How can one define the expression of singing? I think of it as speech so intense that it has to become melody, it has to enter a new sphere of expression. It is a thing of wonder that has been with us, has been a necessity, over millennia in every known culture.

It would certainly not be a surprise to hear that I believe that even in orchestral or instrumental music that does not have a specific programme or storyline, there can be the possibility of a rich narrative, something that is so convincing and personal that strong feelings are conjured up in the listener, who imagines perhaps something private and specific to him or her. The listener might not even know or understand specifically what the performer is trying to express. There may be no words, no background story, but if the expression is strong enough, a narrative is nonetheless communicated. I find it magical that people can tell a story in music with inflection, accent, colour, speed, space and atmosphere. The possibilities are endless – the suddenness of an accent, the warmth of expression, the coldness of expression – elements making up a world that is descriptive, poetic and subjective. How beautiful it is to watch and listen to music being interpreted by people coming together, perhaps just a singer or instrumentalist with a pianist, or many singers and a large orchestra with a conductor in an opera house. To observe how intricate the human relationships are that give birth to performances that command attention is truly fascinating (to me).

When I make music with an orchestra of young people, this process is for me at its most moving level. Teaching about collaboration, listening, adjusting, understanding musical hierarchy – who is most important at any given moment and who is accompanying – becomes a fantastic life lesson, and guess who is learning the most from these experiences? Yes, me, the conductor. In fact, conducting is a never-ending learning curve, or it should be.

In order to communicate music, you have to be able to listen well. Even if you are making music alone, you have to listen intently to the sound you are producing, where it's coming from, where it's going. You have to listen particularly acutely when you are performing, perhaps even more than when you are rehearsing, ready for any new element that might make itself known, a wonderful interpretive inflection you hadn't thought of before, or difficulties of ensemble that need immediate attention. This is especially hard for a conductor, and in particular when a conductor is at the beginning of their career, because it is very difficult to listen when you are concentrating on what your arms are doing! Learning to focus on what is actually happening when you are conducting takes years of experience. The hope, of course, is that you learn how to shape and manipulate the sound and the phrases with gestures and not by talking too much in rehearsal. (Young conductors talk far too much when they start out; I haven't quite got out of this phase myself . . .) Different gestures paint different sounds, and performers have to learn to understand your gestures if everyone is to play together and in the same manner.

The subject of conducting technique makes me nervous, as I have struggled so much over the years trying to find a way of using the traditional fundamentals to fit my body and temperament. There is something pugilistic about my physicality – though, believe me, I have never stepped into the ring. A certain muscular tension pervades, despite me trying my level best almost to dance with my movements and achieve a fluid elegance. I hate watching myself on camera, but in the end I do know that communication, honesty, preparedness, concentration, give and take and generosity of spirit and energy make for the ideal collaboration between conductor and orchestra. The list above has driven me all through my life in music – from those formative days working with my father's students right through to my conducting and television broadcasting today.

The intensive and wide-ranging demands of playing for my father's lessons stood me in the best possible stead for taking on my very first experience of being a répétiteur and rehearsal pianist with an opera company. This was in 1979, when I was nineteen, at the Connecticut Grand Opera, which had fortuitously opened the previous year in Bridgeport, Connecticut, where our family was living. The artistic director was Giuseppe Campora, a well-known Italian tenor who had sung with the likes of Maria Callas and Renata Tebaldi, and in these, his twilight years, was still singing. After jumping in at the last minute for rehearsals of *Cavalleria rusticana* and *Pagliacci*, I was engaged not only as the company's répétiteur and rehearsal pianist, but also as a musical assistant, which included conducting backstage choruses and musicians; the following season I became the chorus master as well. Everything was on a tight budget, so rehearsal for each production was only a week, no matter how complex the opera was. That happened in a lot of small opera companies in the United States at that time. Many times the sets would arrive in boxes and be hung at once, often impossibly creased. We referred to this process as 'instant opera'.

I especially remember playing *Andrea Chénier*, *La forza del destino*, and a wonderful *Norma*, in which the soprano was Gilda Cruz-Romo. Working on these operas was an awakening for me. Despite those short and limited rehearsals, I knew that this world was where I wanted to be. The musical and theatrical experience was far beyond what I thought working with singers could be. It was deeply serious, the characters were compelling, and the singers themselves were marvellous, singing their hearts out and yet projecting specific intentions pertaining to the characters' states of mind; everything they were doing felt real and lifelike to me. One of the highlights of this period was playing *Andrea Chénier* for Maestro Carlo Moresco, or 'old man Moresco' as he was known to some. He was imbued with the undeniably old-school approach to this music, his music; full of flare but noble to the last. It was plain to see and hear the school of Toscanini, de Sabata and Serafin. I will never forget the smile on his permanently grouchy face while he conducted me in the Act I introduction. Another conductor was the Hungarian-born Imre Palló, who conducted regularly at the New York City Opera. After I worked with him on *L'elisir d'amore* and *La forza del destino*, he recommended me for an audition to join the New York City Opera as a répétiteur. By then I had become so intoxicated with this new world that I knew I had to go for this opportunity.

It was 1981, I was not yet twenty-two years old, and I was playing an audition for an international opera company. Beverly Sills was the general manager and Christopher Keene was the music director. I was really put through my paces at that audition. Not only did I have to play the beginning of *Der Rosenkavalier* and other pianistic fireworks, I had to sight-read and even to translate text from Debussy's *Pelléas et Mélisande* from French into English. Well, I was offered the job, and now I had to make one of the most difficult decisions of my life: accepting the position meant leaving my father's teaching practice. I commuted to New York from Bridgeport six days a week, ninety minutes by train each way, often travelling back home very late at night. On my free day my father would take students so that I could play for them. It was a painful decision I felt I had to make. Even though my mother was adamant that I should accept, it took me years to begin to come to terms with the guilt I felt, because I left my father high and dry without anyone who could be his partner for his lessons. It was only many years later that he managed to find someone appropriate to accompany his singers.

Working at the New York City Opera was a wonderful opportunity: just being in a prestigious opera house and with the amazing colleagues who were there at the time – Diane Richardson, John Beeson, Joel Fried, Robert Deckeunynk, répétiteurs with tremendous experience – was an education in itself. It was a den of brilliance, and each one took me under their wing. What was especially rewarding, and for me most unexpected, was that although I was playing the regular repertoire, operas such as *Carmen* and *La bohème*, from the start I was put on many pieces that were outside my familiar territory. One of the most memorable productions I played, although further down the line in 1983, was Massenet's *Cendrillon*. It was the very first occasion when surtitles were being used in New York. I had to learn it from scratch. The opera bewitched me – Faith Esham was beguiling in the title role, the conductor was Mario Bernardi, and the production by Brian MacDonald was gorgeous. In this score, magical effects, pastiche and the most sensual romantic music meld to form an irresistible entertainment.

I was discovering a new kind of music in my life; ever since then I have had a deep love of Massenet's music. *Werther* and *Manon* would become two of my all-time favourites.

It was John Beeson who encouraged me to enhance the piano scores that I was using with more detailed information that came from the orchestral score. This changed my playing over-night, creating a more orchestral sound and including notes that weren't in the piano scores but that the singers would hear from the stage. Unbeknownst to me at the time was that this new relationship with the orchestral scores was silently prepar-ing me for the future.

Another seminal experience was playing Carlisle Floyd's *Susannah*. It is based on the biblical story of Susannah and the Elders, very American in its musical language: open, big-hearted, folksy at times, but such great theatre. Yes, it's a bit melodramatic, and the orchestration is often overblown, but I was completely hooked. Once again, Faith Esham was singing the title role, a role she was born to sing, and Samuel Ramey sang the role of the alluring but malevolent preacher Olin Blitch.

The most unusual and one of the most thrilling of all my new experiences actually preceded *Cendrillon* and *Susannah*: a new production by Hal Prince of Bernstein's *Candide*, billed as 'The Opera House Version'. John Mauceri conducted, the cast was outstanding (Erie Mills as Cunegonde, David Eisler as Candide, John Lankston as Voltaire and Dr Pangloss), and this turned out to be another transformational moment for me. I already loved the American musical repertoire, and here I was working on a famous show that this time included many additions of hitherto unperformed music that had been unearthed by Mauceri (Bern-stein had deleted them before publishing his original score). Not only were the new librettists there at the rehearsals; Bernstein himself also came. Such heady stuff! I had to play the Overture over and over for the staging rehearsals before the orchestra came into the picture, and I remember the ovations I received from the chorus and soloists – back then I had really good fingers! It almost felt as though I were in a movie, but most important of all is that I was learning: Hal Prince's manipulations of the stage, his intricate knowledge of timing, how he directed the singers and what constituted the right delivery.

Two years later and in a similar vein came another illuminating lesson when Paul Gemignani came to conduct *Sweeney Todd*. What I learned in that production working closely not only with him and Hal Prince but also the composer Stephen Sondheim was, I realise now, something that was to shape my way of thinking in the future. They were all concerned with landing the jokes, timing the text to maximum effect, and having the accents only in the most appropriate places. Everything had to look how it sounded, and sound how it looked. They were maniacally insistent.

All through this time, any idea of becoming a conductor never entered my mind. Really. From my earliest days I had never had a shred of desire to conduct, and when some of the singers at the City Opera began to suggest that I should take up conducting because they felt I had the right qualities for it (whatever those were), I never imagined I would have the authority it takes to stand up on a podium in front of a large group of people and dictate. I finally gave in after two of the singers repeatedly kept cajoling me to take up the baton – the Danish soprano Inga Nielsen and her husband the American bass-baritone Robert Hale. Although they were both enjoying formidable careers in Europe, particularly Robert, who was making a huge name for himself in Wagner roles, they still sang at the City Opera. Robert finally persuaded me to take my first ever conducting engagement by introducing me to a frequent collaborator of his who was the music director of a symphony orchestra in Kankakee, Illinois. He arranged for me to direct one item on the programme with just a single rehearsal: Haydn's 'Clock' Symphony (No. 101). This is an intricate work, and I was to rehearse and perform it with people I had never seen before. Experienced conductors can put together a difficult piece like this in one rehearsal; a conductor with no experience, not so much. As well as conducting for the first time, I was playing the Mendelssohn G minor Piano Concerto for the first time in the first half of the concert while the music director conducted. A baptism of fire. I vividly remember that at the rehearsal I started telling everyone what to do, even though I couldn't conduct my way out of a paper bag. However, I did know exactly what I wanted from the players.

Separately, Inga Nielsen remained very insistent that this was the way forward: 'You play the piano like an orchestra, you have to conduct.' She said she was going to propose that I lead her in some concerts she would be giving in Denmark. The concerts comprised several operatic arias and overtures, and then lighter music in the second half. She arranged for me to be invited first of all to the South Jutland Symphony Orchestra. Even when one is an experienced conductor, that type of concert is very tricky to manage because of the many items on the programme and the vast array of styles. I wasn't great, but I wasn't terrible either, and I made a positive impression on the orchestra. I was immediately re-engaged.

One memorable programme included my playing and conducting Mozart's Piano Concerto in C (K. 467) and conducting Strauss's *Four Last Songs* with Inga. Being in the centre of the

29

orchestra for the Strauss changed my life. We often use the word 'lush' to describe rich romantic harmonies, but this was something more. I could feel the composer was revealing his soul in those sounds, in those words.

Relatively soon, I was conducting in other Danish towns, even in Copenhagen, and also in Sweden. These were occasional engagements – perhaps three times a year at most I would be in Scandinavia. Conducting was most definitely a sideline. I was happy with that because the life I was enjoying as a répétiteur and musical assistant was hugely fulfilling. And it was about to bring me an experience that was revelatory.

In the spring of 1983, while I was still working at the New York City Opera, I was asked to be an assistant and translator for Romano Gandolfi, who was coming to conduct a performance of Verdi's *Requiem* that the Connecticut Grand Opera was presenting. Gandolfi was the legendary chorus master at La Scala in Milan, and this was a major event. The Opera Orchestra was enlarged for the occasion, there was a line-up of fine soloists including two from the New York City Opera (RoseMarie Freni and Irwin Densen), and there were the hundred voices of the St Cecilia Chorus of New York. I looked after Romano, whose English was non-existent, including bringing him to dine regularly at my parents' house, and we began to form a close relationship.

It was a very valuable experience to be with him because I absorbed from him the possibilities of what an operatic chorus could achieve. At the rehearsals he insisted that the chorus learned how to sing *sul fiato* ('on the breath'), creating a mysterious *pianissimo*. The effect is built from the bass upwards, creating a kind of veiled, dark, *cupo* sonority similar to the sound of Russian choruses. He achieved an incredible homogeneity that came from this hushed *pianissimo*. It wasn't just a technical feat; it was the fervour of his spiritual conviction that was so gripping in all that he did with this music. At the same time, his technical knowledge of how to obtain that fervour in practical terms, achieving hair-raising effects, was formidable: having the altos sometimes singing the second soprano part, having the sopranos sometimes going up to the high C that the solo soprano was singing (frowned on by purists, but what a sound!), sometimes lifting the tenors up to the altos' part in the big *fortissimo* climaxes, creating a torrent of sound, doubling the sopranos with the altos in the *Tuba mirum* section, doubling the basses with the tenors in the *Rex tremendae* section – and so on. It was a hugely influential musical experience, yet it was also an enormously important practical lesson. He knew how to manipulate or interpret the music to make it as compelling as possible, communicating the essence of the piece. I've conducted the Verdi *Requiem* often since, always grateful for the secrets Gandolfi revealed.

Nothing much had changed at home, but with all that was going on with me, the relationship with my brother unfortunately but understandably became more distant. Though he had a very nice voice and sang in tune, he was more interested in sports, being with his friends and generally having a fun time as teenagers do. He loves to tell the story of when he was out shovelling the snow in front of our house and I was practising the piano and occasionally sticking my head out to laugh because I was inside where it was warm. Not very nice of me perhaps, but we laugh about it now. He went on to become a manager of an automotive parts store and his knowledge is encyclopedic. He also now has four wonderful children and five beautiful grandchildren. A normal life.

That same year, 1983, I received a call to do something completely different: to go to San Diego and do some prompting – for the first time in my life. Nowadays, in many of the big international houses such as the Royal Opera House, Covent Garden, there is rarely a prompter, but at that time most opera companies needed them. The prompter sat in a small, covered box beneath the front of the stage and above the orchestra pit, and their function was to cue the singers just before they started a phrase by mouthing or very quietly saying their words. Sometimes they also helped to prepare the singers for their roles in a production before the rehearsals started – so a prompter could also be a répétiteur. I was engaged as a guest prompter for an opera that I didn't know, *Adriana Lecouvreur* by Cilea, and this was for none other than Joan Sutherland, who was singing the role for the first time – so she needed a prompter desperately. Her husband Richard Bonynge was conducting and Tito Capobianco was the stage director.

This was a special experience on two counts. First, the process of prompting, giving the cue – not only the word but also the entrance – was excellent conducting training, though I didn't know it at the time. Second, I was in very close proximity to Joan Sutherland, who never distanced herself from me for very long. I truly never saw her breathe, and yet she took titanic breaths, but because her face was always communicating directly to the audience, and because she was always in the moment, one never noticed the working mechanism; one never saw the diaphragm, the entire vocal support system that keeps the voice afloat, which with her was like an incredible steam engine. That was such a lesson, and I tell singers all the time that if the face is not fully engaged, the audience starts looking at the motor, at what is *not* interesting. The eyes are everything!

Another remarkable phenomenon – and this is not voodoo – was that every time Joan Sutherland opened her mouth the orchestra played better. The sound of her voice was so inspiring that each time she sang, all of a sudden the orchestra went to another dimension, wrapping their sound around hers. Truly, I was not imagining it, and this was also a big lesson: that a voice can enrapture musicians and affect their sound so that they play more beautifully or more characterfully.

The close relationship that I formed with Romano Gandolfi when he came to conduct Verdi's *Requiem* in Connecticut was the catalyst for a vital new development in my life a year afterwards. It was through an invitation from Gandolfi that I was to take another courageous step and return to Europe, saying farewell to New York and to my family in Bridgeport, at least for part of the year. I wasn't going back to London. I was going to be working closely alongside Gandolfi in one of the major European opera houses – and another chapter for me was about to unfold.

3

LEARNING THE OPERATIC ROPES: BARCELONA – FRANKFURT – BAYREUTH

The Gran Teatre del Liceu stands on Barcelona's La Rambla, an iconic location if ever there was one. In the 1980s, and probably for hundreds of years before that, this street saw a menagerie of promenading people, caged animals and birds of all sorts for sale, and a multitude of flower-sellers. It gave the impression that you could stroll through life, up and down forever, lost in a very pleasant Technicolor dream.

The Liceu, besides being one of Europe's most vibrant opera houses, has had a distinguished tradition of Wagner performance dating back to the 1880s, spurred on by a passionate Wagner Society. Naturally, for a Latin country, the Italian and French repertoires were never short-changed, and all the star singers – the crème de la crème – sang there.

After leaving La Scala, Romano Gandolfi had taken a position at the Liceu as both chorus master and de facto head of music. This involved some administration and – crucially – also regularly conducting operas. He was branching out, and the conducting opportunities now available to him were of course the attraction. When he asked me if I would like to join the company as a rehearsal pianist and musical assistant in 1984, I jumped at the opportunity – not only to work closely with him, but also to become more familiar with Wagner and the operas of Richard Strauss that I didn't know as well (some not at all) as I knew the Italian repertoire. The audience in Barcelona was made up of many Wagner fetishists and Strauss was never too far behind Wagner on the Liceu's billboard.

During my time at New York City Opera, I had realised that, going forward, I would not be satisfied being pigeon-holed when it came to the repertoire that was put in front of me. Just because I had an Italian name shouldn't mean that the German masterpieces were off limits. In classical music, and especially for conductors, there is a tendency to compartmentalise talent. Though it is obvious in my case that I have an innate feeling for the Italian music that is my patrimony, when I was younger I refused to accept that this was the complete story. I am glad that I felt so strongly about it, because those early years of exposure, of maximum curiosity, became the foundation of my career.

The afternoon I arrived in Barcelona, groggy from the flight and apprehensive about being in a new city, I got a phone call from an extremely anxious person asking me to come to the theatre right away. It was a Sunday and a matinee performance of *Carmen* was due to start in an hour's time. A singer had cancelled and the tenor Nunzio Todisco was the last-minute replacement. Maestro Jacques Delacôte was insisting on an emergency piano rehearsal with him, but the house rehearsal pianist hadn't yet shown up and panic had ensued. So I was called in. The rehearsal took place in the smallest practice room imaginable. In fact, the conductor had to stand slightly outside the room in order to wave his arms. The tenor stood right next to me and almost deafened me. I had played *Carmen* at the New York City Opera for innumerable rehearsals and I surprised everyone by how well I could play it. This one short rehearsal not only convinced the people who had hired me that I could be trusted but, more importantly, I convinced myself I was going to be able to handle it.

Almost immediately, I was playing for rehearsals and the demanding solo piano part in Strauss's *Ariadne auf Naxos*, working for the Hungarian conductor János Kulka, a real character. He was short, stocky and fiery. For me, it was the beginning of a love affair with this opera, and such was my revelling in the moment that I felt like Liberace down in the pit during the performances. Next came *The Flying Dutchman*, *Siegfried* and *Salome*, all of which were discoveries for me. I was playing for the most sensational singers I'd ever heard: Reiner Goldberg and Walter Berry in *Siegfried*, Gwyneth Jones and Simon Estes in *The Flying Dutchman*, and Gwyneth Jones (again) in *Salome*. Hers was by far the loudest voice I had ever heard in my life, and her stage presence was mesmerising. I was also playing for wonderful singers in non-German repertoire, and they knocked me off my feet. Imagine: Mirella Freni, Alfredo Kraus and Justino Díaz in *Faust*; Éva Marton and José Carreras in *La Gioconda*; Montserrat Caballé, José Carreras (again) and Juan Pons in *Hérodiade*.

And then there was the chorus, the magnificent instrument that Romano Gandolfi and his assistant Vittorio Sicuri had transformed. Every time the chorus sang a phrase in an opera, my jaw dropped to the floor. Gandolfi would stand in the wings and give instructions to them under his breath. The response was immediate; hushed *pianissimos* followed by tumultuous waves of sound. Watching and listening to this, I was slowly realising what operatic choral singing could be. The burnished sound and homogeneity in each section, the fervour and the precision of this Liceu chorus are the qualities that remain in my inner ear and heart to this day and, together with my chorus masters, what I try to achieve. Most of the members of this chorus had voices of soloist quality. How Gandolfi tamed these vocal lions to achieve such unity was nothing short of miraculous. My singular most indelible memory of my time in Barcelona is how each morning, before going to the rehearsal room, I would steal a peek into the auditorium. It somehow set me up for the day, because gazing at this glorious room was inspiration enough for a lifetime, and the acoustics were a heavenly gift to music.

My stint at the Liceu was actually one of two key European experiences in this formative period of my life. The other was my taking on a similar post at the Frankfurt Opera in 1985. I was desperate to learn the German language, and I knew that the only way to achieve that was to live and work in Germany. I'd had some German lessons in New York City with the late lamented language guru Bob Cowan, but now I needed to really go for it. Once again, the soprano Inga Nielsen, who had secured my first conducting engagements in Europe, came to my aid. She helped to arrange a series of auditions for me: one in Stuttgart, one in Munich for Wolfgang Sawallisch, and one in Frankfurt where Michael Gielen was the music director.

The styles of the auditions were surprisingly different. In Munich they wanted to see my hands flying all over the keyboard, and at a certain point Sawallisch himself came in to check out my sight-reading abilities. I'll never forget the work he chose: *Der Barbier von Bagdad* by Peter Cornelius. No one knows this piece. Sawallisch was dressed impeccably and had the air of someone with the most refined sense of culture. There was a tense atmosphere in the room when he left to confer with his henchmen. These two gentlemen returned with a doom-laden demeanour, so I thought that the audition had gone badly. To my astonishment they offered me a job on the spot, and I thought that was that; I was going to Munich. I had only to do the audition in Frankfurt.

The way the Frankfurt audition was handled startled and impressed me. The jury didn't just want to test my technical facility on the piano in operas such as *Salome* and *Der Rosenkavalier* as they had in Munich. They wanted to hear how I phrased musically expressive but deceptively simple writing such as Pamina's aria 'Ach, ich fühl's' in Mozart's *The Magic Flute*, and how I coped with having to play while a conductor led me in Puccini's *La bohème*, and then with the roles reversed. I was hooked! I immediately sensed that this was a place where I could learn something. I wasn't sure what that was exactly because I was in totally new territory, but I was ready to find out. I turned down the offer from Munich, and for two years, from 1985 to 1987, I agreed to a part-time contract at the Frankfurt Opera – something very unusual for the time. Usually it's all or nothing, but I wanted to continue my other activities, including at the Liceu, and they agreed to it.

The Frankfurt Opera (the Städtische Bühnen) was where I first saw and experienced Regietheater, stagings in which directors create innovative and sometimes highly experimental productions of operas and plays, basing their interpretations on subtext, using abstract design, making intense demands on the performers and, to some degree, imposing a level of distortion in order to tell a very personal story – not necessarily the story in the text. The approach is widespread now, but at that time it was prevalent principally in Germany. I worked with Philippe Sireuil on Strauss's *Der Rosenkavalier*, Ruth Berghaus on the entire *Ring* cycle, and Christof Nel on *Falstaff*, all three conducted by Michael Gielen, brilliantly. Since it was a repertoire house, I was also playing rehearsals for this, that and the other, pieces put on stage with minimal or no stage rehearsals, and so

I was learning new stuff on the fly. Scary, but if you survive it, very good training.

There is no question that Gielen's approach was cerebral, but because I sat so close to him playing for his rehearsals, I was able to perceive many layers of expressivity in his subtle gestures. He was obsessed with the clearest delivery of the text – both the words being sung and the articulation of the orchestral instruments. Transparency of the texture was hugely important to him, and though the danger of the results being cold or skeletal was always threatening, his sense of sweep, of direction, was flawless. He knew how the music went and he had a very particular idea of the way he wanted it to sound.

The productions I saw and worked on were most unusual. Some were incredibly ugly and aesthetically impossible. This confused me, often leaving me baffled, but I have to admit they were always psychologically compelling and/or provocative. Most important for me was to see the hand-in-glove way Gielen worked with Berghaus on the *Ring* cycle. The symbiotic relationship between the conductor and the stage director strongly impressed and influenced me. Both artists were striving for the essence of each scene. Though they were each working in extreme detail, neither lost sight of the forest for the trees. Every gesture, musical or physical, had to be essential, necessary, never decorative or haphazard. The atmosphere in the rehearsals was almost always tense and a certain sterility pervaded the proceedings. (What world had I come into?) Yet the approach was always creative in unexpected ways. After a long process of demanding and repetitive work, the concrete result, for me at least, was that I'd never seen people act so convincingly and sing with such command of the meaning of the often thorny Wagnerian text.

I grew most passionate about the opera *Siegfried*. The tenor William ('Bud') Cochran, a big man, was dressed in long shorts in this production. He looked almost ridiculous, but he most definitely embodied the spirit of the young Siegfried, the rough but sensitive nature boy. His bravado, vocal stamina and sympathetic stage presence were spellbinding. From act to act he grew stronger and stronger, and one was compelled to follow his story. The third act, one of Wagner's most inspired and innovative creations, has always gripped me like nothing else in this cycle.

The other star of this *Ring* was the Swedish soprano Catarina Ligendza. Her voice was neither large nor beautiful in a conventional sense, but what she did with it was remarkable. Her warmth was as natural as it was extraordinary, and to observe close up her musical relationship with Gielen was unforgettable; both tenacious but each approaching the material from opposite ends of the spectrum, Gielen fighting for the clarity of the text and the direction of the score, Catarina fighting for the soul of the music. This apparent tension created something so rich that it marked the production in a unique way. I vividly remember standing in the wings for the final *Götterdämmerung* in the cycle, which was also the final performance of Gielen's tenure. He conducted with such discipline, and yet such freedom, the music delivered rhapsodically in large, cogent paragraphs, and Catarina valiant and ecstatic in the final scene. The audience went crazy. Gielen, the long-serving music director, certainly gave this house a personality, an identity all its own.

The hopping from one part of the world to another didn't stop with Frankfurt. In early 1985 I was approached about auditioning as a rehearsal pianist for the Lyric Opera of Chicago. I had heard that the company rivalled the Metropolitan Opera and attracted the greatest singers in the world, so I was very interested. I knew that the company's long-time music director was an Italian by the name of Bruno Bartoletti, whose interests lay not only in the standard Italian repertoire, but also in the great works of the twentieth century. Mmm. Ardis Krainik was the formidable general manager and, together with William Mason and later Matthew Epstein, she ran as tight a ship as I have ever experienced. They were visionary in their programming. They conceived seasons comprising pieces from every corner of the repertoire, from Handel to new work. In fact new operas became a calling card for the house. I did a gruelling audition and was offered the job. They allowed me to stay just a portion of the season, so that I could combine it with my European work. (It is quite a sore point in my house to this day that my wife Pamela, who came to work in Chicago a year later in the same job, didn't have to audition.)

I adored playing the piano for Bruno. His technique was quite idiosyncratic: a lot of elbows, as I remember; a lot of kneading, and lots going on in his face. The clarity of the beat was a secondary consideration. I quickly realised that if I just looked at his face I would know exactly where I was. The first opera I played for him was Verdi's *Otello* and my fingers flew joyously. The three protagonists were Plácido Domingo, Sherrill Milnes and Margaret Price. Not bad.

So many discoveries were made here: *Kát'a Kabanová, Lulu, Parsifal, I Capuleti e i Montecchi*.

The conductor Dennis Russell Davies was arriving a couple of days later than the cast for rehearsals of Berg's *Lulu*. With such a complicated piece, it was rightly felt that before embarking on the first staging rehearsals a musical 'bash through' of Act I was essential. I was told with very little notice that I was

41

to lead this rehearsal. After recovering from the shock, I managed to get myself together and prepared for this new role, staying up to all hours the night before. Yes, I could play it on the piano, but to lead a rehearsal with the likes of Chicago's reigning prima donna Catherine Malfitano? On the fateful morning I sat down next to the pianist and I was shaking like a leaf, looking warily at this array of stars lined up in front of me like a firing squad, all probably thinking, 'Who is this squirt?' The moment I gave the downbeat and the prologue started, I took charge of myself, of the music and of the high-powered cast. I pulled it off and everyone was more than pleasantly surprised – above all me.

I was playing the piano in rehearsals for a visiting Italian conductor who became interested in what I was doing and what I was thinking about my future. I told him that I was doing a little conducting, but that I was unsure about the whole idea. He explained that he would need to see if I had any aptitude, observing me demonstrating the different beat patterns. We got through one beat per bar, then two, three and four. At five he gave me a wily look as if waiting for me to trip up, then the same with six and the terrifying seven. To his great surprise I survived this inquisition, but at the end of it he said, 'Yes, your arm is ok, but with a last name like Pappano, you'll never have a career.'

After a few years, the Lyric gave me the opportunity to conduct a performance of Verdi's *La traviata*, with a young cast for a vast school audience. The opera house has well over 3,500 seats. There was very little rehearsal as the accomplished orchestra knew the piece backwards and forwards. At the one orchestral rehearsal with singers that I did have, I saw out of the corner of my eye that Bartoletti, Krainik and Mason had come to check me out. In a panic I accelerated the tempo of Flora's C major party scene to a farcical degree. I was told later that during the break some orchestra members had said to Pamela, who was assisting me, 'We saw what was happening, but we'd never let him do that in performance.'

I went on to take over some performances of Bizet's *Carmen*, and was eventually asked in 1992 to conduct a show of my own: Donizetti's *L'elisir d'amore*. Years later came *Falstaff* with Bryn Terfel, and *Salome* with Catherine Malfitano, both memorable occasions. I had grown up in this company's eyes. Of these four operas, *L'elisir* was by far the most challenging. When there are fewer notes, you had better know what to do with them.

A fortuitous and momentous event during those years was my meeting Daniel Barenboim. I became his assistant in 1986, first in Israel, together with the brilliant stage director Jean-Pierre Ponnelle, and then at Bayreuth in productions by Ponnelle, Harry Kupfer and Götz Friedrich. These were more key experiences that formed me; they showed me how an opera conductor can enhance a production and how a stage director can enhance the music, and how if the conductor and director are working harmoniously in – as I like to call it – cross-pollination, the result is unmatchable.

My relationship with Daniel Barenboim began when the Bayreuth Festival (the renowned annual festival celebrating the operas of Richard Wagner) got in touch with me as they were looking for a pianist to play for some auditions that Barenboim, Wolfgang Wagner and Harry Kupfer were holding in Berlin for the casting of the new production of the *Ring* cycle scheduled for 1988. I said yes right away, and on arrival in Berlin I played for two singers, Deborah Polaski and Robert Hale, whom I already knew. Daniel loves to tell the story that during the piano introduction to the extract from *Tristan und Isolde* that Deborah Polaski was singing, he turned to Wolfgang Wagner and said, 'I don't know about her – she hasn't opened her mouth to sing yet – but him I want!' And that is how I became his assistant. What I knew about Bayreuth you could have written on a postage stamp.

Before going to Bayreuth, Daniel invited me to Tel Aviv to be an assistant together with Richard Amner, his long-time *recitativo* player, in a very special staging by Jean-Pierre Ponnelle of the three Mozart–Da Ponte operas.

It was a compact three weeks of intense rehearsals and several performances, in stifling heat, and I loved every minute of it. In these productions, most of the singers were performing at least two roles, in some cases three, and we all felt like a family of players, a troupe. Ponnelle put the Israel Philharmonic Orchestra on the stage in the traditional concert placement, but directly behind the last row of musicians he built a raised platform where much but not all of the action took place. He constructed two covered spaces, like wings, on each side of the stage, for costume changes, exits and entrances, and where characters could hide from each other.

Sometimes characters would walk through the orchestra singing, often sneaking between players (a riotous time was had by all) in the clandestine situations that abound in these operas. On occasion they would run on stage from the auditorium through the audience, creating the illusion that everything was being improvised, that anything could happen at any moment, and from anywhere – very much like vaudeville-style entertainment. It all felt so fresh.

Ponnelle had a supreme understanding of character and psychological motivation. When anything involving chicanery

44

was needed, he was at his supreme best. There was something naughty in his own personality, and he had a colossal ego, so he naturally understood all the self-serving machinations of both the serious and the comic characters. The singers were brilliant: among them the young Karita Mattila, Ferruccio Furlanetto, Karen Huffstodt, Marianne Rørholm and Joan Rodgers.

Watching Ponnelle and Barenboim collaborating so closely was a profoundly enlightening experience for me. Barenboim was with the director every step of the way in terms of supporting the humour, the sensuality and even the cruelty of certain characters. The singers' lines had to be delivered just so, especially in the *recitativo* sections of the piece. This kind of collaboration would have been impossible had Ponnelle not been the musician he was and Barenboim not been the theatre man he was. From this example of teamwork, I learned how much shared creativity is possible, most specifically in the *recitativo* sections of operas.

These sections are where the plot is moving forward, where crucial information is revealed. The characters communicate in a kind of sung speech, accompanied by a harpsichord or a fortepiano, which provides a harmonic context for the words. Recitatives are often rapid-fire conversations, and their wordiness can make them difficult to perform. They need to be delivered with a specific energy and a huge variety of nuance, the characterisation of the words reaching the audience with absolute clarity. When this is not the case, they can be stupefyingly boring. They need to be staged deftly and the singers should sound as though they are creating them on the spot so that the effect is as close as possible to natural speech. This is where the audience will relish the talent and diligence of the stage director working hand in hand with the conductor – or not! Singers love to sing, but *recitativo* is almost always the antithesis of melodic indulgence. To achieve natural speaking rhythms, a singer may often have to sacrifice beauty of sound for pinpoint timing, and there are some singers who resist committing to this.

During one of the final rehearsals of *Don Giovanni*, I was thrown in front of the orchestra without warning by Daniel Barenboim so that he could hear how a passage sounded in the auditorium. This was the duet between Giovanni and the skittish Leporello in the graveyard scene. It goes at a very fast pace, and I discovered that although I knew the opera, I certainly wasn't ready to conduct it. It was the first time I had been asked to do this and although I got through it, I did no more than that. I realised that if I wanted to know operas really well, I needed to be spending more time with the orchestra score and less with the piano score, where so much detail is missing.

Romano Gandolfi once told me how much he regretted not studying the orchestra scores much earlier in his career, as he was now a conductor in middle age playing catch-up, and it made him suffer. Conducting an orchestra is obviously a vastly different experience from playing the piano. You are driving the car, so to speak, and you are responsible for the musical safety of the musicians and the safety of the music itself. You are the guide, inspiration and salesman. This little wake-up call prepared me for what was to happen when I assisted Daniel in Bayreuth the following year, as he asked me to jump into the orchestra pit on quite a number of occasions.

In Tel Aviv there was life and energy in the vaudevillian proceedings, goodwill and humour, and the singers felt secure because they had been fed musically and scenically with a very clear point of view. As a result, there were no inhibitions, no hesitations about how they should perform, about how they should deliver. Seeing that with my own eyes was enormously valuable, and to this day I have tried to create that kind of situation, to provide something concrete and sharply defined for the musicians with whom I work, whether they be opera singers, orchestral players, solo singers or instrumental soloists. Naturally, the singers or soloists will want their say in the final mix, and of course this is another facet of this complex but beautiful journey.

I loved being in Israel: the wonderful climate, the scenery, the people, the food, the sea – it was a window into an entrancing world that was at the time totally foreign to me. I was lucky enough to return there when, in 1992, I became a regular guest conductor and later, for three years, principal guest conductor of the Israel Philharmonic Orchestra. I made many friends, and I treasure the time I had with them. The orchestra comprised a veritable melting pot of Israelis, Europeans, Russians and Americans, and how musical they all were.

Amusing – hilarious even – as these Mozart–Da Ponte operas are, the three share several important serious moments, which are exquisitely interwoven around the comedy to show the other side of the coin, the dilemmas of each character. In *The Marriage of Figaro*, the Countess languishes because she believes her husband no longer loves her and is unfaithful. There is also a political power struggle between Figaro and the Count, servant and master. In *Così fan tutte*, Don Alfonso proposes a cynical bet to the young soldiers (very confident that he will win it, which he does) that their fiancées would betray them if the right circumstances were to arise. When he himself engineers it so they do arise, all becomes very painful. Beethoven thought *Così fan tutte* was scurrilous, and it was certainly outrageously daring

47

for the time. Though the plot might deserve its reputation for shallowness, it is seen today as very modern and contemporary. By the way, the music is sublime.

And what about the iconic Don Giovanni, this character each of us thinks we know for his successes with more than a thousand women? This charming predator is having a terrible day when we meet him; everything is going wrong. It takes two to tango, certainly in matters of love or lust, so how unwilling *was* Donna Anna to be seduced by the Don? She tells a good story to her fiancé Don Ottavio, but her *recitativo* is written so cunningly that some of what she says can hardly be taken at face value. Mozart leaves musical clues everywhere. Does Donna Anna really love Ottavio, and will they actually marry? How much longer can our Don get away with manipulating people before he is punished? Let's remember he is also a murderer. I must admit that I adore Donna Elvira, the somewhat pathetic, deluded former lover of the Don who still carries a torch for him. I find her very touching; she truly loves Giovanni and, yes, she is neurotic, highly strung and easily duped, but she is sincere and her heart is worn totally on her sleeve. She tells it absolutely as it is – very different from Donna Anna.

Mozart and Da Ponte put together three operas that are knowing and psychologically thrilling because of what they reveal about the human psyche. There are truths everywhere. I believe one can learn much from them, and in addition they are tremendously entertaining. They stand together as a cycle of three operas, and as is the case with Wagner's *Ring* or a Schubert or Schumann song-cycle, performing a cycle in its completeness is something unique: a full immersion into the composer's and poet's mindset, the continuous thread of creativity drawing you inexorably into a world that will reflect back to you as a mirror telling the story of the many situations, choices, and roads to be travelled in a life lived.

And so it was to be when I worked on the *Ring* in Bayreuth with Daniel Barenboim and Harry Kupfer. As in Frankfurt, I was primarily playing the piano, but I was now also regularly conducting piano rehearsals, planning the daily schedule (a mammoth undertaking), marking orchestral parts specifically for Daniel, and spending hours coaching the many artists singing their roles for the first time. An uncanny but fortuitous coincidence was the number of British singers in the casting of the *Ring*. These included Graham Clark, John Tomlinson, Anne Evans and Linda Finnie. The inimitable Graham Clark was already a Bayreuth veteran, but John Tomlinson, Anne Evans and Linda Finnie were launching their international careers.

But my first Bayreuth experience involved Barenboim and Ponnelle once again, when I had three weeks in which to learn the piano score of *Tristan und Isolde*. Much of it feels like playing the music of Franz Liszt, so for any pianist it is a dream. It is also extremely complicated and restless music, despite its allure. The thought that I would be playing this music for Daniel sent shivers up my spine, but I persevered. He was not very demonstrative at all in the piano rehearsals and looked over at me only when I was getting it wrong somehow. Trial by fire.

I remember Ponnelle using the orchestra score, not the usual piano score, when he needed to refer to something specific. I can't tell you how rare it is for a stage director to be able to do this. He was a one-man operation in that he also designed the sets, the lighting and the costumes. I spent a lot of time gazing at the sets. His sense of taste, narrative and mood were beyond reproach, each setting so right. I remember the magical golden tree of Act II, and the enormous dead tree trunk and the concerto of grey lighting for Act III, both taking my breath away.

Besides playing for rehearsals, my work mainly involved coaching Peter Hofmann, who was making his role debut as Tristan. This role is fiercely difficult for many reasons. Very few people have the stamina needed to get through it, the notes themselves are very tricky in places and, especially in Act II, it is technically very demanding. Tristan cannot shout his way through this role, though many do. It requires an ability to float the voice in the famous love duet, but also to go to the absolute human limit of expressivity and characterisation, with tremendous generosity. It is that daunting. Peter needed a lot of support, especially with those 'tricky' notes. To sing in tune in this opera is much more easily said than done, and because the role is often very low, it is very easy for the voice to lose its centre of gravity, its home base, making the pitching of certain notes very awkward. Peter did lose his patience once with me after I gave him one correction too many. Another lesson learned.

In the new production of the *Ring*, all four operas (around fifteen hours of music) were rehearsed concurrently, which is not the norm. Daniel couldn't be available for every piano staging rehearsal of each scene as there were simultaneous rehearsals of other scenes. He chose where he wanted to be, where his attention was most needed. He could decide to work individually with a singer, then do an orchestra rehearsal, then dash back for a staging rehearsal. All of us were working three sessions a day for more than two months, Daniel leading by example. Where did he get the stamina?

I had no real technical sense of conducting yet, other than the basic fundamentals, and I had never had anyone watching over me and guiding me in any organised way for an extended period of time. Here at Bayreuth, I was learning how to rehearse in the most meaningful and thorough way, picking up all sorts of information about sound, timbre, musical architecture and text as I watched Daniel rehearse. I began to understand how different ways of using the arms create different responses from the orchestra in terms of sound and attack. I was learning how to link gestures – with the arms, the eyes (!) or the will – to the musical expression. The fine tuning of those elements is an ongoing and revealing process for me.

Daniel was also always thinking ahead, organising in his mind the long-term goals for the project in front of us. Usually it is a conductor's rehearsal abilities that determine whether or not they have a career in music. It's true that there have been some conductors, even prestigious ones, who were relatively low-key or even uninteresting in rehearsals and then turned it on at the performance with good results, but most of us must learn how to rehearse, how to build from day to day. In an opera production this is hugely important, because the rehearsal period is often so long, starting with musical and stage rehearsals with piano, then rehearsals with the orchestra alone, then the *Sitzproben* (the singers and the orchestra together but not on the stage) and, finally, the singers on stage (with all the production elements) with the orchestra in the pit for several more days. If you don't have a point of view about every step in that journey, you lose people: you become uninteresting, and there won't be any improvement or building; the development will reach a certain point and the production will stagnate.

Daniel revealed to me something very important that I often use: how to find musical solutions to technical problems and technical solutions to musical problems, a way of freeing the brain to be more creative. Though music is a joy, producing it involves a host of challenges, many of them frustrating. He made me aware that one has to have a sense of the whole, including an understanding of the entire hierarchy of the written text – knowing who is the protagonist at any given moment, voice or instrument, who is primary and who is secondary, where the harmony is leading, where the real climax is. All this information can be layered and complex, but the conductor has to have digested all these elements to understand and balance the language of the score and, yes, each score has its own language.

Balance in music is very important to me: the different weights of the various choirs or sections in the orchestra, how they must be manipulated to be in either the front seat or in the passenger seat next to the driver or in the back seat. If it's done well, it seems natural. One of the nicest compliments I have ever received was 'The orchestra sounded so full and yet it never drowned out the singers.' That was probably the case because I always force myself to hear the words that are sung on the stage. Even when I am rehearsing the orchestra on its own, I have taken the words into my ear and my mind's consideration, so the internal balance is leaving room for the singers to be added. It requires dominance of the musical material and an understanding of how all the elements relate – and all that was nurtured in my work with Daniel Barenboim. It was indeed nurtured, but to survive in his company (he is an intimidating intellectual force), I had to relate to his mental process, which was strong, specific and, crucially, totally balanced between head and heart. I realise that my own journey is a constant search for this same balance.

4

FIRST MUSIC DIRECTORSHIP: OSLO

It was September 1987 when I rehearsed and performed a full opera for the first time. I was making my opera-conducting debut in Oslo with Den Norske Opera. Founded in 1959 with the great soprano Kirsten Flagstad as its first general director, its full title is Den Norske Opera & Ballett. Once more on Inga Nielsen's recommendation, I was engaged to take charge of Puccini's *La bohème*, an opera I had played and coached on the piano many times. Inga was making her role debut as Mimì, and since she had prepared the role with me, she insisted I conduct it. She had that kind of clout in Scandinavia.

No matter how well one knows this piece, Puccini's ever-popular opera is a minefield for an inexperienced conductor. The first act presents formidable technical challenges: just starting the piece is as treacherous as the opening of Beethoven's Fifth Symphony, and that is saying something. Awkward rhythms must sound fresh and ebullient; knitting the many tempo changes together into a cohesive whole is famously challenging, and controlling the balance to let the singers be heard is hard. At the time, perhaps because I was so pumped up, I wasn't aware of these terrifying obstacles. When I was let loose in the rehearsal room, all my accumulated experiences up to that point came together to create in me an explosive release of knowledge, conviction and exuberance. I remember telling the soloists not only how to sing and inflect, but also how to convey emotion with their eyes, much to the astonishment of the director. I managed to overcome whatever technical deficiencies I had in front of the orchestra because I was riding on a wave, being carried by my love of the piece and my crystal-clear vision of how I wanted it to go. Passion ruled the day. Amazingly, it all went rather well, and crucially I now knew what my future could look like. An unexpected but gratefully received revelation.

I was invited back as a guest for three years before being offered the company's music directorship, a hugely significant moment in my life that would engender a way of thinking about how to build a career over the long term. Being a music director of course means a greater presence throughout any given season, and though one cannot possibly conduct everything, nor should one, the position allows the incremental building of a deeper relationship with the orchestra and chorus (and the public!). It allows you to shape the company's musical development through the repertoire choices you make, and to steer the process of making musical theatre in a specific way. For me, the idea is to develop and grow together with the orchestra and chorus, creating a bond formed by shared ideas, shared energy, many rehearsals and many performances of a wide variety of works.

As a guest conductor, I led *Così fan tutte* and *L'elisir d'amore*, both sung in Norwegian. It was dizzying to follow the quick patter of those two shows in a language totally foreign to me. (The best I could do at the time was to count from one to ten in Danish.) But it was invaluable training. Those comic operas are not anywhere as easy as they might sound, being so rhythmically and harmonically exposed: nowhere to hide . . . What I perhaps lacked in skill might have been partially offset by my silly sense of humour. I grew up on a steady diet of English television's comic heroes, including Morecambe and Wise, Benny Hill, the Two Ronnies, Peter Cook and Dudley Moore, Tommy Cooper and so many more. I'm always ready to burst out laughing at anything that strikes me as reminiscent of those skits I watched for hours.

The comedy of these two operas gave me a clear and joyous path to follow, helping me to guide my forces like some kind of Pied Piper. As I write these words, I am in the middle of a run of performances of Mozart's *The Marriage of Figaro* at the Royal Opera House, Covent Garden. That this piece is life-enhancing has been commented on endlessly, but let me tell you that returning to it, rehearsing it, putting the nuts and bolts together, mining the comedy with a wonderful director, in this case David McVicar, getting the timing right and all the while howling with laughter for much of the day, is an experience I wish everyone could have. Laughter is such important medicine for us musicians. In much of the classical music repertoire, and certainly in the realm of opera, tragedy abounds. I constantly remind myself that I mustn't get stuck in the often predictable morass of tortured emotions. There must be light with the dark. Conduct more comedies, you idiot!

As music director in Oslo, my first new production was Verdi's *Un ballo in maschera*, an opera that was to become very important for me, as its chiaroscuro – its combination of light and shade – appealed to me so strongly. It is influenced by Verdi's time in Paris, where just a few years earlier he had presented *Les Vêpres siciliennes*. There is abundant foreshadowing of his much later comic opera *Falstaff* in *Ballo*; it sparkles and has many frothy moments, even a can-can in Act I, yet it contains some of Verdi's most menacing and foreboding music.

The opening of the Ulrica scene in Act I, where Verdi employs the open low C string on the cello and the deep rasp of the clarinet together in tritone makes one's skin crawl. The softest tremor grows into a roar of demonic energy. An extraordinary freely shaped love duet between King Gustavus and Amelia in the second act has a spontaneous freedom that is remarkable, even for a giant such as Verdi, growing more and more feverish, becoming almost Wagnerian in its sweep and passion as Amelia finally gives in to the ardent pleas of the tenor.

All my knowledge of this opera's inner workings gained from playing the piece for my father over and over helped me in this new situation to give the singers confidence in what I was asking them to do. They felt I knew instinctively how the piece went. (Instinct is an important factor, but no replacement for repetition and experience.) Singers can be suspicious, especially if their roles are difficult, and Verdi roles are famously difficult to sing. They must feel supported but also encouraged, so they can negotiate the many frightening technical challenges and give of their best.

This brings me to the idea of a 'singer's conductor'. It's a phrase that makes me tetchy, the implication being that this type of conductor is ready to serve the whims of each singer, without having an eye or ear on the greater whole. The cliché paints a picture of the conductor totally at one with outrageously held high notes, loud, louder and loudest singing, monstrous ornamentation – in other words kowtowing to the diva of the day. I have very clear opinions on this subject: while I've known that it was often meant as a compliment, I have sometimes bristled when being assigned that moniker.

The vocal mechanics and traditions established by the great singing pedagogues of the bel canto school and their pupils took the physical apparatus (the throat, the vocal cords, the diaphragm, the whole skull) into consideration when guiding voices to produce not only the purest sounds but also, importantly, the most resonant. Resonance and focus will propel the voice over the orchestra and into the auditorium. These vocal techniques not only informed the way vocal music was written but were also a parameter for the tempos that would show the voice to best advantage. I count myself very fortunate to have been around singers for so much of my life because, over years, I have developed a sixth sense about the voice and how crucial the right tempo is for the successful rendition of any given piece. I'm not saying that there is only one right tempo for each aria. Each voice is different: larger, smaller, more agile, less so. The key is sensibility to the voice and singer with whom you are collaborating. Recognising the idiosyncrasies of each voice (all good opera conductors are able to do this) helps guide the conductor to choose the right tempo framework for that singer. The rub is that, in some corners, this is seen as compromising the conductor's sacrosanct individual artistic vision. This ivory tower approach is certainly not for me. I firmly believe that an individual artistic vision, however apparently ironclad, can be enhanced by the new possibilities of one's collaborators.

All the operas I was to conduct in Oslo were debuts for me. The amount of time to prepare became shorter as my workload became denser. This period of seemingly endless debuts is the most difficult in any young conductor's life. You want and need to learn the repertoire, but can you digest it all? Can you learn it in time? Remember that, more often than not, you are facing an orchestra that knows the material far better than you do. No faking allowed. I remember the intense pressure of those days, sometimes only just managing to keep my head above water.

I was particularly challenged by Puccini's *Tosca*. Learning how the orchestration worked and figuring out what beat patterns to use cost me an awful lot of angst. The piece has bigger bones than *La bohème*, feeling more unwieldy in places, especially the parts that are slow but that need a convincing forward tread. It's very easy to write about it, but the difficulties in practice for a novice are very real and very scary. One is dealing with bigger voices, bigger musical gestures and, in this case, pure, unadulterated melodrama that has to keep an audience on the edge of their seats with its fever pitch.

I did finally manage, through endless trial and error, to come to grips with the piece and enjoyed an exciting run of performances, relishing its hot-bloodedness, its violence and its sensuality. The three protagonists of this opera are iconic roles, each given ample opportunity musically, vocally and theatrically to drive audiences into a frenzy. It is all there for the picking. The all-important orchestral contribution is much more symphonic than in *La bohème*, more filmic, driving the lurid plot and conjuring a tonal picture of the Eternal City, Rome, and its awesome majesty, State politics and the Church, and the blood lust engendered by a love triangle fated to spell doom for its participants.

These performances in 1989 were significant because they prepared me for an important opportunity at the end of the run to work with Plácido Domingo for the first time. He came to do a single gala performance that had been sold out for months in advance. There was no orchestra rehearsal, but he did arrive to do a staging rehearsal with piano the day before the show. Truth be told, I could not be available for it because I had been engaged to conduct a concert somewhere else. Not my finest hour perhaps. On the day of the performance, I went to see him in his dressing room thirty minutes before curtain up. He was in his full make-up and Cavaradossi costume, looking stupendous. He sat down at the piano and said, 'Maestro, maestro, hello, hello – I need five things.' So, while sitting at the piano and playing, he illustrated the five passages with his specific needs. And, standing beside him, I sang his music! He had sung the part certainly over a hundred times before, so he knew how it needed to work for him. By singing his part, I took in the details: a pause, a cue, an entry, a timing, a tempo.

As for the performance – I'll never forget conducting it. When Domingo began to sing his Act I aria from *Tosca*, 'Recondita armonia', I thought 'My goodness, it's like conducting him in a recording studio. He really does sound like this!' I was transported just by the sound and the charisma of his voice and the magnetism of his personality. I was young and inexperienced at the time, but since then I have never lost the awareness of that quality and how rare it is.

In 1990, I accepted the offer of the music director post, but just before beginning my tenure I had a transformational experience conducting Massenet's *Werther* in Vancouver. I was working with the stage director Keith Warner for the first time, the start of a wonderful ongoing relationship, and the music of Massenet bowled me over. Since then, *Werther* has become an important work in my life: I have recorded the opera twice and I have conducted it in four separate runs at the Royal Opera House. Once again, there exists that combination of light and dark to which I am always strongly attracted. A respite of lightness and comedy against darkness and tragedy is of course a Shakespearean idea – that the greatest tragedy be preceded by something contrasting, even levity, so that the hand of calamity is all the more destructive.

I was so taken with Keith Warner (his reading of the text and the intensity of his passion for the characters were somehow new to me) that I invited him to come to Norway in 1992 to direct Janáček's *The Makropulos Case*, a production that was a kaleidoscope of colour, neurotic strangeness and, ultimately, pathos – like the piece itself. It was one of three completely new kinds of explorations for me in Oslo. The other two were Janáček's earlier opus *Jenůfa*, which was the first of this composer's works I discovered, and, very soon after I had begun as music director, a world premiere: *Macbeth*, composed by Antonio Bibalo, an Italian living in Norway, with Shakespeare's original text in English. Lady Macbeth was sung by a phenomenal mezzo-soprano with whom I had worked in Bayreuth, Anne Gjevang, and the role of Macbeth was sung by the tenor Louis Gentile. This opera marked the first of what were to be several collaborations with the stage director Willy Decker.

Verdi's *Rigoletto* came up in a new production, and though I knew it well from the piano and had studied the score thoroughly, having the proper rehearsal time to get to the heart of it and discover what a perfect piece of musical theatre it is, I became aware how fundamental a role structure plays in the telling of the story. Not only musical structure but also dramaturgical structure. The controlled release of information and the inexorable drive towards a high point, whether in drama or comedy (this opera has both), create a sense of palpable expectation in the spectator, and all the while Verdi ingeniously manages to produce a string of hit tunes that become ear worms sung by all who hear them.

Strangely, though I went on to conduct some concert performances of *Rigoletto*, until very recently I hadn't conducted this work again, leaving a twenty-nine-year gap! There is nothing that can top this opera, and yet it has constantly evaded me.

Although I had already worked with important directors as a répétiteur and musical assistant, now as the conductor I was discovering for myself how transcendent opera could become by building a vision jointly with someone who had a clear take not only on the staging, but also on the music. My experience of Janáček had been minimal, and *The Makropulos Case* especially presented a style of music that I had not remotely encountered before. It is such a bizarre piece, with a musical environment that is elusive and difficult to evoke, both for the orchestra and the conductor. I had never come across anything as problematic for the players, particularly the string parts, which are high and technically awkward, but which must somehow sound natural. Just being able to get it together is a feat in itself. Once past this excruciating stage, I started to realise how alluring this music could be, and eventually I couldn't get enough of it. As with *La bohème* and *Jenůfa*, I rode the waves by throwing myself into the story, and then little by little I began to understand how Janáček's music, with all its repetitive phrases, works like a hypnotic drug. There is something primeval that governs the entire atmosphere, and yet the music can also be tumultuously romantic. A motoric tug that gives the overall pulse to the drama, like a dance, must be followed carefully. I remember fondly Warner's startling and entertaining production and the fearless performances of Anne Bolstad as Emilia Marty, and also Solveig Kringelborn in the title role of Jenůfa. How strange that I never conducted another Janáček title.

It was in September 1990, in the very month that I had begun my mandate as music director in Oslo, that my manager, Peter Wiggins, who represented me for almost three decades, arranged a dinner with two people who were keen to meet up with me after a performance of the first opera of the season, *Un ballo in maschera*. Bernard Foccroulle, the then new intendant (general manager) of Théâtre Royal de la Monnaie in Brussels, and his casting director, Bernd Loebe, started to talk to me over dinner in what I thought were surprisingly encouraging terms about a potential music directorship at La Monnaie. I couldn't believe it – La Monnaie, one of Europe's foremost opera houses with a reputation for innovative work, particularly with regard to productions. 'This isn't for real,' I said to myself when I got home afterwards. Remember, I had only just started at Oslo. Peter Wiggins, who had been introduced to me by William Mason from my time in Chicago, was very canny in the way he searched out potential music directorships. My whole career trajectory was guided by his intuition.

The overtures from La Monnaie were being made so soon after I had begun in Oslo that, although I was excited at the prospect, the possibility of accepting felt a long way off: I had a three-year contract with Den Norske Opera. But things took a turn and I was able to go to Brussels earlier, after only two years. The intendant who had engaged me for Oslo, Bjørn Simensen, had left the company for a big job running a newspaper just before I started, and I found out months later that I was not his successor's man. By my second year, the new intendant, Sven Olof Eliasson (a former singer), was programming ambitious new productions, among them the *Ring* cycle, with another conductor whom he knew much better – and that person had been my predecessor! This was all arranged without my knowledge and when I got wind of it, I furiously decided to quit. I cut my contract by one year and I was available to start in Brussels in 1992.

I must emphasise that this was very painful for me. I loved working at Den Norske Opera. I loved the orchestra, the chorus, the place, the air, my apartment overlooking the fjords in the distance, even the food, and certainly the beer after performances. Because I had been conducting concerts in the provinces and developing a strong relationship with the opera company in the three years when I was regularly guest conducting before I took on the job as music director, I felt at home in Scandinavia. In my two years in the post, I had developed a strong rapport with the company. I was not yet a good conductor by any stretch of the imagination, but I was learning how to build productions from the ground up. So, although Brussels was a vital career move, an opportunity I had to take, leaving Oslo a year earlier than originally planned was extremely unfortunate. The music business, especially in the theatre, can be very Machiavellian. I certainly learned a big lesson.

The Belgian theatre previously run by Gerard Mortier was not known for its presentations of the traditional Italian opera repertoire. Rather, there was a strong leaning towards the operas of Mozart, but not only the familiar ones, as well as baroque opera, French opera, twentieth-century repertoire and new works. This is not to say that Verdi was not performed, but the bel canto repertoire, Puccini and the other *verismo* composers had been practically non-existent in previous seasons. That Foccroulle and Loebe were considering me to take over seemed at the time a signal that the Italian repertoire needed to be moved up to the front of the queue. La Monnaie was celebrated for its bold presentation and its focus on inventive but extremely beautiful productions, creating events that had their own individual aesthetic identities. That I could bring a strong hand in the Italian repertoire was of great importance for them.

On a happy note, from time to time my parents managed to come and see me perform in Europe. A visit to Oslo was particularly special as they were in great form at the time and I was performing Puccini's *La bohème*, which was of course a family favourite. My own visits to the States unfortunately became less and less frequent, and although I telephoned very often from abroad (astronomical telephone bills), the close family bond inevitably took on a different aspect. Over the many years, I never managed to change this, to find enough time to visit the family. This is an enormous source of guilt.

5

LA MONNAIE, AND SOME
CAUTIONARY TALES OF TRAVEL

I had no idea at the time what kind of city Brussels was. Being the seat of the European Commission definitely gave it a certain gravitas, and the whiff of officialdom was in the air. Before taking on the job, my short visits were taken up primarily with planning, so I got acquainted with the theatre and the offices of various people that I needed to meet. A lot of stairs. The theatre's offices were situated on the upper floors and were quite crowded; they resembled a beehive. Everyone seemed extremely busy and quite stressed, a familiar theme in this world.

Brussels is a bilingual city where both French and Dutch (Flemish) are spoken. Bernard Foccroulle is Francophone, but the bulk of his staff were Dutch-speaking. What surprised me was how easily they went from one language to another. They all spoke beautiful English too, and most were fluent in German. I didn't know at the time that Belgium has a substantial German minority and that German is one of the official languages. A stimulating environment by any measure, but I found it diffi- cult to pin down the identity of the city. The languages you hear spoken are pulling you south and then pulling you north, but I went with the flow and, anyway, my head was spinning with the quality of the restaurants to which I was being introduced. Matters culinary are a very important part of life in this corner of the world and my collaborators were making sure I became hopelessly seduced. I have so many lovely memories, and my waistline became the proof of my discoveries.

My meetings with Bernard Foccroulle and Bernd Loebe were fascinating. There wasn't a detail of an upcoming production that wasn't forensically analysed: the combination of voices, the aesthetic environment, the sequence and the fit of the season's layout. Though I obviously had quite a bit to say about the music and the voices, Loebe was already way ahead in having his own clear suggestions and the reasons behind his choices, so discussion was lively but always constructive. Foccroulle had an intellectual grasp of all the elements and a vision of how these elements could coalesce to make a convincing evening of musical theatre. I realised quite quickly, thank goodness, that sometimes it was better to shut up and just listen to these brilliant people. Everything they said entered into my brain, giving me much food for thought for when I was 'in the trenches' – the rehearsal room or the theatre itself.

In casting, special attention was paid to what the essence of each singer's presence was. Was the quality emanating from them the right one for the given role? It went far beyond the vocalism and the general appearance of an artist, and it had nothing to do with whether the person was a star or not. What made it all the more interesting was the fact that both my colleagues had an amazing knack for divining potential in someone, even if their career was only just getting off the ground. Neither of them was born into the world of opera. Bernard was and is a fine organist and composer, and Bernd was a journalist and critic. How different the three of us were, but that was our strength.

Everything was so carefully curated that I felt all grown up in this setting, being shown an enormous amount of trust. The choice of stage director was mainly Bernard's domain and the decision was typically deeply considered and researched so that when discussions began with a stage director, they were not given carte blanche but were met with challenging questions. In the end it was all in the details.

I was most fortunate to find an apartment just above the Sablon on rue aux Laines. Quite smart actually. My newly bought second-hand grand piano fitted nicely and there was a lot of light. A progression of three good-sized rooms gave on to a tiny little cocoon of a bedroom at the back of the flat. The birdsong was deafening in the mornings but I'm a big fan to this day. Birds are the world's most natural musicians. I was able to walk to work, enabling me to move my legs and not just my arms, and I grew to understand how important it was to register my surroundings. I wasn't transient any more; I lived here.

The best decision I made concerning Brussels was asking the American pianist Pamela Bullock to be the head of the music staff at La Monnaie. We had previously met in New York when I was a pianist at the New York City Opera in the early 1980s. We later became colleagues and very close friends, working together periodically in Chicago at the Lyric Opera. The music director depends a great deal on their staff, not only on their pianism, but on their people abilities also. This last quality can make or break a rehearsal period. Pamela plays the piano wonderfully, knows the ins and outs of most of the operatic and lieder repertoire, and knows how to get the best out of people, offering support and encouragement. In those days she was even willing to bang out notes for singers who hadn't learned their roles properly. She was such a positive force and lovely to be with. I can't begin to describe the joy I experienced when she was playing works, such as Wagner's *Tristan und Isolde* or

Die Meistersinger von Nürnberg, that I was conducting for the first time. She was rhythmically so solid but knew intrinsically the correct ebb and flow of the music, and yet she was always with me, even when I would occasionally go into the deep end musically speaking. She definitely made me look a lot better than I actually was.

Pamela had enormous operatic experience, having started by working in the American provinces in places where time was very short but expert conductors such as Anton Coppola and Anton Guadagno would miraculously whip everything into shape in just a few days. The level of singer was usually high as these companies often managed to get older stars who were starting to slow down but could still do the job. Pam met and worked with many of them – importantly, she heard the right sounds. These were real voices. When she went on to the Lyric Opera of Chicago, and in 1990 to the Bavarian State Opera in Munich, she knew exactly what she was doing and what was going on. A perfectly built career. Take heed, young répétiteurs and fledgling conductors.

I made my debut in Brussels with Richard Strauss's *Salome*, the opera based on Oscar Wilde's play of the same name, interestingly enough written originally in French, which gave it a particularly seductive yet poisonous flavour. Pamela and I were sent to Salzburg where Luc Bondy's iconic production was being premiered by other forces before coming to Brussels. It was what we call a co-production, a fact of life in today's opera world, which allows companies to share the product and the cost. Opera is enormously expensive as it involves so many creative teams, even before the chorus and orchestra are included. Co-producing is a way to minimise costs, but of course the sharing parties (there can be several) must decide who gets to inaugurate the new production. Usually, the house that conceives the project gets the first go, meaning also that the problems of something new (and there are always problems) will have to be worked out and resolved during this first run. The inheriting houses will be saved multiple challenges as, by the time they put on the show, most if not all of the technical issues will have been worked out, and they can collaborate with the stage director (if willing) to develop the show further. A marvellous opportunity for any stage director to refine his work, and very lucrative.

Hearing the Vienna Philharmonic conducted by Christoph von Dohnányi blew my mind. The sheer opulence of the sound and the maestro's keen ear for detail and balance shook me a bit. Though I had played *Salome* at the Liceu as a rehearsal pianist, now I was expected to transfer my knowledge to what is an essentially symphonic piece of music theatre. The orchestra as protagonist. As I have always done, I immersed myself in study, gradually coming to terms with the seemingly endless complexity. However, it slowly dawned on me that this kind of piece becomes less complicated when you understand how to organise your study. By that I mean with a score such as *Salome* you must be aware of the orchestral groupings; the musicians are often doubling each other, playing the same notes to create texture. This takes up space on the page, giving the impression of complexity, where there is actually none. While following the all-important harmonic journey, you learn to distinguish what is fundamental to the harmony and what is window-dressing. And with Strauss there is an enormous amount of window-dressing.

His supreme gift as an orchestrator took him on unbelievable flights of fancy, showing off the kaleidoscopic possibilities of the

69

orchestra to illustrate the details of the libretto, creating breath-taking sonic pictures. By grasping these elements and digesting the compositional process, you learn to master the material. So much of Strauss's writing (as he himself suggested) must be rendered with the lightest of touches; the feeling should be that it is all totally natural. No sweating allowed. You can begin to consider achieving this only after many tortuous hours alone with the score.

In Salzburg I watched the rehearsals carefully, so that I would be well prepared for Brussels. I heard Bryn Terfel for the first time. He was singing John the Baptist (Jokanaan) and his presence on stage was a wonder to behold. The voice was sent down from heaven: rich, expressive, big. He certainly had competition with Catherine Malfitano as Salome and Kenneth Riegel as Herod. Both were stage animals who used their voices as the ultimate communication medium. The electricity was frightening with these three on stage. Bondy's production was a huge success. He, together with his designers, created a highly sophisticated world, coolly capturing the excess of Herod's court, guiding the singers subtly as he turned the screw and ratcheted up the tension to an unbearable degree.

I was fortunate enough to have Catherine Malfitano for the Brussels revival, and I couldn't wait to get stuck in. I remember how fascinating the orchestra rehearsals were, as I revelled in the descriptive writing. I could do it! I created a bit of tension with the orchestra almost immediately by asking them to sit in a formation they were not used to. I prefer to have the woodwinds in front of me rather than on the left side, which is the traditional German system. I felt I could breathe with the players better with the winds closer to me and the strings could achieve much better ensemble. It was a battle for a while, but I prevailed. The Jokanaan this time was none other than José van Dam, the most important Belgian singer in the world. Quite a bit older than Bryn, he brought an astonishing sense of line, fluidity and sheer vocal beauty to the role. He had sung and recorded the role with Herbert von Karajan, and now he had me in front of him ... He was delightful and wonderfully encouraging, and though I thought I knew something about singing, I realised when listening to him I had a lot to learn. There was a serenity in his singing that was unique. Nothing fazed him, he just brought me along with him on this magical vocal carpet ride. We weren't floating, however; he had all the required authority to convey the rock-solid faith of John the Baptist in the hugely confrontational duet with Malfitano's feline Salome near the beginning of the opera.

It's a big understatement to say that the orchestra can be quite loud in this work. The onus on the conductor to make the singers audible for at least most of the piece is no walk in the park. You must be creative with the score, delay *crescendos*, speed up *diminuendos*, sometimes even change *fortes* to *pianos*, without killing the frenzy that is part and parcel of the piece. It must shock. I sweated and sweated (sorry, Richard) to achieve this with a very large orchestra in a relatively small theatre. We were packed like sardines in the pit and the delirium of the performances was something completely new to me. A powerful narcotic.

In this first season, I happily returned to Verdi's *Un ballo in maschera*, this time in a new production staged by Guy Joosten, at the time an up-and-coming Belgian director, and towards the end of the season I made another debut with Wagner's *Die Meistersinger* in an existing production by Kurt Horres. This last entry into yet another contrasting musical environment affected me deeply, and I have returned to the piece often over the years. It is a piece essentially about music, how it works mechanically, its traditions, the whole art of composition through the ages. Through the character of Walther, a young knight, Wagner reveals to us the new, the yet to be discovered. It is a comedy where music of Bachian rigour sits next to music that seems to fly, replete with modern psychological complexity. Wagner is debating his own place in the musical pantheon, where novelty will at first be met with suspicion and scorn. This was his life for many years. Along the way he draws inimitable and unforgettable characterisations.

My fondest memory of this time was observing the stage relationship between José van Dam as the open-minded Hans Sachs, the cobbler and poet, and Dale Duesing as Beckmesser, the frustrated and irritating town clerk. Let me first say that I never got over being a part of Sachs's monologues as sung by José. The hypnotically mellifluous sound of his voice, the bitterness of his reactions to others' folly, the light-heartedness of much of the role, all these elements came together in a characterisation that was totally honest, open and generous. Dale provided much of the comedy, but though the role of Beckmesser is inherently unsympathetic, he somehow managed to inspire affection for the character. His manic movements and virtuosic delivery of the text created the perfect foil for José. They were so completely different in their stage energy that the contrast was very humorous and often very moving.

In Acts II and III of this opera, the conductor must deal with huge choral forces and, especially in Act II, music of enormous complexity. I've always felt at home with choruses; somehow just the idea of a chorus brings me joy. In this production they were running around the stage and sometimes quite far away from me, obliging me to reconcile precision with theatricality. This part of my work never becomes easier; each show offers new challenges. What one can do is to be very vocal in the early rehearsals about how the possible chorus positioning could affect the delivery of the music for good or ill. At the same time, one mustn't be afraid to experiment; they are called rehearsals for a reason.

Starting in 1992 and continuing for ten years, I came face to face with many new operas and I met scores of talented people – soloists, orchestra musicians, chorus members, music or stage staff and front-of-house staff. This is perhaps the greatest gift that a conductor can experience, the opportunity to make music and theatre with hundreds of people on a given project. What a beautiful metaphor for community, for family.

It is only now that I realise just how important several of the productions I conducted were, and how I was formed by them. Among them was Debussy's *Pelléas et Mélisande*, directed and designed by Herbert Wernicke, a dizzying world of strangeness, mystery, beauty and violence. This opera I came to kicking and screaming; Bernard had to talk me into it. I had imagined that it was boring and intellectual. How wrong could I have been? I fell madly in love with it, nothing else coming close, or at least that's the way I felt at the time. To this day I haven't been able to return to it. It is a notoriously difficult sell at the box office. *Pelléas et Mélisande* did though come up at the ROH in 2007, brilliantly conducted by Sir Simon Rattle. Its symphonic undertow and the natural speech patterns of the singers on top is like nothing else. One day . . .

Puccini's *Il trittico*, made up of three one-act operas, is also something that seldom comes up, as it is hugely expensive to stage, cast and direct. I was fortunate to work with the

Norwegian director Stein Winge. I don't believe at all that the pieces are interconnected as some commentators would argue, so capturing the essence, the individuality, of each one can be an elusive business. Stein had an unerring instinct for what was right and wasn't afraid to wear his heart on his sleeve. José van Dam, very funny in the role of Gianni Schicchi, and Sonia Theodoridou as a heart-breaking Suor Angelica made the experience unforgettable.

Also directed by Stein Winge was *Lady Macbeth of Mtsensk* by Shostakovich, a piece that mixes tragedy with hilarity, burlesque with murder, brass bands along with the most moving slow music. Nadine Secunde in the title role was ferocious in her intensity. I remember that conducting this piece could be extremely demanding physically; certain passages made me feel as if I was going to have a heart attack any moment.

Dealing with an enormous outlay of energy and developing the knowledge of when to hold back is something that I struggled with for many years. Energy is a very good thing of course, it lifts everyone and everything, but the control of this important ingredient, trusting those in front of you to understand what needs to happen at any given moment rather than showing them every last detail, is crucial. To this day I have constantly to remind myself of this, on occasion talking myself away from the edge of the precipice. Writing about this inevitably conjures up memories of my parents constantly overdoing things.

My relationship with Willy Decker deepened as he came to direct Verdi's *Otello* and *Falstaff* and Britten's *Peter Grimes*. Willy was obsessed by the idea that Otello must renounce his Christianity as he falls ever deeper into his paranoia. He must hurtle back to his Muslim roots, shaking off all the trappings of Venetian society. This isolation made for very disturbing and powerful theatre. The cast was terrific: Vladimir Galouzine in the title role, Tom Fox as a subtle Iago, and Susan Chilcott as a radiant Desdemona. This opera always brings me back to my father. It was his greatest ambition to sing Otello, and though we went through it many times in the studio at home, he never got to do it on stage. Working with him I learned just how much of a challenge a role can be. The weight of the emotions can weigh down the voice, and though that extra depth can be a plus, it means the journey to the very difficult high notes is that much more treacherous. Willy's argument becomes very strong when you listen to Otello's Act III aria 'Dio mi potevi scagliar' and realise that, in the accompaniment, the four-note melismas that drone on obsessively and almost hypnotise the protagonist are Middle Eastern, not Italian, or Western. He was right. Observations of that kind are revelations.

Willy's production of *Falstaff* was totally different; set in a train-station café, with a very dirty Falstaff, a *clochard*, presiding over everything. José van Dam as Falstaff was surprisingly sleazy and rough, while Susan Chilcott sparkled as Alice Ford. These two late operas are Verdi at his most sophisticated. I don't pretend to have gleaned everything from these first attempts, but one has to start somewhere. I have come back to both pieces over the years, especially *Otello*. They are at the summit of the operatic firmament and for a conductor everything is there. This is what makes them so challenging and so constantly alluring.

In show business, timing is that special ingredient that every performer must know how to use. I'm not talking about rhythm or tempo here, but the knowledge of when exactly to drop the punch line, or to land the chord, or to dose out the naturally accumulating tension. Any actor, comedian or musician is playing with this all the time. To some it comes naturally; for others it is learned. These two Verdi operas are dramatically very lean; Verdi left no fat, no padding. Leading them requires an ability to achieve what needs to be achieved in a remarkably tight time frame, where luxuriating is totally misplaced. *Otello* has a ferocious inner drive. The arc of this work feels most definitely as if it is to be expressed in one long breath. *Falstaff* celebrates rhythm in all its life-enhancing wonders, much like *Die Meistersinger*, using the Italian language courtesy of the genius librettist Arrigo Boito as a springboard for all kinds of musical hops, skips and jumps. There is precious little lyricism in the piece (which means it is not an audience favourite), but when it does occur, it bathes you in its warmth and humanity.

The *Peter Grimes* production was a towering achievement for Willy. With a superb and atmospheric set designed by John Macfarlane raking up towards the back of the stage, and a beautifully painted backdrop that reminded me of Ponnelle's Bayreuth *Tristan*, the staging was from the first scene dangerous, provocative and inviting. The image of Grimes carrying the coffin of his young charge in the opening courtroom scene still haunts me. The detail of the work with the chorus – so difficult to achieve – was sublime. Despite everything being impressively technically accomplished, the show had genuine grit and weight. William Cochran was in every way larger than life in the title role. He was frightening, appearing in the tavern floodlit from behind, making his entrance in shadow so menacing. The effect took your breath away. His final mad scene was incredibly individual, though he was note and pitch perfect. Without overly twisting the music like a pretzel (a temptation in this scene), he managed to risk everything to share with the audience the devastation of his character's breakdown. The extremes of loud and soft (the secret here), were phenomenal.

Susan Chilcott was Ellen Orford. An amazingly disciplined performance; her singing was ravishing and yet it had backbone, never becoming maudlin or sentimental. This part was made for her. I had never heard music like this before, so clever, so theatrically unerring yet lyrical; and, like Verdi before him, Britten drives without mercy to the finish. The cruelty of village society as portrayed by the chorus was truly disturbing – almost demonic. I was so thunderstruck by this production and Willy's passionate way of working that I brought the show to Covent Garden years later.

Verdi's *Aida* is famously tricky to stage. It demands not only the best singers – dramatic voices with the capability for exquisite refinement – but also requires a directorial vision that must go beyond the public's collective memory of the iconic MGM depiction of ancient Egypt. Much of the atmosphere of this opera, the air it breathes, is startlingly ethereal. It seems to float, as if in a dream, and in fact the piece has often been staged as an extended dream sequence. In contrast it has scenes of implacable martial power, making the juxtaposition of intimacy and grandeur truly theatrical. I knew in my heart of hearts that Robert Wilson would be the right man to take this on. The minimalistic and quasi-ritualistic body language he demands from the singers is in itself a harking back to an imagined ancient time. I will be the first to say that the singers were not overjoyed to be hemmed in like this, especially as the roles are vocally so strenuous, but the way Bob lights a show that embraces the singers, bathes them in glowing and arresting colour is unique. However, we had to wait until we got to the main stage to be able to realise what his true intentions were. You cannot create lighting effects in the rehearsal studio, and this uncertainty understandably caused some impatience in the cast. The shimmering blues, the desert yellows and the stark whites definitely captured for me a world so far away. Johan Botha sang the role of Radames beautifully despite his irritation with the production, and Norma Fantini was a sympathetic and passionate Aida. I remember clearly that Bob wasn't happy with the Triumphal Scene in Act II. He hadn't created enough space to allow the scene to look truly majestic. The chorus looked bunched up and cramped, and he had no way of changing the design so late on. Nor did we have the money! We later brought this production to London, and though I was totally convinced, the press and much of the public were not. Boos notwithstanding, I was very proud of the production because I believe it reflected the music to perfection.

Susan Chilcott was a fixture at La Monnaie. Aside from the pieces I've already mentioned, she played and sang the feistiest Composer in Richard Strauss's *Ariadne auf Naxos*. Impatient, passionate, young! Her voice soared in the high-lying passages. Interestingly enough, this part was originally conceived for a soprano, but has now largely become the jealously guarded property of high mezzo-sopranos. She also sang the role of the Governess in Britten's *The Turn of the Screw*. Based on a novella by Henry James, this opera is perhaps one of the strangest in the repertoire. The atmosphere is somehow poisonous, and working day after day on bringing it to life put us all in very bad humour. Susan, though not immune to this (and she was pregnant), was able to transcend the uncomfortable subject matter and revel in its weirdness. There is a CD recording on a small Belgian label that gives an idea of her ability to embody completely this misguided character. Keith Warner's production was brilliant, often leaving details to the spectator's imagination, making the fear and paranoia unbearable. But he also knew that the director has to have a strong point of view about what is actually happening in this puzzling piece; he rightly believed that it can't all be 'mysterious'. He strategically revealed shocking information to keep the audience on the edge of their seats.

Working with just the thirteen orchestra musicians demanded by Britten not only helped me to get to know my players better, but also made me yearn more and more for opportunities to work with smaller ensembles. The chamber music environment stimulated me to listen better, to hear better, and the amount of detail I could achieve was astonishing, each player bringing a soloist's individuality to the score.

I was asked to conduct the world premiere of *Wintermärchen*, an opera by Philippe Boesmans, another fixture at La Monnaie. It was a take on Shakespeare's *The Winter's Tale*. Luc Bondy's production focused on keeping the audience curious and off balance. Archaic and ultra-modern settings intertwined. The music was scintillating and mercurial, jumping stylistically from quasi-Monteverdian allusions to febrile personal modernity. The Belgian rock band Aka Moon, who use complex rhythmic structures in their music, also featured in the mix. Amazing. Susan Chilcott played Hermione to Dale Duesing's Leontes, she aloof and ravishing at first, then loving and sympathetic; he a whirlwind of paranoia and suffering. His was one of the single greatest performances I've witnessed. Susan was taken away from us much too soon. She battled against breast cancer for several years before succumbing at the age of forty. What a loss. A true artist and individual, she was a big part of my musical life. I miss her.

Having had an initial immersion in Wagner's *Tristan und Isolde* in Bayreuth, I was desperate now to lead my own production. Bernard and Bernd were reassuringly on board with the idea and we even had a cast in mind and Bernard, a stage director.

The painter Achim Freyer, like Ponnelle, was a one-man band: sets, costumes, lights and staging. And what a space he created. The stage was steeply raked, leading down to the pit as if we the musicians were both the lower decks of the ship of Act I and the sea combined. The top of the pit was covered with a jalousie, a sheet of angled slats, making us invisible to the public. On both sides of the proscenium, there were glorious paintings evoking the sea and the storm of the stage proceedings. Behind me Freyer built a ramp on which the singers could bring the action into the auditorium, in particular for the tumultuous Act III entrance of King Marke. A sort of shell was created to cover the top half of my body. By the end of Act III, the oxygen levels down in the pit were woefully inadequate. The musicians were surrounded by electric fans to keep some kind of circulation going, but I was also suffering higher up on the rostrum. I remember having to talk to myself to keep calm in the furious fifteen or so minutes before the final *Liebestod*. Soon after this production, I ended up in hospital with stomach ulcers. This music can do it to you: the restlessness and the passion are almost always playing out on the edge of human possibility.

Anne Evans and Ronald Hamilton were superb as the hapless couple. Anne was so warm and fiercely determined, though she did have 'issues' with the puppet-like wigs and make-up that were Freyer's go-to style. Ron was masculine yet expressive in his demeanour and his voice was perfect for this role.

I was probably over-parted, but I felt as though I had just climbed Everest, and I was so proud. This piece would follow me, or I it, for the next twenty years. You are never through with this one.

The list of titles goes on: a wonderful, hard-hitting, Mediterranean *Marriage of Figaro* directed by Christof Loy, and Loy also directing *Der Rosenkavalier* with Felicity Lott singing the Marschallin. I was in safe hands. She was able to conjure surprising vulnerability yet never let you forget the aristocrat that is this character. The role of the Marschallin is quite short, but Felicity made every phrase, every word, memorable. Another piece I haven't visited again, unfortunately for me. Together with the director Klaus Michael Grüber, an extraordinary man with whom I had worked previously in Paris, we made a highly original triple bill staging works by Arnold Schoenberg: *Erwartung, Begleitmusik zu einer Lichtspielscene* ('Accompaniment to a Film Scene') and *Verklärte Nacht*. Anja Silja sang her famous portrayal of the Woman in *Erwartung*, and for *Verklärte Nacht*, staged as a ballet to hypnotic effect, Bernard engaged the dancer and choreographer Anne Teresa De Keersmaeker, the tenacious founder and director of the Rosas dance company.

My final show as music director was Berlioz's *La Damnation de Faust*, which is not an opera at all, but can become a theatrical event nonetheless. I was outrageously lucky once more with the casting of José van Dam as Méphistophélès, Susan Graham as Marguerite and the young Jonas Kaufmann as Faust. Right before the stage premiere in Brussels, we gave a concert performance at the Semperoper in Dresden. Just seconds before his first phrase, José stood up so slowly and diabolically that I was compelled to take a huge intake of breath. He scared the life out of me. I discovered that even the smallest but focused gesture can in itself be what theatre is all about.

One of the great advantages of working at La Monnaie was that I was able to plan and conduct a number of symphonic concerts with the orchestra – it was part of the house mission, and although there were only a few each year, they were important for all of us. On several occasions I had Martha Argerich as piano soloist as she lived in Brussels at the time. I was needing to bridge the gap between the copious amounts of opera and the relatively sparse symphonic activity that I had encountered, so a lot of new repertoire came my way. Study, study, study.

During my ten years at La Monnaie, being in situ for the lion's share of each season, I was still able to accept some outside engagements that were to prove very important. Especially remarkable – and challenging – was the notoriously controversial production of *La traviata* by Klaus Michael Grüber at the Châtelet Theatre in 1993: it was almost entirely staged in a murky darkness, with just a small sphere lit from within that Violetta would gaze into as if in a trance. All the singers were young and not very well known, including Giusy Devinu, who sadly, like her character Violetta, died before her time. The management felt that having a young fresh cast would be attractive to the Parisian audience and perhaps advisable as Grüber needed them to work painstakingly alongside him in great detail to take on his experimental ideas. The stars of the time might not have been so willing.

Grüber was perhaps the most sensitive man I have ever met. I don't mean touchy, just full of feeling and emotion, a wonderfully warm human being; I adored him. Sadly he had alcohol issues, and that, naturally, could affect his work. The pervading gloom of most if not all of the production, even in the two party scenes, was too much for many people. I, on the other hand, was absolutely convinced by it. Curiously, though I tried to conduct the tempi I had grown up with in this piece, my performance came through as very dampened, toned down – dare I say, dull. Gorgeously played by the Philharmonia Orchestra, the music didn't, couldn't, sparkle. I'll never forget getting booed for the first time, and my parents had come over from America to be in the audience that night! When Grüber came out on the stage to take his individual bow the theatre exploded. I've never to this day heard a sound so violently loud in a theatre, so indignant and angry. It prepared me for what can and does happen in an opera house.

Some years later, in 2003, when I brought over La Monnaie's production of *Aida* by Robert Wilson to Covent Garden, it was loudly booed too. Though I wasn't booed myself that night, I was of course shocked by the reaction, though at the same time I have to admit it all felt very exciting: I remember saying to James Naughtie as I came backstage that night, 'The theatre's so alive, isn't it – it's *alive*! Something's happening here!' No one likes getting booed. It leaves the most acrid taste and can seriously rock an artist's confidence for future performances. I say, 'Just don't clap' if you don't like something.

Three years after *La traviata* came another Parisian adventure, again at the Châtelet. Stéphane Lissner, the very successful general manager of the house, obviously trusted me as what he offered was a high-powered new production of Verdi's *Don Carlos* in the original French language version of 1867, which had been rarely performed. When I say high-powered I mean that the cast was of the top international rank: Roberto Alagna, José van Dam, Karita Mattila, Waltraud Meier, Thomas Hampson and Eric Halfvarson, together with the splendidly idiomatic Orchestre de Paris. I prepared for a year and a half, looking at all the different versions, all the scenes that were dropped at the Parisian premiere because of the impossible length of the evening, all the permutations. Verdi was never happy with this opera and kept tinkering with it for years.

Yes, there is an original French-language musical version, but I discovered very quickly that some of the music that Verdi rewrote for the later Italian premiere is far superior, harmonically richer and theatrically more telling. I am not dogmatic about these things and not interested in original versions per se, so I decided therefore to make a hybrid version that comprised the original but with several detours. I believe it made sense and was certainly true to the spirit of the piece. But in this business, any time there is some musicological tinkering, the experts come out in droves to scream bloody murder, and they did! How ridiculous. Opera is not supposed to be a history lesson. There must be room to mould the material, especially when it involves something as problematic as *Don Carlos*. There is no definitive version of this opera. This subject gets my blood boiling . . .

Luc Bondy was once again the director, staging the intimate scenes with great care despite the fact that each one of the singers was a star, each with their own convincing ideas. Putting this all together was far from easy, not helped at first by the fact that there was most definitely a sense of rivalry and competition in the air. When the artists are trying to outdo each other in performance, the intensity can be fantastic, and that's how it was, but in rehearsal this can be tiresome. I must be honest and admit that with hindsight both this job and *La traviata* were perhaps a couple of rungs above my stage of development. In their completely different ways, each one was too highly charged and under the microscope of the opera-going public and press for the amount of experience I'd had at the time. If one looks at the DVD of the *Don Carlos* production or listens to the CD, the performance is really very good indeed, but I know what the struggles were.

In fact, as a cautionary tale, both those experiences in Paris need to be coupled with my debut at the Royal Opera House, Covent Garden, which had actually taken place back in June 1990, just before I took up the post of music director in Oslo. I jumped in at very short notice for *La bohème* to replace Sir John Pritchard, who had recently died. There was a slew of performances – fourteen in all with two different casts – and it was an unmitigated disaster. I knew the piece inside out, but I had seven different tenors in the first seven shows because the tenor who had been engaged for them cancelled after the first night, and it was a revolving door of replacements. The point is that I wasn't experienced enough to handle that kind of situation, reinventing the music from night to night for each individual singer. Although I never saw the reviews, I was told at the time that they were sensationally bad. I felt like a leper walking through the halls of the opera house, as if everyone was avoiding me.

I call this a cautionary tale because it was an intended career leap. When you are young and you have your first music director job, you aren't there for twelve months in the year, so you guest conduct in between, and you hope to guest in places that are more prestigious than your home house. But if you do that too early and too ambitiously you can get into serious trouble. Yes, the situation was unusually fraught on this occasion, but that was no excuse. It was too early for me to be in such an illustrious theatre.

In a way, I had the last laugh as nine years later, in 1999, I was nominated as the next music director at Covent Garden, having never set foot there since that tragic run of *La bohème* performances. Quite a lot of young conductors have had this kind of experience, ambition getting the better of them.

Yet sometimes this kind of situation can work out for the best. While I was guest conducting at the Berlin State Opera in 1993 – *I Capuleti e i Montecchi* by Bellini, a piece I absolutely adore – I was telephoned by Ioan Holender, the intendant of the Vienna State Opera. This was a Wednesday afternoon, and he said, 'I have just spoken with Daniel Barenboim. On Sunday we have the premiere of a new production of Wagner's *Siegfried*. The conductor Christoph von Dohnányi has gone into hospital and is too ill to conduct now, and Barenboim just told me he himself can't step in but that you know the piece better than anybody. I don't want to ask one of the usual suspects – can you take over?' I was almost catatonic at the other end of the phone, and I said, 'Can you call me back in ten minutes?' And for the next ten minutes I just sat there like an idiot, in a stupor. I heard myself saying when the phone rang again, 'Yes.'

That night I went over to Daniel's house, looked at his personal score, and took it with me to use in Vienna. When I arrived in Vienna the next day there was the Vienna Philharmonic Orchestra waiting for me at a closed dress rehearsal, no audience. The tension was palpable. They hadn't played the opera for a long time and unbelievably Dohnányi had never conducted it before, but I felt I knew how he might approach this score. He is quite a cerebral conductor and I thought he would give a fluid and transparent performance, meticulous in detail and driven by the text.

By the end of the first act, however, having taken into account the way I thought it would have been rehearsed up to that point, I realised that what I was trying to do wasn't working at all. I knew the opera very well and had already extensively coached Siegfried Jerusalem, who was singing the title role, in Bayreuth. But I wasn't conducting the score as I knew it, and I felt I couldn't continue. When Mr Holender came to see me in my dressing room after Act I, I said, 'I can't do this. I'm going home. I just can't do it – I shouldn't have taken it on.' He implored me to do the second act and managed to persuade me to stay. About ten pages in, I said to myself, 'This isn't working for me', so I stopped and I worked on a passage. I did that every twenty or so pages, and after I got to the end of Act II, I rehearsed Act III in the same way. When we had finished the rehearsal seven hours later, I turned to the concertmaster and asked him, 'Herr Küchl, tell me what should I do: should I stay or should I go home?'

'Well,' he said, 'who else are we going to find at this short notice?'

I took note of everything I did right and wrong in that rehearsal, and over the next two days I figured out how I was going to make the premiere work. To this very day, I have never been so calm and collected as I was at that first performance of this new production. I went in there and just conducted the hell out of it. Never having conducted a Wagner opera before, never having conducted at the Vienna State Opera before, and having had just one rehearsal. I can honestly say that it was a real triumph – not least taking into account the fairy-tale nature of the whole story.

So does that completely contradict all I was saying before about the danger of doing something too soon? I did have the advantage that I had worked in such depth and detail on the opera in Bayreuth but, even so, it could all have gone spectacularly wrong. Instead, it went spectacularly right – and that transformed my reputation, because the whole matter of my being considered solely an Italian-repertoire specialist went out of the window. I could now be taken seriously in another domain, and that was a tremendous boost – not only for my confidence but also for my development. I haven't done anything like that since – I'm not that stupid. But it did happen at a very important juncture in my growth. Now I must return to counselling caution.

The success with *Siegfried* led to a number of offers from Ioan Holender – a revival of *Manon Lescaut* was already on the books for the following year, but then I was offered in 1998 and 1999 respectively Verdi's *Les Vêpres siciliennes* and an opera that greatly interested me, *Palestrina* by Pfitzner. Both new productions – and a gift to any conductor. As well as my commitments at La Monnaie, I had accepted a lot of engagements conducting the top symphony orchestras in America: Cleveland, Chicago, New York, Boston, Los Angeles. I was performing a lot of music that I had not tackled before, so there was a huge amount of learning I was having to do. The young conductor's plight. I am a fast learner and a strong sight-reader, but I remember hitting the wall in the late 1990s. It all became too much for me, and I started having to cancel engagements.

The feeling is one of overwhelming stress and insecurity. The idea of not being adequately prepared for something was for me the worst kind of nightmare, proof of being an imposter. My stomach was never the strongest and I remember it being in knots constantly during these tumultuous first years of my conducting career. Among the cancellations was this *Vêpres siciliennes*. It was a very important new production by Herbert Wernicke, a great stage director, and to this day I am still mortified that I cancelled, because he wrote me the most heartfelt nine-page letter trying to convince me not to. But I knew I just could not learn the opera well enough in time, and so I thought I was being responsible giving the theatre eight months' cancellation notice. Ioan Holender was very upset and took away *Palestrina* from me as a result – and he was right to do so, as I had shown that I could not be relied on.

Here was another lesson: not to take on too much. You get greedy and you think you can do anything, but you can't. I survived it, but apart from that *Manon Lescaut*, I never returned to the Vienna State Opera except, ironically, to take part in a gala evening that Ioan Holender himself arranged to celebrate his retirement in 2010. He had since forgiven me, and on that night I conducted both Plácido Domingo and Waltraud Meier with no rehearsal whatsoever. It was so much fun. Conductors have to be very careful because the body and the mind can become assaulted with way too much information – and the emotion of it all can land on you like a ton of bricks. The big operas and the big symphonies take a huge toll and that does not include the learning and digesting that is necessary in preparation for the real thing. My advice is not to be in a rush. Savour these first experiences.

A very important and happy development in my personal life at this time was that Pam Bullock and I fell in love, eventually marrying in 1995, both saying 'Oui' in the Town Hall of Auderghem, Belgium, replete with a gendarme wearing a sash and brandishing a sword, and a very fine harpist for the ceremony. The fact that Pam and I entered at the opposite end of the building from where the haughty gendarme was expecting us had our guests in fits of laughter, but on this sunny morning on 27 February, the union was made official. I can report that we're still going strong. This relationship has been what has kept me sane through all the tumult; Pam's intelligence and musicality, charm and infinite patience guiding me every step of the way.

6

A NEW DIRECTION:
THE ROYAL OPERA HOUSE

I could easily have carried on in Brussels for several more years. I had developed a shorthand with the orchestra and chorus, and I knew how the opera house worked. I loved my colleagues and there was so much repertoire still to explore together. However, when I found out that the Royal Opera House had my name on a list of five possible candidates for the music directorship to succeed Bernard Haitink, I was stopped in my tracks. You can't ignore something like that or be aloof from it. Covent Garden, as we call it, is not just another opera house, it is one of the top five in the world. To be in the running for such a prestigious institution certainly woke me up.

Before I knew it, the orchestra committee came to listen to a performance of *Lady Macbeth of Mtsensk*, and I was summoned to a meeting in London with Michael Kaiser, the then chief executive, and Colin Southgate, his chairman of the board. I had known Colin for years as his day job was as president of EMI records, the company with which I had a growing relationship. One friendly face at least. I was all dressed up and very serious, not myself at all, as they interrogated me on why I might want this job, and how my philosophy of music theatre could best be described. Being far, far away from the music felt so alienating and artificial and I'm sure I came out with platitudes that even I wasn't convinced by. I did say, however, that I was a very hard worker and that I loved the sense of potential family in a company, that the size of the opera house itself would be a big change for me, going from an 1,100-seater to 2,200 in London, and that would have on an impact on my repertoire choices.

Without naming names, the rest of the list was made up of the top conductors of my generation, most of whom had more illustrious careers at that point than mine. Somehow, and to this day I still don't know how, I was chosen for the job. This was in 1999, three years before the succession would actually take place. What followed was that my Brussels life went on as usual but now I was inundated with meetings, phone calls, trips to London to see performances, much as had been the case with Brussels, only more of it. I will never forget how gracious, generous and warm the reaction to my new appointment was by the whole staff at La Monnaie. My last concerts and opera performances were the crowning moments of ten of the most important years of my life, and the appreciation I was shown by audiences and colleagues alike I will always carry with me.

During the three years' hiatus between being nominated and taking over, I wasn't scheduled to conduct one note at Covent Garden. Strange, but that was how the calendar had been arranged for a long time before that. In the opera world, artists are often booked three or four years in advance. Completely different from actors, who often don't know until a few months before or even less if a play or a film is going to happen. I was most fortunate as two projects came up that allowed me to get to know the ROH orchestra a bit. The first was a recording with Plácido, together with the soprano Deborah Voigt, of Wagner duets, from Act II of *Tristan und Isolde* and Act III of *Siegfried* to be specific. Big stuff by any measure. We recorded in the splendidly sumptuous acoustic of Watford Town Hall and I was given a chance to get to know the musicians of the

Covent Garden Orchestra. What they brought to this music in knowledge, experience and warmth of tone was invaluable to me.

The record did well and we were asked to make a follow-up of other Wagnerian excerpts, this time exclusively from the *Ring*. Plácido was really enthusiastic to get stuck in, no matter the hurdles; he has always had an insatiable curiosity for new and challenging repertoire. To hear a voice of that quality sing this music is a gift. Sure, perhaps his German pronunciation is not perfection, but who cares, when you hear such ardour, such heroic singing?

The other project was the soundtrack for a film of Puccini's *Tosca* starring Angela Gheorghiu, Roberto Alagna and Ruggero Raimondi. There were a few things that almost scared me off this project. The original idea was that I record the orchestral track without the singing so that the singers could sing 'live' during the filming. The recording sessions would also be filmed (highly unusual), using a special intense white light that would render an atmospheric monochrome that would then be somehow interwoven into the glorious colour world of the film telling the actual story. The heat from those lights was unbearable, the orchestra and I almost passing out in Abbey Road Studio No. 1. Of course, as good Brits, we got on with it, but it was rough. The getting-on-with-it part was very important now that I look back on it all. I could have become very self-conscious about how I was obviously being sized up by my future orchestra, but I didn't. The main thing was to make a good record. There we were on the same wavelength.

The singers decided quite quickly that singing 'live' over and over again while filming different takes was not something they thought they could achieve, so I eventually did record with them in situ. It has happened to me very seldom that I have had to record something for a soloist who would then record their part later in overdub. I hate it with a passion, and I don't think I'm very good at it either. The give and take of collaboration is everything. I say this, but at the first session with Ruggero Raimondi, a veteran of the role of Scarpia and one of the great singing actors, he lost his voice almost immediately. He hadn't sung for a couple of months as he'd been recuperating from a minor operation, but somehow his voice, rather than being rested, just shut down. So, I was forced to record almost his entire role without him there. Luckily, I had sung the role together with my father and innumerable sopranos over the years so I knew how it went. Not that you would have wanted to hear the sounds that emanated from yours truly. I was relieved at how well it worked, but I did hate doing it.

I have conducted *Tosca* quite often over the years, and this film version brought a new dimension. My tempi were relatively more spacious, not slow per se, just more grandiose, more Roman. Completely different from how I conduct the piece in the theatre, where I'm more visceral, more obviously theatrical. One can compare the two DVDs.

Naturally, deciding on the piece with which to inaugurate my tenure kept me up nights. Totally unexpected by almost everyone, I chose Strauss's *Ariadne auf Naxos* in collaboration with director Christof Loy. I've written about how this piece is a chamber opera, using a virtuosic ensemble of musicians, thus giving me the opportunity to get to know my first-chair players really well. The opera addresses so many issues around creativity, composing, putting on a show, improvisation, the myriad obstacles, sponsorship, all clothed in wondrous-seeming chaos. A comedy and a tragedy, together. My own personal tragi-comedy started on day one of rehearsals when, early on that very morning, I had to have an emergency root-canal dental procedure. If you could have seen what I looked like at that first rehearsal . . . Once I was able to get stuck in, I just got on with my job, not thinking for one second where I was and what the stakes were.

This piece speaks directly to someone like me whose preoccupation is getting the show on by hook or by crook. Though this show was a huge success, we had several heart-stopping moments in rehearsal when an important and visible stage lift continually gave up the ghost, costing me precious minutes of rehearsal time. I thought we'd never open. When we did, after my entrance bow, I turned around to the orchestra and my electric-powered music stand popped up by itself to neck level. It was hysterical for sure, and the musicians were in stitches, but I had to figure out in seconds (though it seemed like minutes) how to fix it, which I did. Phew. Opening night! The youth of this piece, conveying the spirit and talent of the young Composer, is like a drug for me and always has been: the backstage goings-on a true picture of my daily life.

I had several dreams I wanted to fulfil, among them debuting Berg's *Wozzeck*. It came second, right after *Ariadne*. This time the director was Keith Warner, with Stefanos Lazaridis as set designer, and Matthias Goerne in the title role. And I was pulled in by *Tristan und Isolde* once more, this time with Christof directing again, and featuring Nina Stemme and Ben Heppner. The list goes on and on.

The job, though, is not just about fulfilling dreams, as wonderful as that is. Every opera house will be compelled to choose a particular work for a variety of reasons. It might be the desire and availability of a big star or combination of stars, the necessity of keeping offering fresh operas to the paying public, the continuous introduction of new names, the work that will entice the star conductor, the line-up of the entire season seen to be offering enough contrast. Where I think we have been particularly successful these past years is in creating events. Choosing operas that draw the big singers, and that therefore draw the public. Titles such as *The Trojans*, *Otello*, *Les Vêpres siciliennes*, *La forza del destino*, *Andrea Chénier*, *The Ring* . . .

During my first couple of years in London, I didn't have a list of tangible changes that I wanted to implement. I felt I was so different from my predecessor that the general atmosphere would be quite different anyway. Naturally, the pieces you choose for yourself ultimately define you, but I don't like to be defined, and perhaps that is why I chose from the German repertoire to begin with at the Royal Opera House. With my Italian name, the expectations were that I would certainly focus on the Italian repertoire, but I didn't, at least not for quite some time. Yes, my other two operas that first season were *Madama Butterfly* and *Falstaff*, but then I concentrated on twentieth-century works (Prokofiev's *The Gambler*, Shostakovich's *Lady Macbeth of Mtsensk*, Berg's *Lulu*, Szymanowski's *Król Roger*), contemporary pieces (Birtwistle's *The Minotaur*, Turnage's *Anna Nicole*) and the German and French repertoire, with just a smattering of Italian operas. I was interested in pieces that were more symphonic, where I could revel in the sensuality of the orchestral writing. That was fine for a while, but one day I said to myself, 'Why are you avoiding the obvious?'

The Italian repertoire constitutes the majority of the works in any given season in any given opera house in the world. I came to the realisation that this music was so in my blood that I needed to take greater care of it, show my love for it more, conduct revivals and not just new productions of these works.

I immediately put into practice a completely different way of choosing titles for myself, now including more revivals and new productions of Italian operas. In our business much of the Italian repertoire is considered a second-class commodity, easily put together and not as important as the 'big' pieces. The revivals of certain of these works don't attract the top singers and especially not the top conductors. My new plan was, besides being a personal homecoming for me, a way to show that the music director was now fully invested in keeping the highest musical standards in these all-important and popular works. *Il barbiere di Siviglia*, *La bohème*, *Tosca*, *La traviata*, *Rigoletto*, *Il trovatore*, *Turandot*, *Lucia di Lammermoor*, and *Madama Butterfly* are the backbone of every theatre's repertoire and deserve the music director's attention. The only one I haven't got to is *Lucia*. My great loss.

I have now whole-heartedly embraced the music of Rossini, Bellini, Ponchielli, Giordano, Mascagni and Leoncavallo, as well as Verdi and Puccini, and I return to their creations often.

This makes me ruminate about how Wagner loved Bellini's music, in particular his way of spinning a haunting melody. We know that Wagner admired the bel canto style of singing that prized purity and beauty of tone, and he wanted his singers to incorporate this style of singing into his own works. Likewise, it makes me think of conducting Giordano's *Andrea Chénier*. I hadn't realised how much *Tristan und Isolde* is in this score. Having conducted both Bellini's *Norma* and Wagner's *Tristan und Isolde* has enhanced my way of approaching not only the connections between these two composers, but also between them and so many others.

Another important realisation on this subject and the concept of influence and inspiration concerns Verdi's musical provenance. I had always thought that Verdi's music was just a natural next step on from Donizetti, his immediate predecessor as the greatest incarnation of Italian operatic creative talent. Though they share many things, primarily an indebtedness to the solidity and energy of Beethoven, it is actually Rossini, the Rossini of *Semiramide* and *William Tell*, the grand operas, that really invented Verdi. The thrusting musical gestures, the potent rhythmic development and the daring dramaturgy appear many years prior to Verdi's heyday. As Verdi himself grew older, he also took greater notice of the developments Wagner was applying to the structures of music theatre and to the enrichment of the harmonic palette. At Verdi's death the score of *Lohengrin* was on the music stand at his house at Sant'Agata. Puccini always had the score of *Tristan* at hand. And all these composers looked back to Mozart and Da Ponte for inspiration in how to create fully fleshed characters. This is why I love the job I do and the way I have been able to structure it. Every day I see connections, influence, inspiration, theft(!), homage, history being made or being rewritten. To conduct Beethoven's *Fidelio* is to open the door to the realisation that myriad other composers were shell-shocked by it, ultimately inspired to fantastic flights of creativity. A continuum.

I have bandied about a lot of operatic titles already, but it is not a given that they can all be done at the highest possible level. I have been beyond lucky to have had an orchestra with which to collaborate that not only understands what opera is or can be, but also has the technical and musical proficiency to meet any stylistic challenge. It has been proved to me repeatedly that this orchestra is ready to reinvent itself with each new musical landscape.

I write a lot about productions because I am immersed in them, but I know that certain members of the public don't understand or don't accept certain conceptual decisions, in particular with regard to the setting of a given piece. Many people are traditionalists, and if it says in the libretto that a scene takes place in a castle or a forest, there must be a castle or a forest depicted on stage. Fair enough. However, stage directors nowadays often tend to conceive productions in spaces that are psychological rather than literal, creating an environment that is full of suggestion, poetry even, but open to interpretation. This can be confusing if the spectator is not willing to make a creative leap together with the director. One has to ask oneself if the historical trappings are decorative or essential. In some pieces the defined sense of place should be respected. I don't think you can take *Tosca* out of Rome, *Turandot* out of China, ancient or otherwise. But do the sparser modern spaces make the relationships clearer? Sometimes I think they do.

This conflict for audiences most often happens when there is updating of the action. Directors are constantly trying to elucidate the similarities between the often archaic worlds depicted in the libretto and today's societal struggles. There are many connections, as humanity is bound to make the same mistakes over and over, but many people need the security of a historical context, otherwise for them the evening is ruined. I am not one of those people, but I can say that a director must deal with the material they have, tell the story clearly, updated or not, and use the music as it was intended, as a conduit of narrative, energy and emotion. While it is true that some directors want to tell a different story, their own story, if it is at the cost of destroying the coherence of the music, and the sense and spirit of the drama as conceived by the composer and his librettist, then I am definitely not on board. I have found that the more musical a director is, the safer the ground you tread on, no matter the aesthetic style.

My main preoccupation has always been and continues to be wanting to see characters communicating. There is nothing more visceral. Are they listening to what the other character is singing about? Are they reacting and being reacted to? The type of interaction with a stage director that inspires this attitude in our singer colleagues is essential to my existence. Though I immensely appreciate visual depictions of beauty and poetry, I am not actually very interested in pretty pictures; for me it is about the people. The opera house cannot just be about pre-serving a given visual and design style that harkens back cen-turies. It must be constantly renewed: established styles should be respected but also challenged.

Admittedly directors have been coerced more and more into thinking differently about matters visual. These days opulent traditional productions are almost impossible to afford given the extreme cost of materials, in particular for the costume changes expected for soloists and chorus alike. Budgets have been slashed year on year and so the thinking veers toward the 'out of the box' variety. Though I don't like the budget slashing, the creativity it has engendered has overall been a good thing for opera. The focus is now squarely on the complete dramatic package.

Because there are so many technical preoccupations for singers when they sing and act a role, helping them consider what exactly it is that they are supposed to be communicating through the words is not as easy as one would think; constant reinforcement, reminding, coaxing are needed to shape a clear and convincing version of what needs to be transmitted, to the other characters and to the audience. Replacing opulence with specificity of expression is for me only a plus, and it has been a characteristic of a whole slew of outstanding singing actors who can hold the stage with their concentration and preparedness, all the while celebrating their vocal talent to the fullest. That's the goal for me.

7

ROH PRODUCTIONS: SOME HIGHLIGHTS

During my time at the Royal Opera House, Covent Garden, I was most fortunate to work with a very broad and diverse array of stage directors, so there has been a wide variety of approaches – some really adventurous and some more traditional. An interesting phenomenon is that directors, together with their designers, often tailor their aesthetic approach depending on which theatre the production is destined for. In countries such as Italy and the UK, audiences tend to be more conservative, in contrast to Germany or Austria, where the director's vision, no matter what, is paramount. I'm not so sure the audiences in Germany and Austria are demanding iconoclasm from the artistic teams, but the music press certainly is, and the theatres seem to go along with it, fulfilling the expectations of the intelligentsia. When the components of conceptual music theatre all add up, enormously compelling work can be achieved, and I am admittedly terribly jealous of the lavish government subsidies these theatres receive. They can risk so much in the name of innovation because they don't have to worry about ticket sales to the same degree as we in the UK most certainly do. My personal problem with conceptual productions is that, aesthetically, beauty and poetry seem to be in such short supply. I hate grunge for its own sake. A cheap way of mirroring today's society? I don't buy it.

When it comes to my collaborators, certain names keep cropping up. Richard Jones, who has a zany aesthetic sensibility, is absolutely precise about timing, marrying movement to the music in often very funny ways, and demanding only essential gestures, economy and potency above all. Keith Warner, who is extremely theatrical and grand in his imagination, is brilliant in guiding singers about the meaning of the words in hellishly complex Wagnerian texts; their understanding of what the phrases mean becomes a fulcrum of their performance. Christof Loy produced a wonderfully sassy and ultimately very moving *Ariadne auf Naxos* – very much in the spirit of Strauss's opera, with opulence and simultaneous elements of pure silliness, surprising us with his heart-melting staging of the duets. His *Tristan und Isolde* divided opinion much more with its conceptualisation of the playing space. However, the performances he drew from his cast and his overall vision were totally committed to the essence of each word and each note Wagner wrote. David McVicar is so versatile, and in the classical style of Handel and Mozart so brilliant in his virtuosity and speed of thought; his *The Marriage of Figaro* is a personal favourite that I keep coming back to, as does he. His handling of the explosive class politics of this score was the key to bringing out the theatrical power of Mozart's and Da Ponte's 'domestic' comedy. Also in the classical mode but far grander was his production of Berlioz's *The Trojans* – a first for both of us, and a piece that haunts me. One more time . . .

Damiano Michieletto, a relatively new name on the horizon, staged Rossini's *Guillaume Tell* soberly but very clearly, using a set that featured a huge felled tree in a mountain setting. Representing what at first seems the crushed Swiss natives, it gave no clue that the tree would dramatically resurrect at the end of the opera when freedom from the cruel Austrian occupation had been achieved.

A detail that somehow got by me and my team was the semi-natural earth that the singers had to perform on. Besides being quite tricky to negotiate, it was acoustically a disaster, rendering the music often dry and muted. I'm still kicking myself on this one.

Michieletto courted controversy in one of the dance scenes, of which there are several (it is a *French* opera). A young maiden is being at first gently pushed from one Austrian soldier to another, the music 'militarily' barrelling along apace until the pushing becomes more and more violent. A rape ensues, made all the more disturbing by the juxtaposition of the very jaunty music. Theatrically, it was a daring and hugely powerful statement, but it was met with disdain and contempt from a vociferous part of the audience and most of the press. It is a shame that one scene negated all the considerable good work, but no one said that the theatre was a place for the meek.

Michieletto very much embraced his Italian heritage in *Cavalleria rusticana* and *Pagliacci*. He is one of the few Italian directors who are conceptual in approach, but I begged him to return to his roots for these pieces as they are *italianissimi*, and that's what he did, cleverly managing to weave the two stories of the operas together, and creating a palpable southern atmosphere, using the expected clichés in a fresh and convincing way, and avoiding empty grandeur.

Christof Loy, a director I greatly admire and had worked with many times at La Monnaie, seemed to me the obvious choice to produce Strauss's *Ariadne auf Naxos*. Christof's knowledge of the music in any opera he directs is prodigious, and like any good director he is preoccupied with what lies underneath the text, delving into the subtext to create a concept for a production. While he is acutely aware of established traditions, he and his teams always manage to come up with a sort of hybrid of the old and the new. (To break with tradition you have to know the tradition.) He loves singers and singing, so he is aware of what the singers need in order to give of their vocal best.

For the Prologue of *Ariadne*, Christof and his set designer Herbert Murauer created a sumptuous setting that brilliantly captured the atmosphere of an 'upstairs/downstairs' for all to see (the servants downstairs, their masters upstairs). The downstairs was a somewhat grotty space with all the confusion of pre-performance – the tenor screaming about his wig, the soprano erupting like a cartoon diva, the soubrette flirting with her players, the composer of the evening's opera in despair with all the last-minute changes, the arrogant Major-Domo making startling changes to the soirée, and a burgeoning love story. Does this sound confusing? It is. The evening is supposed to comprise a 'serious' opera part with characters from Greek mythology, then a lighter comic part with *commedia dell'arte* characters. The Major-Domo announces that at exactly 9 p.m. there will be an unmissable fireworks display for the illustrious guests of his master, therefore the entertainment will need to be shortened, and the tragedy and the comedy will need to be performed together. You can just imagine the chaos.

Of course, chaos onstage requires virtuosic stage direction and a keen eye for detail, making sure everything 'tells'. Christof was definitely in command of all of it. I almost prefer this part of the show to the second part. When it's all on its feet and running, you feel you are part of an amazing improvisation act, yet it's rehearsed to within an inch of its life. The hugely entertaining jumble that is the Prologue is a pretty good picture of the struggle for artists to be taken seriously by the people who are paying them to perform. Artists are not puppets, nor slaves, but they must remain flexible, otherwise they starve.

Christof has a special affinity for directing the women's roles. His sensitivity to every textual or musical twist and turn is awesome. It paid special dividends in the scene in the Prologue between Zerbinetta, the showgirl sung originally by Marlis Petersen, and the young Composer, played in travesty by Sophie Koch. For the first time in his life, this boy becomes aware of sensual feelings and is awakened to what he thinks is love. Even though the showgirl gets around, to put it mildly, she has a heart of gold, and Loy was so subtle and patient with the timing of how they could come physically ever closer – the knowing worldliness of Zerbinetta and the impulsive, restless nature of the Composer, desperate to succeed and yet ripe for learning a life lesson, matching Strauss's music and Hugo von Hofmannsthal's text to perfection – leaving me room to weave the sinuous and intricate melodies and counter-melodies around the two characters, and launch out of this scene into the explosive finale.

In the Opera part – where the entertainment in the posh house takes place and the tragedy and the comedy are simultaneously performed – Christof's work with Petra Lang, debuting in the role of Ariadne, was supremely subtle in the way that he approached the character's sensuality and suffering, the vulnerability of this woman who has been abandoned by Theseus and is later overwhelmed by Bacchus. Through a series of relatively slow-moving arias, Ariadne has to work through her insecurities, a quasi-psychological cleansing, in order to be able to love again. The way Christof brought Petra Lang through that textual and musical minefield was sublime. This psychologically self-indulgent process is set to music that is often profound but becomes very challenging if singer and conductor don't retain a sense of direction through this series of slow tempi. Christof certainly helped guide both of us, giving us specific targets to hit along the way.

Christof set the action of the opera in a space that could almost be a fantasy version of a drawing room, a world dimly lit, very spacious with big doors, and yet somehow retaining its intimacy, thanks to Jennifer Tipton's perfect lighting. It was a very beautiful and vivid psychological space in which Ariadne could suffer. No one had any real need for the rock that she is supposed to be lying on in the libretto. She languishes all the more in this more modern location, but one that is infinitely more poetic. The extreme beauty of the setting was crucial because when the comedians came onto the stage mid-scene with Jeremy White's Truffaldino wearing a biker's leather outfit and Zerbinetta in a tiny mini-skirt, the way this impossibly out-of-place group looked as they barged in after the prima donna had been singing one dirge after another was so ludicrous that it caused a real shock. It was hilarious. The material is all there in Strauss's music and Hofmansthal's libretto, but the way that Loy and Murauer were able to surprise the audience and how Loy staged the comedy players' dance routines and the mini love affair between Harlequin and Zerbinetta was the work of a true master.

———

Richard Jones was the director for the new production of Shostakovich's *Lady Macbeth of Mtsensk* that we first put on in 2004. I had first conducted the opera at La Monnaie in 1999, when the combination of its smouldering, brutal, violent, sexy music, coupled with wildly zany parts where the music parodies a circus, brought a completely new dimension to my idea of theatre. The difficulty of the score and the great challenge it presents for all the performers is a vital part of the theatrical experience. For the conductor the challenges include very tricky ensembles, testing everyone's rhythmic sense; dealing with often huge forces and the logistics that go with that; and the need for a film-score conductor's precision of timing even in the intimate scenes. Precision is a word that I associate with Richard Jones – but I don't mean precision in a cold way. He has the courage to demand that the singers be absolutely precise about their expression. These words – expression, feeling, passion – they are bandied about so much in the music world, but for Richard it isn't enough to do something with passion and great feeling alone. The expression has to be exactly specific to the given moment. That is surprisingly hard to achieve and it requires repetition and a degree of soul-searching on the part of the singer, leaving behind inessential baggage.

Richard often creates a choreographed physical language that is tightly minimalistic and therefore all the stronger for its economy. He works to achieve the utmost with the minimal amount of reiteration, so that a given gesture will be specific to one moment and to that moment only. It might later become a riff, but it initially calls attention to itself because the physical language is so sparse. Richard works very carefully on timing. When you are rehearsing one of his productions it can feel almost as though you are rehearsing a Broadway show, because the aim is for a kind of pin-point accuracy, as though we are all dancers. This gives huge vitality to the proceedings, but it doesn't mean that his characters are like robots. In *Lady Macbeth* he ingeniously used robotic elements for parody, most especially when he was working with the chorus: for instance, the stupidly mechanical movements of the police in the police station rendering them automaton-like, emphasising this cynically ironic and biting vignette by Shostakovich on the ineptitude of the police in Russia. He also used mechanical movements for the scene at Katerina's and Sergei's wedding when everyone was drinking vodka directly from the bottle. The lunge backwards was very funny, and it was timed to perfection with the chorus's fugal entrances.

Richard loves creating laughter at the most seemingly inappropriate moments. Katerina (the Lady Macbeth of the title) and her lover Sergei brutally kill her husband Zinovy – in Richard's production she gives Sergei an axe to finish the job. After the grisly act, a shift in lighting reveals Katerina carrying a plastic supermarket bag dripping with blood. Obviously Zinovy's head is in it and although the moment is beyond terrifying, every night it got the hugest wave of laughter from the audience.

Richard Jones's meticulous timing, his going for the unexpected, his tight control over the soloists' emotional intensity and his pungent humour made for a harrowing yet highly entertaining evening. His audacious innovations embodied the fundamental mix of horror and humour that Shostakovich has in his score: the violence, conflict and tragedy are all heightened by the stark contrast of comedy.

For all the opera's stinging irony and dazzling daredevilry, *Lady Macbeth of Mtsensk* is a profound tragedy: the final scene is barren desolation, and Richard evoked it with great pathos. After Katerina and Sergei have been convicted of murder and are prisoners doing penal labour in Siberia, Sergei begins an affair with one of the other convicts, Sonyetka. When Katerina realises what's going on and all the other prisoners jeer and taunt her, she is devastated and sings a plaintive monologue about a forest and a lake where the water is pitch black. There's almost nothing for the conductor to do there except just listen to the soprano intone her hopelessness – and how wonderful Shostakovich's theatre is here when just a few notes from the singer and a held pedal note in the bass can create the most moving stillness, in such contrast to what has gone before. So much of this opera is deliberately over the top, with the feverish sensational quality that was part and parcel of the young Shostakovich's burning talent at the time. Inspired by Nikolai Leskov's story, that talent exploded like a volcano. But this scene near the end is not young; it's old, it's worn and beaten down as the tragic Katerina Ismailova experiences her final humiliation, and plans to kill herself and Sonyetka together. That Richard was able to show this with such heart-rending simplicity and pathos drew my genuine admiration.

The set design by John Macfarlane was a brilliant combination of a kind of embarrassing 1960s aesthetic with a very Russian grit, everything looking as if it was badly in need of renovation. In fact the production's most memorable *coup de théâtre* was an onstage renovation of one of the rooms. During the scene change, when there is an enormous passacaglia, an immense piece of music that ignites after Katerina has murdered her father-in-law and builds up after several minutes to a deafening climax, an enormous wall is repapered, and it's finished just as the passacaglia ends with extra brass bands blaring in boxes at the side of the theatre. Again, Richard gives us strikingly telling entertainment while he is pushing the story forward at the same time – taking us into a new chapter. The entire sequence that culminates with that renovation – Katerina murdering Boris by putting rat poison in his mushrooms and then pretending to be oh so distressed at his death, Boris's very Russian solemn death scene, writhing in agony, chewing the scenery, and then the outrageous appearance of the priest doing a popular song-and-dance routine with the men's chorus just as he is about to give Boris the last rites – all this is grist for Richard Jones's mill. He makes sense of it all and we are inexorably pulled along for the ride.

A vital constant throughout all three runs of the production, in 2004, 2006 and then again much later in 2018, was Sir John Tomlinson in the role of Boris. He was scary, unhinged and menacing, and the thought of reviving this show without him was unthinkable. I must also pay tribute to two Lady Macbeths, first Katarina Dalayman, and then in the revivals Eva-Maria Westbroek. How powerfully they embodied this intensely frustrated, unhappy housewife, psychologically tortured by her lusting father-in-law and married to a weakling of a husband who in turn is also subjugated by his belittling father. She is in a way dwarfed by this man's world that demeans women so brutally; she's not a murderess but becomes one because she is totally hemmed in, isolated and treated with a cruelty that is inhuman. We know the clichés of this kind of story. However, that doesn't mean it doesn't happen, and it very much still does. Look how the world is struggling today for women's rights and the fight against the abuse and physical torture of women. In all the performances we gave of this tremendous work the Royal Opera Chorus acted and sang their hearts out. Both the orchestra and the chorus are the crucial motor behind this weird and very uncomfortable opera.

From the moment *Lady Macbeth* was first performed it caused controversy. Stalin himself was scandalised and set out to ruin Shostakovich – even putting his life in danger. The upward trajectory of this phenomenally gifted composer's career was basically halted for a long time after that. I think Richard's production had all the brazenness and bravado and daring the piece begs for, and I feel very proud of what we all achieved because, in the end, the music and stage elements came together so well. It was the first production I did with Richard Jones, and it was the start of a wonderful ongoing collaboration between us.

———————

For my second new production at Covent Garden I had invited Keith Warner to direct an opera I had been especially longing to conduct: Berg's *Wozzeck*. His preoccupation with what the characters were thinking – not only with what they were singing, but with what was going on deep inside them at the same time – struck the strongest chord with me. Keith and I bonded immediately, and so after our work together in Oslo I was determined to catch him for *Wozzeck* at the Royal Opera House. This opera has become iconic, a magnet for conductors and directors alike.

Wozzeck is a poor, pathetic, downtrodden soldier, mentally unwell, treated abusively by his Captain, exploited by the army Doctor who does psychological and physical experiments on him, and cuckolded by the Drum Major who sleeps with his partner Marie, who has borne a child by Wozzeck. Though the opera has the tight dramaturgy of Büchner's original play, its scenic structure is laid out musically using traditional dance forms, much like a Bach partita. This gives Berg the skeleton that he then can nourish with a variety of musical environments, building the greater overall dance of the drama, scene by scene. Berg successfully used atonality and followed the advanced language developed by his former teacher Arnold Schoenberg to express the harsh reality and cruelty of some scenes but, crucially, he was not imprisoned by this style. He was not afraid to come back to Mahler's late-Romantic musical language when it suited him, to create moments that are uniquely moving.

This is not the forum for an in-depth discussion of twelve-tone technique that Berg was to use in later works. Suffice it to say that Schoenberg was searching for a way that composers could be freed from what he thought were the exhausted possibilities of diatonic and chromatic harmony. In his new method he made all of the twelve pitches within an octave equal: no dominant, subdominant, tonic, and so on. The music would be conceived rather on tonal rows, twelve equally important notes arranged in the order of the composer's liking that would form the basis of melodies and chords in any given composition, acting as a template, a blueprint for creativity. Sounds very dry, doesn't it? It can be. Having performed several of Schoenberg's orchestral works, however, I can tell you that the case he makes for this new way is utterly compelling.

Keith, like me, was doing *Wozzeck* for the first time, and as his productions often have dark set designs, on this occasion I said to him and his stage designer, the late Stefanos Lazaridis, 'Why don't you do something in white instead of black?' So they came up with a space that couldn't have been whiter, a laboratory where the Doctor – a loony and very menacing character – does his experiments on Wozzeck. There were glass cases filled with earth, plant life, what looked like animal life, and other more gruesome images. Wozzeck suffers from severe hallucinations, and these are embodied in what he sees in those cases – he sees both what is actually there and what he imagines to be there.

Keith carried this idea forward later on in the opera after Wozzeck has murdered Marie. The nearby lake is represented by a huge glass case full of water over which Marie is killed. Wozzeck returns later in search of the murder weapon, but the allure of the water and his intensely fraught state of mind lead him to give up and resort to drowning himself. When I think of how this was achieved, it still startles me. Naturally, Wozzeck had to get into the glass case to complete the image. Matthias Goerne, who sang the title role in the premiere run of performances of this production, had been a champion swimmer for East Germany when he was younger, and he said to us, 'If you give me an oxygen pump and you are able to hide it, I'll stay under water with my eyes open for the six or seven minutes during the following scene when the Doctor and the Captain come by and during the orchestral interlude after that.' This is what the audience was to stare at, a horrific sight and wrenchingly uncomfortable, yet all this underpinned by some of the most moving music ever written for the theatre. The staging of this scene was one of the greatest *coups de théâtre* I have ever seen in any drama.

Another extraordinary stroke of brilliance from Keith was in the second act, in the tavern, where Wozzeck sees Marie dancing with the Drum Major. The entire chorus and little dance band were squeezed into the smallest, most claustrophobic area next to the Doctor's laboratory. The cramped space made movement almost impossible, and yet everyone did move, and how, creating a devilish vortex of drunken dance and psychological unwinding as it went on, spiralling out of control, driving Wozzeck mad, planting thoughts of murder to avenge his jealousy.

Altogether Keith's theatricality often manifests itself through an extremely physical acting style, one that hits you right between the eyes. Strong stuff, exemplified in one scene by showing Marie's little boy hiding but witnessing the Drum Major having violent, brutal sex with his mother, the painfully squalid nature of the encounter sadly rebounding on a helpless child. In contrast, the stillness of Marie when she reads from the Bible in the third act, pathetically hoping to find comfort and forgiveness, brought a much needed respite from the fever of the other scenes. The huge intensity of this opera was graphically depicted by Keith and Stefan in their production; in fact because of the whiteness of the walls there was an antiseptic quality that wedded powerfully with the bloodiness, the psychological mayhem and, ultimately, the moral decay of the characters.

Particularly in an opera that is as complex musically as *Wozzeck*, the conductor and stage director have to have a genuine understanding. The director has to be able to give the conductor time during the stage rehearsals to keep putting the music together again and again, because to make it absolutely precise together with the staging demands so much repetition. Keith was most generous in allowing me to work on the music as much as possible, and actually we worked musically together with the singers because he always had something to say about the delivery of the text. Keith has a profound understanding of text and subtext, very much like both Christof Loy and Richard Jones, and also like them he has great sensitivity towards the music. As well as opera he has an encyclopedic musical knowledge encompassing the symphonic repertoire and also the American musical, not to mention what he knows about the theatre repertoire in general. As a partner then, I have had someone who brings a wealth of valuable and inspiring knowledge to the proceedings.

These brilliant directors are very different from each another, with different views about how their productions should look and with very different approaches to how they want their singers to act, but all of them have true musicality in common – for me perhaps the most important quality. I have been blessed to be able to work with people like this and I have learned so much about the operas from them. It is uncanny what fine directors can mine from a piece you think you know very well, and these experiences have made me who I am. And they have also made me very fussy about who I work with. I have high expectations of directors because I have been spoiled.

8

WORLD PREMIERES AT THE ROH

Every opera company worth its salt must do everything it can to keep the repertoire alive. A part of this mission is to uncover neglected pieces of bygone eras, bringing them to life, making a case for them, convincing an audience of their worth. The bel canto repertoire in particular has been much expanded in the last fifty years, often revealing jewels that had lain hidden for centuries. Performing these titles in concert form rather than fully staged has helped many operas gain traction with audiences and producers. A lot of the music is of a high quality but, interestingly enough, it is the sometimes woeful deficiencies of the librettos that have sealed the fate of these works.

Surely the commissioning of new work is even more important than musical archaeology. It is more than challenging in the twenty-first century to write theatre music that is fresh, somehow speaks a new language, communicates emotion and is dramaturgically interesting, but this for me is the Holy Grail. I am fully aware that an uncomfortably large percentage of the opera-going public clamours for the tried and true standard repertoire and sadly not much else, but I'm certainly not cowed by this. In fact, it spurs me on to relish convincing audiences just how fascinating contemporary opera can be. With new music, audiences might have to contend with all manner of strange sounds, unusual singing and complexity with a big C, but for me this is a good thing. It is a part of today's living language, the challenge of everyday contemporary life with its bullying noise and unpredictability.

Opera composers of today have the same preoccupations as their predecessors: what subject should they write about; literary or contemporary; fact, fiction or myth; political or domestic; fairy tale or horror story?

During my time at the Royal Opera House, I have conducted two strikingly different new operas, works that approach the idea of music theatre from opposite ends of the spectrum regarding story, sound world, and general atmosphere and presentation. The first of the two was Sir Harrison Birtwistle's *The Minotaur*, with a wonderful libretto by the poet David Harsent, a retelling of the Greek mythological story of the Minotaur (half man, half bull), Theseus and Ariadne, which was performed for the first time in April 2008. This story was tailormade for Birtwistle as he had been preoccupied with myth for decades, its archaic tendrils inspiring him to dig deep into a sort of shared memory of a history none of us has ever lived.

I know it sounds strange in my description, but the music that he drew forth for the subject was not only primal and dreamlike, but also vividly human. The music churns as the sea churns, wave on wave, but slowly, menacingly, keeping you aware of the terrible depths below. In some of his previous operas the orchestral part was often overwhelming, producing a wall of sound that was most definitely impressive, but also oppressive at times. In *The Minotaur*, a greater ebb and flow of the dynamic range was achieved by the composer, the score undulating from the bottom up. What I mean by that is that Harry orchestrated using every possible combination of bass instruments to create a thick molasses of moving musical matter that acts as an unstable foundation to everything that goes on above. It is eerie and hypnotic, but then there are flecks of light. It felt to me as if the opera was somehow conceived to sound moonlit. I certainly don't mean this in a romantic way but poetically and theatrically, a dreamscape.

Supplementing this dark foundation and alongside the traditional string section and the much expanded woodwind section, was a dizzying array of percussion instruments, so numerous that we had to put many of them in the boxes on each side of the orchestra pit, thereby giving a bird's-eye-view to the audience of the kaleidoscopic inventiveness of the composer. It was theatre in itself watching the players negotiate their often freakishly demanding parts. In passing, a small anecdote: throughout the orchestra rehearsals, even up to the general rehearsal, Harry kept tinkering with the detail of the percussion parts, so much so that by the end of it I had no idea what he had taken out or added or enhanced. So much for my orchestra score . . .

I find that because a vast amount of contemporary music is focused on the orchestration – the colour, the timbre, the combinations of sounds – the danger is that the fascinating aural texture can often mask, dare I say it, a lack of actual musical content. Luckily, Harry was way too talented and wise for this to occur. I think many were surprised at how lyrical the writing was, in particular for the role of Ariadne, amazingly sung by Christine Rice, floating her voice high above the orchestra in the most mysterious and captivating way. She managed to weave in and out of the orchestra in the most confident and alluring manner in this admittedly unusual music, allowing it to express its deep significance to the audience.

Drama abounds in the ritualistic chorus scenes. Ritual has always invited an artistic response that celebrates rhythm in all its primeval glory. From the *King Kong* film to Puccini's

Turandot, it's the same. Harry challenged the conductor here. The music becomes highly complex and unrelentingly rhythmic and barbaric. The Innocents are sent through the labyrinth to be sacrificed to the Minotaur, the drama demanding music of the utmost savagery. It was up to me and my second conductor (we needed another one), in this case my wonderful chorus master at the time, Renato Balsadonna, to try to achieve a level of precision that made sense of it all. It was a truly scary ride. Though the chorus and orchestra were sharing the same basic rhythmic groove, which was complicated enough in itself, a group of drummers strategically placed around them on stage was at the same time hammering out at full volume a completely different set of ritualistic and attention-seeking rhythms. You can just imagine the chaos at the first rehearsals, and the racket. There are two of these scenes, the second when Theseus challenges and kills the Minotaur. Both scenes are highly explosive.

Throughout this process I was astounded at the willingness, courage even, that the chorus and orchestra displayed. These two groups spend most of their time playing or singing music by people long dead, but it is also true, and I have seen this again and again, that they are somehow programmed to 'get' new music, no matter how difficult or weird or obtuse. This is our time and it is our music. We perform it with glee, even if we might not love learning it. The greatest gift given to me during this time was that Harry sat next to me during all the preparatory music and staging rehearsals. Can you imagine what an inspiration that was for a conductor? I had myriad questions for him as I felt almost lost at the beginning, trying to decipher his musical language, having had no previous experience with any of it. But it was more than that: despite his legendary matter-of-factness over technical matters, it was his aura that gave me so much strength and courage to search within myself to find the keys to communicating his world. It was as if he was from another time and sphere. A couple of weeks in, he paid me the greatest possible compliment: 'You know, you conduct this like music!'

Conductors spend a tremendous amount of time trying to get everything together, and of course that is important. People are paying money to see and hear a polished product. No matter the complexity of any given work, there has to be another level to aspire to. This is particularly difficult in modern music because of the special mathematical challenges one is faced with: polyrhythms, innumerable strands vying for attention, and the often necessary fixation on transparency of texture. Every composer that I have worked with wants their music to have ebb and flow, contrast, atmosphere and drama. This takes an extra level of study and digging on the part of the conductor, but I welcome this kind of work because ultimately I'm the one selling it to the public.

Despite the gruesome strangeness of the title character, Sir John Tomlinson once again delivered a towering performance, managing to capture both the Minotaur's frightening animalistic qualities and his hugely expressive and ultimately heartbreaking human ones. He did this both through his singing and his body language in a series of dream sequences where he is given the gift of speech. Guided by the perceptive stage direction of Stephen Langridge, in an appropriately austere arena created by Alison Chitty, atmospherically lit by Paul Pyant, John frightened us and yet made us pity him, his enormous voice baleful and deeply personal. The sounds he conjured before uttering actual words were hair-raising and certainly painful to listen to. (I mean that in a good way, John.) The music became almost timeless for the Minotaur's death scene, and I believe it can be compared with Boris Godunov's. I'm sure John's experience in that role gave him crucial insight.

Although I had previously done quite a bit of new music, I certainly wasn't associated with it in Londoners' minds. *The Minotaur* was therefore very important to lay that perception to rest, at least for me personally. I got so much out of being in this world; it stretched me, made me contemplate the many ways music and theatre can be made. I think any conductor would agree that having direct contact with this kind of music, wrestling with it, communicating it, is fundamental to one's own development in music of all genres. Your perspectives are enhanced, your ears become more open and discerning, your storytelling ability is enriched, and it is to be hoped that your relationship with the audience, whether it is modern-music sceptic or not, develops into one of mutual trust and engagement.

Mark-Anthony Turnage's opera *Anna Nicole* was premiered in February 2011. To say it was a step in a different direction is an understatement. In conversations with Richard Jones over the years, he was always of the mind that for a modern opera to be truly contemporary it had to be about the present. Without wanting in any way to diminish the importance of Birtwistle, Boesmans and Bibalo (my three Bs), I saw his point. When Mark-Anthony and his librettist Richard Thomas pitched *Anna Nicole* to us, we at the Royal Opera House were at first taken aback. It certainly offered us an opportunity to bring to the stage something of today, subject matter that was still very much in the news and therefore remarkably prescient. I will

121

admit that it took half of the rehearsal period before I was able to jettison those 'what were we thinking' thoughts.

Anna Nicole Smith, a young girl who grew up in Mexia, Texas, went on to have more than her fifteen minutes of fame, becoming a pin-up model (breasts outlandishly enhanced), an actress, a reality-TV personality and an aspiring heiress. She married an eighty-nine-year-old oil billionaire and then, as far as the media were concerned, all bets were off. She became grist for the journalistic mill and for a time she seemed never to be out of the spotlight, portrayed more and more as a gold digger in caricature. The tawdry goings on as the family aggressively contested her right to her husband's estate after his death played right into a certain kind of sensationalism for which a sector of the media was salivating. The American public too became drunk on voyeuristic reality TV, the more embarrassing the better.

How does this become an opera? The answer is character. Anna Nicole was certainly an opportunist, pursuing fame at any cost, anything to escape the stain of her 'white trash' upbringing. Tragically, what she saw and experienced in the cliché-ridden limelight of the world of show business was far more destructive than her beginnings. She became addicted to various narcotics, was manipulated by a whole slew of unsavoury characters and, before her own death at the age of thirty-nine, lost her teenage son to a drug overdose. Composer and librettist knew that the focus of the piece had to remain ultimately on the likability of Anna. We could laugh at her as we followed the cartoon-like scenes around her physical transformation, and giggle as she sassily clawed her way to the top, but we had to remain on her side all the way. This they achieved brilliantly.

Several months before rehearsals started in earnest, a few workshops were held to sing and read through the piece, provoking lively discussion about structure, tempo, length and language. This last item was hotly debated. Richard Thomas had written a no-holds-barred text full of expletives, and though it was hilarious fun to hear such outrageous words sung by opera singers, it was also a bit embarrassing. At least at the start. There was no question that this was indeed the language environment of the situation and its characters, but I knew I had to prepare everyone – chorus, music staff, and so on – for what was ahead. I explained the story. I also explained that I was aware that for some people the subject matter and the accompanying foul language would be uncomfortable, but I told them that all of us on the team were one hundred per cent behind the project, that I would be there from day one, and that they were going to work with one of their favourite directors, Richard Jones.

How do you cast a title role such as this? There was never any question; it had to be Eva-Maria Westbroek. The real Anna Nicole was reportedly a very sweet person, but she made some bizarre choices in her life, driven by the rebel within her. A dream role, I think. Though some of the part is written 'operatically', vocally speaking large chunks of it are written in a quasi-pop-music idiom, needing just the right approach. Eva-Maria was game for all of it, even the prosthetic breasts and the pole dancing. She was radiant in the role, and was hugely sympathetic, as she is in real life. We couldn't have done it without her. Other terrific roles were that of the mother, an imperious Susan Bickley; the oil billionaire J. Howard Marshall, played outrageously by Alan Oke; the lawyer Stern, the smarmiest version of the amazing Gerald Finley I've ever worked with; and Peter Hoare as the overwhelmed talk-show host Larry King.

The opera also featured a host of other character parts: lap dancers, pole dancers, and a rock band. Mark-Anthony grew up, much as my orchestra and I did, with the pop and soul music of the 1970s, and we share a love of jazz, too. He cannily used these idioms to create a raucously splashy, sexy, unmistakably American musical environment. It's not just faux pop music, however. The whole 'show' is underpinned by an orchestration that reveals his encyclopedic technical knowledge and his showbiz nous, using dissonance sparingly but tellingly. One of the things that struck me most was his use of two soprano saxophones. This instrument, usually heard in mellow, soft-focus musical situations, is here often played *fortissimo*, a sound you will never forget. Fantastic. Hillbilly music makes an appearance too. Strikingly, Mark-Anthony contrasts this garish world with unexpected slow ballads that are strategically placed (like any good opera) to hit home. Genuinely poignant, they stop the action and make us reflect, especially with the two death arias, Anna Nicole's and her son's. Really tough stuff. Of course there is a drug-fuelled party scene replete with onstage rock band. My players were John Parricelli on guitar, John Paul Jones on bass guitar and Peter Erskine on drums. I had died and gone to heaven. Richard Jones's choreographer was Aletta Collins, who got the soloists and chorus to really turn it on in this scene. We had a blast. I was most definitely bouncing around as well in the pit.

To an even greater extent than in *Lady Macbeth of Mtsensk*, Richard Jones together with Aletta could revel in the cartoonish dance-heavy scenes. This was as close to a West End or Broadway musical as the Royal Opera House was going to get, and the rehearsals, though fun, were punishing. The timing of everything had to be spot on. Naturally, my work with the orchestra to a great extent had to reflect this. We were a turbo-charged pit band and we had to be all razzle-dazzle, meeting the obscene patter coming from the stage punch for punch, the band feeling they could let their hair down. The trajectory of the piece leads us on a more distressing journey. The opera becomes darker, desperation creeping in. Though it became a difficult watch for the audience, it was an opportunity for all of us to find other colours, other tempi – a relief from the relentless sleaze. The ending, though inevitable, was devastating.

I hope this demonstrates how even a story like this can be told operatically, and can move us. What Turnage was able to do was to sew many disparate stylistic elements together into a convincing and entertaining spectacle and wasn't afraid to wear his heart on his sleeve.

9

MUSIC DIRECTOR

The most tangible manifestation of what a music director does is obviously leading performances from the pit. Here all the trial and error, values, opinions and decisions taken in a collaborative effort come together in a statement that should be clear, compelling and entertaining. In addition to rehearsal and performance, there are many elements and people, in today's opera environment, that a music director is required to engage with.

My first contract at the Royal Opera House had me conducting a minimum of five operatic works and one ballet project with an overall presence of six months per season, which was often stretched to seven. Compared with most music directorships internationally, this is a lot.

The planning for a given production, especially a new staging, can often take place three to four years before the event. The Royal Opera House is competing with the other opera houses of the world to secure the top singers, conductors and stage directors, so it has to move way in advance. Logically this means I know what I'll be doing down to the fine details this far ahead of time. There are positives and negatives regarding this way of working; to have everything lined up is a good thing, but it leaves little room for change or spontaneous decision-making.

Long before the music director can begin to be artistic about anything, they have to be practical. Is there enough rehearsal time? When do the different singers have to be present for their respective parts in the opera, both for preliminary music rehearsals and the staged ones? Is there enough time for the stage director to rehearse before the orchestra joins? Do all the rehearsals allow both the music director and the stage director sufficient time for their needs? Does the opera we want to perform fit into the projected season's overall choice of pieces? Do we have too many operas of that style or genre in the season? Will it be suitable to programme just after a particular opera and just before another one? Will it make a strong contrast of colour to other operas being performed during the year? The music director has to take all those questions into consideration, and they have to do so in close discussion with many other people.

The closest relationship I have had is with the casting director. Peter Katona, who has been with the Royal Opera House for four decades, has a famously shrewd ear for singing and conducting talent both young and established, and a keen awareness of all the elements of opera performance. He enjoys ideal relationships with conductors, handling the stars with great finesse and the up-and-coming ones with true understanding. He and I have been in accord that the casting of an opera performance starts with the conductor. If you have the right conductor for a project, a true theatrical musician, you have the foundation on which all the other elements can coalesce. Of course you have to be painstaking about getting the right singers and stage director too, but the conductor is the key piece of the jigsaw puzzle. Several decades back, before I became experienced as a music director, I used to believe that you should start by planning the singers and if you have great ones, then the success of the performance is basically assured – but this is not actually the case. As wonderful as the best singers are, when you put them together with an equally outstanding conductor, then you really have something.

After determining the conductor, the business of envisioning the ideal mix of singers and stage director takes a great deal of very careful consideration – and once again this is where Peter Katona has been such a pivotal creative colleague for me. He is also the long-term detailed planner for the ROH, thinking four years in advance most of the time about the process as well as the casting, and directly bargaining with demanding stage directors and conductors who may have their own strong ideas about who should sing which role. Not an easy transaction. To keep up to date on the talent that is out there, he travels around the world looking for top singers and the conductors to lead them. This also affords him the opportunity to see how production styles are evolving elsewhere. Knowledge is power. He is a judge in many of the major international vocal competitions, and so most of the finest younger singers will have sung to him repeatedly in different locations. He would alert me to the people he thought should immediately come and do a work session with me and together we'd discuss the results.

I have been blessed with so many wonderful combinations of singers I wouldn't know where to start to list them. Suffice it to say that the combinations have always been carefully thought through and in the end it is the ingredients in balance that count. When I started at the ROH in 2002, it was thought that the structure at the top needed to be rejigged. I needed an artistic collaborator with whom to discuss anything and everything. While I was in the trenches, so to speak, someone needed to implement in practical terms the decisions taken for each production.

The director of opera is an unusual position that rarely exists outside Covent Garden, but for us it totally works. I have collaborated with three excellent people in this job: Elaine Padmore, Kasper Holten and now Oliver Mears. Their focus has been mainly around the stage directors, their teams and the upcoming designs and technical demands for new shows coming in. This is an *artistic* position; it is not only managerial. They will have been deeply involved in choosing the artistic team, and the schedule for any given season. They have to keep an eagle eye on the budgets – not easy when costs are going through the roof. Attending innumerable meetings is a part of this. Keeping everyone informed and onside is paramount for achieving solutions to our budgetary issues. And we have plenty of those.

The director of opera has to travel a lot to see productions all over the world and has to maintain a close relationship with leaders of other houses, networking and also hoping to build consortiums of co-producers. As his predecessors did, Oliver Mears monitors rehearsals, watching the development as a show comes to the stage, and often quietly gives notes to the director, suggestions or food for thought. Oliver, like Kasper before him, is a stage director himself and so speaks the same language as his often prickly colleagues. As a trio, Oliver, Peter and I give the final go ahead for the big artistic decisions, repertoire and teams. We're very different one from the other, so the discussions can be interesting . . .

The board, though not an artistic body, needs to be kept aware of the artistic goings on. As they are going to be our cheerleaders, it is imperative they know what they're cheering for, and where the money is going. The director of opera provides this information, together with myself.

Tony Hall (Lord Hall) and Alex Beard have been the two splendid chief executives during my tenure. Although at the

ROH the role is not an artistic position per se, the CE is a crucial facilitator who, taking care of the whole house's finances – opera and ballet – focuses the board of directors so that it can support our artistic work with a degree of knowledge and conviction about what it is we are doing. The CE has to lay out a financial strategy to the board, and here the relationship with the chairman is vital. Together they form a juggernaut with sound judgement but also artistic ambition. That is the key. Over several years Sir Simon Robey helped guide and support both Tony and Alex; together they created one strong board after another. It is not lost on me that I have been able to do my job because of what they do. Over the years I have much appreciated their sharing of information, giving me a heads-up on our relationship with the government, the Arts Council and prospective sponsors, and keeping me aware of ticket sales and the real world. And in the real world we've shared many dinners and bottles of good wine.

Having been a part of a music staff for many years myself, I have been very close to the exceptional team I've had over twenty years. Besides playing the piano for me, these enormously experienced people, some conductors in their own right, have supported me through every production, offering advice, encouragement when all seemed lost, lending their ears to thousands of rehearsals, making a vital contribution to the final product. My job has been to provide the approach, offer the point of reference; each one of them brings their own particular way of looking at things, and they all listen differently. This is good for me. In trying to understand their comments I am forced to figure out why they are thinking along these lines. That is the first step in attempting to correct a balance problem, a tempo, a pacing issue.

It is staggering to think that some of this team have given as much as three or even more decades of devoted service to the house, among them David Syrus (now retired), Christopher Willis, Paul Wynne Griffiths (retired 2023), Mark Packwood, Richard Hetherington and Susanna Stranders. They are joined every two years by an infusion of new talent through the Jette Parker Artists Programme, an extremely valuable scheme that gives not only outstanding young singers but also gifted young répétiteurs, conductors and even budding stage directors opportunities to learn, working alongside international performers, directors and the music staff for a two-year period.

I constantly work with the répétiteurs alongside the experienced team. Even the prospective conductors must play the piano well. I try in every staging rehearsal to dedicate a part of my attention to them in the hope of moulding them into proper theatre musicians, whether they have conducting ambitions or not. When they play the piano for me, I demand that they think orchestrally, that they listen carefully to the text being sung, and when the music stops, I make them listen to what the stage director is saying. I'm pretty full on with them, but they have all shown they can take it, and I make a point of listening to their comments once the orchestra comes into the picture. So it's an exchange of sorts.

The stage staff – the assistant stage directors, the stage management, the technical staff, the lighting technicians – are an invaluable part of the music director's daily life, and I refer to them and work with them every single day. The interconnection is what defines this house.

The chorus master is the second most important musical position in the opera house. The workload is enormous as many operas feature chorus participation and the preparation to get everything learned needs careful scheduling. We must never forget that the chorus is singing from memory. Near the beginning of my tenure the chorus numbers had been cut down, leaving a complement of only forty-eight regular choristers. That is not very many, though admittedly there are some operas where this number is sufficient. The big chorus operas, such as *Turandot*, *Lohengrin*, *Peter Grimes* and *Nabucco*, need considerably more numbers, up to seventy, eighty, ninety even. For those pieces we have a pool of extra choristers that need separate training before they are put together with the regulars, which means that there is not a lot of time for them to meld musically before staging rehearsals begin.

Again, in this domain I have been most fortunate. My first chorus master was Terry Edwards, a legendary figure in the English music scene. A man of enormous experience, he was a canny musician who quickly got the best from every group he worked with. After Terry came Renato Balsadonna, who had worked with me for many years at La Monnaie: a wonderful musician, a very fine pianist, and a fluent linguist in French, German and of course his native Italian. He created a wonderful culture of sound and theatricality in the chorus. He is now a fine conductor.

And now we have an American, William Spaulding, who worked at the Liceu Opera in Barcelona and several theatres in Austria and Germany, among them the feted Deutsche Oper Berlin where he also conducted. (I seem to be surrounded by conductors.) I like that he has Mediterranean and Germanic experience as I do, so we are on the same page about so many things. He is a scrupulous musician and extremely intelligent and our bond is very strong. It has to be. The chorus goes from strength to strength. Not only is this one of the most musical choruses that I know, but I am constantly bowled over to see how game they are on stage as actors, dancers – well, you name it, they can do it, all the while maintaining the rigour of a great ensemble.

The recruitment of orchestral musicians can be a long and arduous process, both for the house and the candidates. I get involved at the second-round stage and sit in on auditions with many different panels for the various vacancies. I adore sitting with my musicians in those auditions because not only can we exchange opinions about what we've just heard, but we can also talk about music in general. I crave this, and with their experience they have a massive amount to offer. I get to know them better and better personally, too. This makes a huge difference when you stand up in front of them and wave your arms.

Opera is extremely expensive, and as the government subsidy for opera in the United Kingdom is woefully low, there's a tremendous amount of fundraising that needs to be done. This is overseen by what we call the Development and Enterprises Department, and over the years its importance has increased; today, it is crucial for the survival of the house. It isn't enough solely to ask corporate bodies and private persons if they will support specific projects – we have to approach them, entice them to make them feel personally involved with the Royal Opera House, so that they are inspired to make their generous support ongoing. The one-off donation is great, but we want donors to stay with us. How do you entice them? A complex question, but part of the answer is by creating events specially for them. This is where I often come in.

Exclusively for our supporters I have done numerous masterclasses with young singers and young pianists, members of the Jette Parker Artists Programme, some given in the private homes of our donors and sponsors as well as in the ROH. Besides being lovely social events, the sessions stimulate interest in exploring how opera singers create and express their characters. I work in depth and in great detail with the young singers, pushing them to embody every facet of the character of their piece, imploring them to engage their eyes as well as their voices. The singers' resilience is most definitely tested, but they are proving to me and the audience that they can learn while trying to survive. This is theatre in itself.

Doing these masterclasses with young singers is one of a wide-ranging series of events I have curated for a group of donors called The Maestro's Circle, in which I give them opportunities to look at my work close up, whether it's discussing aspects of conducting, pontificating on a given opera, chorus music rehearsals or orchestra rehearsals with singers. That inside information, believe me, inspires people. They want knowledge, and they want to continue learning, so this has been an invaluable way of keeping sponsors and donors close to us. I have made many friends and become close to many of these people. For both my wife Pam and me this has been a wonderful added dimension.

The Royal Opera House, Covent Garden, is a multifaceted conglomerate, and if the music director is doing their job, they are deeply, not just peripherally, involved with everyone in this complex edifice. I'm not sitting in an ivory tower just learning my scores and creating art in my head. I am working on the ground, as my parents did before me. For me, it's the same thing. My aim here has been to be the central point of reference artistically in the opera house, the person who is setting the example for what kind of a house we want to be.

Halfway during my Covent Garden tenure, my agent Peter Wiggins decided to move back to the United States and we mutually agreed that it would be best for me to make a change. This can be a very insecure moment for any artist, but I am lucky that Nick Mathias and Thomas Walton at IMG Artists have been doing a splendid job, in particular with getting me back to the great symphony orchestras of the world.

In 2012 I was greatly honoured to receive a knighthood in the New Year's Honours List, for services to music. I thanked the Royal Opera House at the time for providing me with a platform to make music and drama with a world-class orchestra and chorus and the then Prince of Wales most kindly offered me his personal thanks. Carmela Maria and my brother made the trip over the pond for the ceremony; my mother beaming and posing for every photographer that came anywhere near.

10

THE CONDUCTOR AND THE SINGER

One of the reasons I do get along well with singers – and I am including the ones who can be quite headstrong and opinionated about how they want things to be – is that I have accrued a knowledge and understanding of the many physical and technical challenges they have to face up to and deal with. Matters of tempo are especially sensitive. Every singer has a specific lung and breath capacity, and the conductor must find out what that is relatively quickly. Conductors can stretch singers for the benefit of an interpretative idea, but not beyond their capabilities so that they come crashing down. The conductor must understand the different way voices work according to their size: bigger voices need more time to breathe, and some bigger voices will have difficulty singing very quietly, so you are constantly helping them to find ways to create variety with the dynamics, but ideally never to the detriment of the music. We all breathe in our daily lives, but singers cannot afford to be cruelly exposed, and so, justifiably, they are very sensitive about tempo and the whole matter of breathing.

So, what is the right tempo? There are many factors, of which the most important are: the specific harmonic movement of any stretch of music – how slow or fast the harmony is moving; the contours of the melody – its shapes, and the lengths of its phrases; and how all this links up to the syntax of the words that are being sung. On top of that, every language has its own musical rhythm – there are big differences here between, for instance, Italian, German, French, Russian and English. Italian and French and Russian are in themselves very different in shape and sound but they share a natural fluidity. The differences between them and German are considerable. German-language pronunciation and declamation often is vertical in its emphasis. Italian, French and Russian phrases tend to feel as though they move over the bar-line horizontally, whereas German phrases need to feel as though the backbone of the rhythm is somehow always present.

If the conductor is not aware of all this with a singer who is very much in contact with the language they are singing and who also has very clear ideas about their breath control (or maybe limitations of breath control), problems will present themselves. Singers immediately sense when they and the conductor are swimming in different waters, if the conductor is not breathing the same way or not feeling the phrases the same way, or if they feel the conductor is not conducting in the same language. This could be because the conductor is not familiar with the language; it could be because the conductor is lacking in knowledge of the voice; or it could be that the conductor feels the music differently from how the singer feels it. The fact is that the singer has to be on stage performing, and the conductor has to find some way of honouring their own conception of the music in tandem with the singer's specific abilities. A method has to be found for balancing one's conviction about how the music should go with what the singer is not only capable of achieving, but also what they can be convinced is the right thing.

It's a hornet's nest – a highly complex operation, and it takes years of experience to learn how to handle it with a degree of *savoir faire*. Conductors can and do get into trouble with singers, but it isn't always the conductor's fault. Singers can sometimes be shoddily prepared – you'd be surprised – so, sometimes part of the conductor's job has to be to instruct the singer even on such fundamentals as rhythm, notes and intonation. It's not so much fun, but it's better than trying to fight ingrained mistakes from the past. The opera conductor, if the job is done properly, really does have to be fully aware of all the many layers entailed in leading people with the most precarious and human of instruments.

Under normal professional circumstances you have music rehearsals with the singers involving no staging, then during staging rehearsals you observe and learn the tendencies of the singers. That's important, and I don't use the word 'tendencies' negatively: I am talking about each singer's personal idiosyncrasies that you can latch onto to help you guide and support them. You take that on board, you know the language, you know about breathing, you've got it all together ... and still you don't see eye to eye on the tempo. What then? Well, if you really are aware of all the issues, more often than not you and the singer will have been working in a felicitous manner, and the singer will have been overjoyed that you have been concentrating as much on the words they are expressing as the notes they are singing and the melodies they are fashioning.

I try to see what the singer looks like as the music is being sung and the drama acted, and ask myself if it adds up. Does it make sense for the moment, does it make sense for what is being said, does it make sense within the geography of the production – and I am meaning the tempo, the colour, the temperature and the conviction of even just a single word, let alone a whole scene. I use the truth of the theatre, the entire experience of the singing and acting, as the basis for my consideration –

and if I find it convincing in its sum, then I will certainly bend to the desires of the singer, because even though I may not feel it in my bones the way that particular singer might interpret something, I can see that it works in the context. My hope is that this can work the other way round too – that if I can make a case that something specific is perhaps not working musically, to support the drama better, I defend my corner, and hope that the singer will be convinced. This can sometimes take time, but I'm known for hammering on.

I assure you that this can and should be done in a friendly and constructive manner. I have been very fortunate indeed over the years as I have got along splendidly well with singers and have been able to be a support for them when they have needed it most. This has been vital when a singer has been preparing and performing a role for the first time and understandably has a lot of questions and maybe a lot of anxieties and insecurities including vocal ones. These are tricky to deal with. At times singers might even get into vocal crises and lose confidence. The truth is that they don't really hear their voices in the way that they are projected to someone else, so they constantly need an expert ear to guide them. As a conductor and as a music director I have always felt strongly responsible for helping the singer as much as I possibly can. They are on the front line and, believe me, singing opera is a high-wire act, which is why I adore and admire these courageous artists. I have learned so much from them, starting of course with my father, Pasquale.

There is a flip side. What I have never had time for are singers who are not generous with their art – those who are seemingly uncaring about who they are singing for, and that means both the audience and the other singers in the production. People pay to come and see an opera, and it's crucial that we performers never just phone it in, so to speak. We are living a privileged life surrounded by great music and great opportunities to connect with the audience on the deepest level, therefore nothing short of a hundred per cent will do. I cannot understand or tolerate capricious behaviour in a singer. An opera is totally dependent on collaboration, and no matter how important the diva or the divo, the complete show on the night is all about how they are integrating with their colleagues, in the context of the stage director's production and the conductor's musical vision. When, for example, a singer starts not showing up to rehearsals for no particularly convincing reason, I have no patience with it. However, I have great tolerance for singers' sometimes nervy behaviour because what they do is tremendously demanding and the public's expectations can be truly daunting. This I understand better than most people – as long as they are generous in their art. This has to be our credo.

Given the astonishing level of support staff available on any given production, I think some people would be impressed to learn how deeply most singers have thought about each moment in the score of the opera they are performing before they partake in the rehearsal process. The stage director and the conductor cannot simply ignore this; they have to respect it and ponder how this person's preparation might enhance their collective vision for the whole. The artistic leaders must mould, coax, cajole, push and encourage every step of the way, but it is a two-way street.

What a wonderful thing we are lucky enough to be able to do. The opera rehearsal process is something engaging, so full of energy and discovery. It doesn't have to be a period of five or six weeks as with a new production – it can be done in two weeks, and with some people sometimes it can be done in a few days, as long as the focus, the concentration and the desire are there. I'll never forget how Plácido Domingo could do this. Because of his schedule being so extremely dense, he couldn't offer many days of rehearsal, but my goodness when he was in the rehearsal room as well as rehearsing on the stage, his focus on what was going on was like a laser. You had a hundred per cent of this tremendous talent and a man of vast experience – you weren't starting with a blank canvas as you might be with somebody else. You were from the start at such a high level that you achieved remarkable things very quickly. But there are very few people who can do that.

Plácido was as intense in the recording studio as he was in the theatre – and so am I. For me the recording of opera is not the restrictive and edgy burden that it is sometimes portrayed as being, and for more than a quarter of a century I have derived wonderful inspiration making records with many of the greatest singers of recent decades. It's an art form in itself.

11

RECORDING OPERA, AND THREE GREAT MASTERWORKS

In the many recordings I have made with singers, I have found that, despite the worry of exhaustion and the wear and tear on the vocal cords from the necessary repetition in the pressurised conditions of studio sessions, each individual has been tireless in the pursuit of an often elusive convincing final result. From the time I made my very first recording conducting a variety of soprano arias with Inga Nielsen back in 1985, in collaboration with the Helsingborg Symphony Orchestra in Sweden, I became fascinated with this phenomenon, this inexhaustible energy that carries singers through. It would be inconceivable to demand that kind of repetition in a normal rehearsal situation in the theatre, where there are so many non-musical preoccupations, yet when it comes to leaving a lasting sound document, something that is not ephemeral, the singer's ego kicks in, producing huge amounts of adrenalin, and the singer flies. I've made it a lifelong study to figure out how to aid and abet this, and along the way I've learned to develop a positive 'rhythm' in the sessions, often pushing the singers relentlessly to follow a line of thought, an interpretive strategy, knowing that they will have the energy and stamina to express it to the highest degree of intensity so that we can together achieve real drama. If everyone is secure about the mission of each session it can be hugely exhilarating. Remember, there is no visual component.

The microphone picks up indifference before it captures anything else, and so the singer has to be specially convincing in the studio. With each section that we record I try to create the dramatic or poetic atmosphere by first sharing my thoughts with the orchestra, describing the action of the moment in very basic terms, and reading through the material for that day with the players. More often than not, an orchestra will be meeting the music for the first time at the first session, so you are literally starting from scratch, sight-reading at first, and subsequently moving towards putting them together with the singers, and ultimately building the performance. To say that this process has to be done quickly would be a huge understatement, but good musicians are quick and they can glean mostly everything from my often simplistic, bordering on comical, description of what the drama needs to communicate, and a couple of read-throughs. No take should be just about repetition. The orchestra must not only support the singers; it must also exude character, and always propel the action. The word 'accompaniment' fills me with suspicion; I will never let the orchestra just accompany.

There is no question that a recording should sound polished. The ensemble has to be precise, the words should be clear, and everything has to be well balanced – but for me that's just the starting point. It's true that there never is enough time at your disposal in the studios, but if you are going after the right things, the use of the time usually, even eerily, works out. If the music seems to jump off the page when you listen back, then you're getting somewhere.

Recording gives the artists an opportunity to bring the music to life with experimentation, with reconsideration. Yes, you are under the microscope, but that is an opportunity; it's not a negative. It's like being in close-up all the time – terribly risky, but gorgeously revealing.

Very important for me in recording opera is that I get to be the de facto stage director. I have had wonderful times working with gifted stage directors in the opera house, but in the recording studio the process is not at all the same. The lack of the visual element means you have to convey time, place and specificity of character through interpretation, with accent, colour, tempo and atmosphere playing key roles. That's my domain.

Making a recording is much like making a film. I like to record in very long takes. I do a complete run-through of the scene we are recording, warts and all, to achieve the continuity and context of the action. I might well then do it all again with some prompts from the record producer before listening. After that, if it's necessary, I go back and do retakes of short passages to perfect them. Because of the availability of singers through the period of the sessions, rarely in a studio recording of an opera does one record the piece in playing order. Typically, one can do a scene from Act III, followed maybe by the last scene of the opera, then an early scene in Act I, and so on. This is where it gets very tricky. If the conductor doesn't have a clear idea of the whole, its structure, its dramatic and musical journey, they will lose all sense of coherence and the inevitable increase of intensity will never feel right – inexorable – as it must. I have never had a problem feeling in the final edit of any of my recordings that the coherence isn't there. I don't know where it comes from, other than I think it must emanate from the way one studies: the way one puts it all together in one's mind, one's heart, one's soul, one's belly, when one is alone with the score at hand.

I used the term 'final edit', but to get to that point there is considerable work done in post-production. Hand in hand with the producer, who also maintains the direct contact with each singer, several versions of the eventual truth are put together, and, believe me, there are often competing interests. One constant is that the singers ask to be ever louder in the sound mix, sometimes at the expense of any real orchestra detail or heat. The producer and I have to try to consider everyone's individual demands while making sure that the whole is vivid. In practical terms this usually means fighting for more orchestral presence and detail alongside the visceral thrill of Hollywoodised star vocal performances. The recording engineer is driven mad during this period, but it does work out in the end. You just have to nurture it right up to the day it goes to the factory.

Through the first fifteen years of my recording career, my partner in crime was the EMI producer David Groves. He was a scrupulous listener in the studio, keeping me focused on the task at hand, and a wonderfully calm presence when things got tense, as they always did. He was a brilliant organiser of complex schedules and a very fair musical ally in the editing process, which by its very nature can be so subjective. And the singers loved him.

During my time as music director of La Monnaie, Peter Alward, the artistic boss of EMI Classics, gave me the chance to conduct a work I loved dearly but that was not in the house's repertoire at the time. With the orchestra and chorus of La Monnaie and a superb cast headed up by Angela Gheorghiu, Roberto Alagna and José van Dam, it was a great joy to put Massenet's *Manon* down on disc. The smaller roles were taken by outstanding singers at the beginning of their careers, all of whom would go on to bigger things. I am a lifelong fan of Massenet's music because he so effortlessly and so subtly balances the dark and the light of his musical paintings. He is not afraid of extremes either. Though *Manon* is a tragedy, with passages of exquisite pathos, so much of the music is light and sparkling, often making you feel as if you are conducting a vaudeville show. Such is the fun of this music: I'm thinking of those lovely little ensembles with the three grisettes dotting the piece, and the sometimes raucous chorus scenes, creating a genuinely French *esprit*, champagne corks popping everywhere. *Opéra comique!* Massenet was brilliant at pastiche, in certain scenes writing music that is faux eighteenth century, deliciously capturing the flavour of the time and the place, but his true genius is in his uncanny ability to weave all these stylistic strands together. The distance between comic opera and grand opera is immense, but this music is convincing at both extremes and fills in all the gaps along the way with arias and duets that are to die for.

For me, a particularly successful decision on the part of the composer (and very different from Puccini's *Manon Lescaut* of nine years later) was that we do get to see, albeit briefly, Manon and Des Grieux in a blissful domestic situation before everything goes horribly wrong. That arching melody at the beginning of Act II is so free and open. I adore it.

Puccini was jealous of Massenet's piece and he didn't appreciate his opera being compared with it. This is perhaps why the Italian left out the domestic scene and plunged us straight into the more heated melodrama, his territory. What always makes me smile is that at the end, as Manon dies, her last phrases are strikingly similar in both operas. Puccini's general approach was considerably more torrid; he was at the time totally under the spell of Wagner's 'new' highly symphonic operas. Admittedly, his own voice does manage to shine through, but his debt to Massenet is also beyond question: just listen to the pastiche of faux eighteenth-century music in his own Act II. The cherry on the cake has to be that he must surely have realised what a great melodist beat him to it by nine years.

We recorded in an unusual location, the Cirque Royale in Brussels. Yes, a circus. The faint smell of animal droppings notwithstanding, it turned out to be ideal – not too reverberant. I had done a *Carmen* production there, so French music was in the air. The lightness and delicacy of the La Monnaie orchestra's playing, and the colour and sparkle of the chorus's singing brought an ideal authenticity of style. Building the performance was a labour of love from all sides. We had the great fortune to have our intendant Bernard Foccroulle playing the organ in the great St Sulpice scene, using an instrument that is very similar to the one that would have been in use at St Sulpice during the time of the action. No, we didn't bring the organ to the circus; we went to the organ. The vocal sparks really flew between Angela and Roberto – competitive in a good way. They were young and in love in real life. What more could you want? The French language brought out the best in them, both producing the requisite tenderness, refinement and panache. The duets sizzled.

The thorniest aspect of the piece has to do with the underscored spoken dialogue that pops up from time to time, de rigueur in works written for the Opéra-Comique. These episodes are so difficult to time. There is a certain amount of music to support a certain number of words, but either one of these elements performed too quickly or too slowly can seriously rock the boat. Repeated takes . . . The other thing one has to realise is just how awkward it sometimes is for opera singers to speak rather than to sing. The placing of the operatic voice is inherently unnatural for conversational speech, so it is very easy to sound comically mannered. Even Maria Callas had difficulty with this. With these two brilliant, impulsive protagonists, José van Dam was the anchor. His little aria advising his son to find a wife and have a family instead of becoming an Abbé in order to forget the memory of Manon – he made it into a masterwork. It was paternal, and yet foreboding – and strong. A warning. Giorgio Germont in true French garb. It was a real shame that I couldn't do more of these French opera recordings at La Monnaie, but I am really proud of the one we were fortunate enough to have come our way.

When Alain Lanceron, the then new head of Warner Classics (formerly EMI) and expert in all things operatic, asked me about recording Verdi's *Aida*, I was on the one hand filled with excitement and on the other filled with trepidation. If ever there was an iconic title to be recorded, it would be this one. So many superlative recordings have been in the catalogue for years and years – conducted by the likes of Toscanini, Karajan, Solti, Muti, and . . . and . . . and . . . I certainly had great trust in the forces involved – another superlative cast, and my new orchestra and chorus in Rome, the Orchestra e Coro dell'Accademia Nazionale di Santa Cecilia, but the piece is so exposed, so well known, there is truly nowhere to hide. A great preoccupation I had was about the hall where we would be recording, the new Sala Santa Cecilia. Would it be the right space for this extraordinary opera? I use the word 'extraordinary' because it is like no other. Primarily known for its gargantuan chorus scenes, it boasts other scenes of surprising intimacy and refinement. Its many offstage effects and special peculiarities I knew from the outset would be a challenge for any sound engineer. Could the hall do justice to these contrasting elements?

It actually took all of five minutes to realise that I had something that was potentially ideal for this enterprise. A crucial concept is that, though the arias, duets and trios are intimate scenes, they must sound as if they are being performed in a gigantic space. The idea is not contradictory; there must be an aura of gigantism. We know relatively little of ancient Egypt, but our imagined ideas of its reputed grandeur must always be in play. Verdi suggests a vision of this unfamiliar world both in his ingenious acoustical effects and in his most peculiarly individual and seductive musical language. Bombast plays its part, but the melismatic character of many of the melodies and the rarefied nature of the harmonies evoking a faraway land are the essence of the opera's atmosphere. It is no coincidence that Puccini, who himself later conjured up the colours of exotic distant realms, was knocked off his feet as a teenager when he first saw *Aida*. This was the original inspiration; this was to be his path.

For the diverse acoustical spaces in *Aida*'s world, the Santa Cecilia hall offered substantial height and breadth. It has huge balconies surrounding the orchestra, and as there is no organ behind the orchestra, as in many other halls, the open spaces extend way up towards the sky. Both the feeling of size and the perception of distances needed for the offstage effects sat comfortably and naturally in this space.

The opera makes tremendous vocal demands on the singers, with notoriously difficult phrases and Verdi's infamously precise dynamic markings. Often it is the case that in this piece the most subtle dynamic markings have not been considered – sometimes because singers have not been able to manage technically the amount of very soft singing they are required to do,

149

and often because *Aida* is thrown on to the stage with woefully little rehearsal. I knew I had to try to address this issue somehow, to try to be as true as possible to what Verdi intended. Every conductor says that – but of course it all has to do with the ingredients that you have to hand. I knew that the orchestra – with the sweetness of its string sound, the bravado of the brass section, and the woodwind players' inherent knowledge of how Verdi's melodies go – would sound absolutely terrific. I also knew that, although the chorus doesn't sing opera in their day job as a symphonic chorus, this music is in their blood. To be able to put together a dream cast, with the ideal singers for each role – Anja Harteros, Jonas Kaufmann, Ekaterina Semenchuk, Ludovic Tézier, Erwin Schrott and Marco Spotti – all available at some time or other during the two-week recording period, was a rare propitious start for this particular opera.

Thinking back on it, when Jonas Kaufmann and I recorded 'Celeste Aida' and he was able to sing the high B flat at the end with a breathtaking *diminuendo*, as so few tenors can, the whole recording moved onto another level. Everybody heard what it was that we were aiming for; it was encapsulated in that one phrase. Because the orchestration of this aria is often so sparse, Jonas sang almost the entire piece softly, secretly. There is undeniably more to the role than this one aria, and he also relished the opportunities to produce those trumpet tones that show the warrior in him, creating the complete picture.

When you listen to Anja Harteros's Aida, you realise that she isn't a dramatic soprano as is often cast for this role but a lyric singer – I would use the term *lirico spinto* – with the flexibility of a lighter voice, ideal for the more lyrical sections, of which there are many, but also with the steel for the more eruptive parts of the role. Though of Greek heritage, Anja is German. I was surprised at how much she invested in the text, not only in the pronunciation, but in what lies underneath. Perhaps one can tell that she might not be Italian, but her sense of commitment to the drama in the words was absolutely tremendous. In the final scene when she and Jonas trade treacherously difficult phrases all the while capturing an innermost intimacy as they say farewell to life, they pay a tribute and homage to the history of singing in the Italian operatic tradition. This from two Germans.

Ekaterina Semenchuk is a flame: her Amneris had all the flair and fire that Verdi said he was looking for, and underneath the aristocratic surface you were never in doubt that she would do anything for Radames' love. As indeed she should, she let loose in the Act IV trial scene. The warm, noble yet dramatic quality of Ludovic Tézier in the relatively short role of Amonasro, Aida's father; the nobility in the authoritative sound of Marco Spotti, the King; and the dangerous voice of Erwin Schrott, the political high priest Ramfis, are all hugely impressive on this recording.

Having that trial scene take place unseen offstage while Amneris is on stage in full view listening in and desperately wailing in protest is a fantastic idea of Verdi's – the idea being that Amneris feels the tension of the trial to a much greater degree when it's happening in an adjacent space than she would if it were right in front of her. She is driven into a frenzy. Here is a particularly strong instance of the crucial necessity for spatial effect in this opera. (Sidebar here: I recently conducted Robert Carsen's new production of *Aida* at Covent Garden where he placed the trial onstage. I have to admit that it was overwhelming in its impact.)

The greatest challenge for distant effect is the opening of the Nile scene at the start of Act III – one of Verdi's most wondrous inventions, and one of the trickiest moments to perform in the entire opera. The first violins have a riff over three octaves, marked triple *piano* and muted, and difficult to control technically; the cellos play very softly with harmonics; and the flute plays an exotic-sounding melody with trills – all creating a trance-like atmosphere full of tension in a mysterious location on the shores of the Nile where Aida is to have a secret rendez-vous with Radames. In the distance you hear the prayers of the Egyptian priests and priestesses in the temple, where Ramfis is about to consecrate Amneris on the eve of her marriage to Radames – she has been given to him by her father, the King, as a prize for his winning the battle against the Ethiopians. We had to find an extremely faraway space for the chorus in order to create the necessary effect. With the use of television and sound monitors and my blood, sweat and tears to try to get it all together from what felt like three kilometres away it was a daunting experience. It was our first real taste of distancing in the extreme – something I relived a lot during the Covid time.

We were very fortunate to have the participation of one of the Rome police bands – the Banda musicale della Polizia di Stato – for the stage band in Act II. They are an accomplished and very large band. I had collaborated with them for concert performances of *Un ballo in maschera* in the Verdi 200th anniversary year of 2013, and then again for Berlioz's *Grande Messe des morts* six years later when we had over 160 players with them and the orchestra together, not to mention a huge chorus and solo tenor as well: a tremendous clamour! They give a very big and punchy sound to the Triumphal Scene in *Aida*, an important addition to the gargantuan pompous grandeur, though even they had to be somewhat distanced as required by Mr Verdi, so finding the right spot for them took a few goes.

The sense of mission and teamwork everyone had in that recording was truly special. All the performers and the recording producer and the sound engineer, Stephen Johns and Jonathan Allen respectively, worked together assiduously to capture the atmosphere of each scene. I know I have used the word 'atmosphere' several times now about this opera, but it really is so important. We were using a dynamic and spatial range that I think is very impressive, going from the most delicate whispers to thunderous intensity – and menace too, which the power of this bellicose Egyptian society must convey.

One of the reasons that this recording was so successful, winning many awards, is that, after we had finished, Stephen Johns and Jonathan Allen put aside a great deal of time in the studio with me to go through everything forensically, investigating every turn of phrase, every long paragraph of music. Because of the cavernous recording space, certain details are bound to be lost in the halo of the sound, so important orchestral details must be given greater focus to keep the listener's attention and interest.

There are a number of different philosophies of sound engineering: one approach is to make everything sound opulent, sexy and glamorous; simply put, in your face. Another is to make the sound more refined – which is certainly more difficult to bring off. Of course it depends on the music and the performance that you are recording, but what we aimed for was the more refined and subtle approach to the balance, with the singers front and centre, and the orchestra creating an aural embrace for them, never covering the intent and specificity of the singers' performances. It never ceases to amaze me that you find that quite often you decide to use first takes of the various scenes (if the ensemble is good enough) because of the brand-new energy, the 'this is it' attitude that you have as you start off for the first time. There is always a danger in recording that as you repeat again and again, for whatever reason, you can lose the initial blaze. When you listen back to this happening it can be deeply humiliating, as you realise you were in truth going backwards.

Just as was the case with *Aida*, I was both very excited and yet also apprehensive at the prospect of recording *Madama Butterfly*. I was excited because I knew that Angela Gheorghiu had all the vocal charisma to perform this enormously demanding role and I knew that my orchestra and chorus in Rome had the sound and style of Puccini in their veins, even though they don't play opera in the theatre. I was apprehensive because of the iconic reputation for over forty years of another recording of the opera, also made on the EMI label (now Warner Classics): the John Barbirolli performance with the inimitable Renata Scotto as Cio-Cio-San. She was one of the very greatest of all singing actresses and my admiration for her is boundless. The warmth Barbirolli elicits from the orchestra is a wonder to behold. My concerns were not allayed by the fact that the recording had also been made in Rome, though with the Rome Opera Orchestra and Chorus. I was certainly inspired by this recording, but I knew that trying to in some way copy it – the tempi, the shaping – would have led me into a musical black hole. Recordings are snapshots of their time, so I had to stay firmly in the present.

Puccini creates a musical setting that from the first note plunges us into a tightly focused sense of place. The opening fugue, with its unforgiving rhythms and whirlwind tempo, is in itself a *coup de théâtre*, hurling us into another world, far, far away. This opening was technically very challenging for me. It invites over-conducting, and for someone impulsive like me it can be a trap. The conductor is not playing the notes; they must create the right environment for the musicians to be able to play the notes with precision and with character. I remember pushing and pushing for greater intensity and rhythmic concreteness, an almost samurai sense of discipline, but at first it just seemed to be stuck. Once I figured out that perhaps loosening the leash a bit might help, things started to gel, the players feeling just enough freedom, space, to make the music live. When I listen back it does sound on the edge of being frenetic, painting a pretty good picture of the scurrilous marriage broker Goro, but perhaps a shade too quick. This process was not easy for me; I was getting in the way as if I wanted to play the notes myself. This is not how it works. However, the struggle did help me realise that throughout the piece I was manically preoccupied with and fighting for a convincing musical portrait of all things Japanese, focusing less on the romantic aspects of the score, but rather on the finer things, the smaller things, the details. Madam Butterfly says: 'Noi siamo gente avvezza alle piccole cose, umili e silenziose' – 'we are people who are accustomed to small things, humble and silent'. For a person who had never been to Japan, Puccini had an ability to capture the sounds and the sentiments of that society's philosophy that is astonishing. With just a few Japanese tunes in musical boxes at his disposal, and every now and again using some traditional folk tunes he had discovered, he miraculously created a Kabuki-like sense of proportion, all the elements beautifully stitched together. I tried to conjure this up by striving for a certain classicism in the orchestra, clean lines, transparency, and an avoidance of overt *italianità*. Call it minimalist if you like. As I write this, I am only now aware that I was at the time subconsciously aiming for the polar opposite of the beloved Barbirolli recording. To this day I'm not sure if I was on the right track or not.

The culmination of the first act is an extended love duet that slowly unspools to reveal a host of musical and psychological wonders. Cio-Cio-San has been denounced by her uncle the Bonze and she is devastated by this public humiliation. Pinkerton, in a rare display of sensitivity, comforts her, pulling her away from the mocking voices of her relatives, and draws her into the night. The burgeoning sensuality feels as if it is in slow motion, dreamlike, and surprisingly erotic. It is Cio-Cio-San who unexpectedly takes the reins and step by step augments the intensity of this moment, the tempo gradually pushing forward. She genuinely loves Pinkerton and the sheer sincerity of her emotions and her surrender to him become almost unbearable for the spectator who knows this is for her a trap, the exquisite music for the two reaching a *Tristan*esque level of beauty and excitement, layer on layer.

The sensuousness of Angela Gheorghiu's voice is truly remarkable. Her voice seems to seduce the microphone and she is indefatigable in the studio recording process, unique. Her totally natural sense of the Puccini style, with the give and take of the language and how it goes hand in hand with the phrasing of the music, is a lesson. What a terrible shame she has never performed the role on stage. There was an unspoken understanding and real chemistry between her and Jonas Kaufmann, completely in keeping with the relationship between Madam Butterfly and Pinkerton, and appropriately his singing was completely in contrast to her searching, mysterious and heart-breaking poetry. He was ardent, free, devil may care, reckless – American! This was essential for this tortuous drama to convince. The genuineness of one and the clichéd shallowness of the other.

The heart of the opera is Act II. There is a bitterness that pervades the scene at the top of the act, and Suzuki, Cio-Cio-San's maidservant, personifies this as she intones a droning prayer, with a certain dryness in the orchestration, muted strings and flutes, bringing stark relief from the splendours of Act I's closing duet. This prayer is accompanied by repetitive chords, an ostinato, lending it a hopeless, airless quality. (Puccini went on in his later operas to use this device to create a particular required atmosphere. Compare *La fanciulla del West*, *Il tabarro*, *Gianni Schicchi* and *Turandot*.) Three years have passed since Pinkerton abandoned our young heroine, but her sense of unrelenting hope and belief in the return of the man she loves, despite the caustic negativity of Suzuki, gives her a newfound steeliness and resolve. She aggressively berates Suzuki and paints her a picture of how it will be when Pinkerton returns in her aria 'Un bel dì' ('One Fine Day'), Puccini's fragile yet visionary orchestration climaxing in an overwhelming expression of faith, that final high note going directly to the heart.

Cio-Cio-San's very first phrases in this act, 'Pigri ed obesi son gli Dei giapponesi!' ('Fat and lazy are the gods of Japan'), are very interesting because Puccini uses a penetrating and chilling theme to underscore Butterfly's disdain for the Japanese deities. This music is uncomfortable to listen to, the theme poisoning the atmosphere, each utterance getting louder, faster and more combative. She has found a new faith, her husband's American faith and, with echoes of the American National Anthem woven into the musical fabric, she hurls insults at things from her past. Angela is very strong here. The interplay between her and the warm-voiced Enkelejda Shkosa, our Suzuki, works beautifully, and the blending of their voices in the Cherry Blossom duet (very difficult by the way) is ideal. The role of Butterfly encompasses everything. The singer must in turn sound youthful, coy, innocent, fragile, strong and ultimately heroic. It becomes intensely dramatic over its trajectory and few singers can truly meet its frightening demands. I was indeed very fortunate to have Angela for this.

As with all Puccini's music, and despite my 'classical' approach, the small turns of phrase, the telling delay or nudge forward, the exquisite lingering on a key word or harmonic shift, these are the elements that really set this music apart. The skills needed to be able to navigate this shaping of the phrases or of the moments take years to master. One of the main factors a conductor has to deal with is the banal-sounding 'getting it together'. The level of sophistication of the orchestration and the demand that the phrasing go hand in hand with the text means that your artistic work can begin only after there is an acceptable level of coherence in the ensemble. To get to this point takes time, and then you have to be an imaginative colourist, a conjurer of all things exotic. Puccini wrote this music for an opera orchestra familiar with his style, but my Italian symphony orchestra met the challenge wonderfully, surprised at every turn by just how fabulous this music was to play, that shattering and ambiguous final chord really shocking them, as it should.

I believe *Madama Butterfly* is Puccini's greatest masterpiece, and I have continued to think about it a lot over the years. The way it portrays the suffering of this girl and the tremendous strength and conviction of her love until the end is unbearable, to the point that I can't watch it in the theatre. As the Consul Sharpless predicts in Act I, Butterfly is definitely the creature that has been pierced and killed to be put in a collection.

12

OPERA AUDIENCES

Over the many years of the Royal Opera House's existence, audiences have had the privilege of having the world's very finest singers and conductors to hand. The musical side at Covent Garden has always been strong, and therefore expectations have always been high, and – one hopes – gratified. When it comes to opera productions and generally anything to do with the visual side of the opera experience, the audience historically has been relatively conservative. There are still many people who want the presentations to be traditional, as they were fifty or a hundred years or so ago, and I certainly understand that impulse. It's a desire for authenticity, and that is not wrong at all, but I can't help feeling there is a degree of laziness, perhaps born out of the fear that instinctively closes the door to new ideas. This subject stirs passions and I've had some 'lively' discussions with patrons about their bewilderment when their opera is not delivered exactly as it says on the tin.

Theatre cannot stand still, and therefore sometimes a new and perhaps more challenging approach to stage design is something an audience should be steeled for when they go to the opera. I think an opera house must be a place of artistic challenge; it is not necessarily and indeed should not always be a comfortable place to be in. I think the opera house is a place where innovation should be expected, both with new operas and with the core repertoire of operas from the past, works that we know and love. I also think it is the responsibility of the stage directors and opera managements not to seek distortion of story lines and visual styles solely to be provocative. I strongly believe we should always be trying to tell the story that the composer imagined, but maybe strengthening the story for our present time with a degree of new thinking, enhancement, liberty. However, the spirit of the original must always be respected. The greater the work, the more there is to plumb, to consider and to discover.

People often judge a stage director's work only by what they see in the stage design: if they find the set aesthetically pleasing they will like the production. For me opera is much more than this: there has to be a strong and challenging statement too, sometimes emotive, sometimes political, sometimes laugh-out-loud daring, preposterous and/or entertaining; choose your adjective. Still, there are audiences and there are artists too who dig their heels in, rejecting novelty and experimentation, and so at times there is going to be conflict, hatred and anger on both sides of the footlights. As long as something strong has been delivered, then strong opinions will naturally follow, and this is as it should be. You will have the music critics sometimes agreeing with the perception of the general public and sometimes disagreeing. It might transpire that the show is a public success and a critical failure, and vice versa.

Interestingly, because London has so much music press on hand – the daily and weekly newspapers' correspondents, the music magazines, the opera magazines and various internet magazines – you rarely have all bad notices, or all good notices for that matter. As an artist you have to learn to take it all with a pinch of salt. In the past this was not at all easy for me, but in the end you need to be convinced by your own ideas and you need to know in your heart what you have done – both right and wrong. You have to follow your convictions but you absolutely must work very hard to implement them. You must never be lazy and assume that they will succeed under their own steam. No one is that accomplished.

———————

As I write this, I am thinking about how much of what I have been focusing on in these chapters had to be put on hold because of the Covid pandemic. Ironically, the trauma of Covid-19 has proved to be a powerful motivator for the Royal Opera House. It has been moving to see the mettle and resolve of the component parts of this institution in this time of great uncertainty and anxiety: the orchestra and chorus, the leaders of each of the groups in the house – the chief executive, the chorus master, the casting director, the director of opera, the head of operations – and their staff, plus the board of directors, and thankfully the sponsors who, incredibly, have stayed with us right the way through. Together they have been determined that this awful disease will not beat us. Many institutions have failed in this period, but the Royal Opera House is surviving. Covent Garden might be a beacon and crown jewel of the English arts scene, but it certainly doesn't follow that it should automatically survive. It has fought and continues to fight to survive this horror tooth and nail. The financial toll has been crippling, but we push on.

Different things happened during the shutdown. One quite amazing feat was the orchestra's and chorus's remarkable success doing virtual performances, separately and together, with each member recording on an individual track that was then put together into a composite recorded master – an incredible and extraordinary achievement by our audio production department. We joined many arts institutions in doing this, kept the morale of the house high during this desperate time, and, crucially, kept contact with our audience. In these circumstances the worldwide web was a godsend.

For my own part, the Covid-19 pandemic led to an opportunity to expand something I was already very passionate about. This is something that goes back to 2006, when the BBC had asked me to do an interval feature for their televised relay of David McVicar's then new production of *The Marriage of Figaro*. I remember only looking straight at the camera, explaining the main points of the opera, and playing illustrations on the piano. Well, the BBC was so pleased that I could sound moderately intelligent but didn't have an Oxbridge accent, didn't give off an elitist vibe, and managed to come over naturally, that they then asked me if I might be interested in doing a series of programmes about Italian opera. Astonishingly, I presented three features, spanning opera from Monteverdi to Puccini. What actually happened was that they wrote up a script of what they wanted me to cover, and I took it and turned it completely upside down and sideways, driving my directors Flavia Rittner and Dominic Best crazy, so that I could make it my own. As before, I talked to the camera and played illustrations on the piano, singing a lot as I went along. The real joy of the programmes was that we did them as a travelogue – we visited the most beautiful places in Italy that had connections with the music I was discussing. The series was called *Opera Italia*, and it was the beginning of a new facet of my musical life.

I had no idea I could pull this off, but I did and had a ball doing it. The series was very popular, to our delight, and it was followed up by more programmes. I have improved in front of the camera since those early forays – it takes practice, as everything does – but right from the start I felt that this was very valuable as a direct means for bringing opera to the general public – not just to connoisseurs. If I had to analyse my approach, I would say that my mission was not only to enthuse, but also to demystify the subject of opera itself. Unfortunately, many people are afraid of opera and classical music in general, but I felt that if I could take away the mumbo-jumbo and the cold listing of fancy terminology and show what a thrilling and vivid experience it is, I would get the message through. I used the terminology but explained it simply, trying to make everything as natural as possible for the person who knows little or nothing about opera, yet also at the same time stimulating for somebody who does know something, even a lot, about the subject. The key was to pitch it right. Opera is visceral, and with just a little preparation, the right information, the spectator can experience the full power of it. Yes, sometimes the storylines can be improbable, sometimes the political situations can be tortured, but people are singing up there on stage. It's crazy and wonderful, and it's all wrapped in music, more often than not glorious music.

I have come to feel now that being a talking head is my duty. If I can do it, then I must. The BBC and I decided to do a follow-up with a series of four meaty programmes about voice types, *Pappano's Classical Voices*. What was truly revelatory making both series was the amount of stunning archive footage available featuring the greatest of the great singers. The *Voices* series allowed me to tackle for the viewer the specifics of vocal technique. I have been interested in this subject since working with my father all those years ago, but it is a subject with many caveats, and there are a lot of opinions out there. I wasn't there

to tell people how to sing – each singer has to find their own way
– but there are principles of bel canto, and I loved showing how
the greats, including Franco Corelli, Maria Callas, Giuseppe Di
Stefano, Janet Baker, Renata Tebaldi, Birgit Nilsson, Feodor
Chaliapin, Tito Gobbi, Mario Lanza and a host of others, used
them to create vocal magic.

During the pandemic, I found myself at first twiddling my
thumbs, not knowing what to do, until a temporary scheme
was proposed that alongside other events I could do mini-
masterclasses from my home. This entailed me looking at a
camera from the piano and talking about opera. Sounds familiar? I adored it. A camera was installed in my music room
and operated remotely from far away and I explained scenes
from many different operas, orchestral pieces from operas, and
sometimes over several of these episodes I would go through an
entire opera. They are all on the Royal Opera House YouTube
channel. I am particularly proud of them because I think they
are informative and I don't get many opportunities to teach like
this. The series was called *House to House*, and I introduced it as
'from my house to your house'. I wish I could do it every week.

———————

A key word that springs up all the time on the British arts scene
is 'accessibility'. It's a word that I have a little trouble with, in
that it implies that artistic institutions are not naturally accessible, that they are an exclusive club. How I despise that perception. Much has been said about the high ticket prices for some
operas and for certain seats at the Royal Opera House, Covent
Garden. Well, if you plan in advance and apply for a ticket early
enough, Covent Garden is financially accessible to nearly all.
The Royal Opera House has created events in very affordable

smaller spaces, and the educational work that the house does, which is substantial in its proportions, has reached out far, wide and diversely through the country.

Is it hard to get a ticket at the last minute on a night when a very famous singer is on, or when it's a hot show on the bill? Yes, because there's a demand. You have to think ahead. Younger members of the public can take advantage of schemes to get them into the best seats for a show at an incredibly low price if they sign up, and thousands have.

Try getting into a London Premier League football game. Almost impossible without a season ticket, and outrageously expensive. Quality restaurants are also difficult to get into and there is only one set of prices for anyone who walks through the door. At Covent Garden and at other opera houses there are a wide range of seat prices, and acoustically some of the best seats are at the top of the theatre, where they are the cheapest.

All this information, today wrapped up as 'communication', has perhaps become the most important tool for any arts organisation, and you cannot just preach to the converted, which often happened in the past. You must now strive to reach out to people who perhaps have never ever been to the opera. Give them information, help them explore, dazzle them.

Renewing the audience is perhaps the greatest challenge we face and there is a lot of hand wringing in our sector. Competition out there is fierce in the entertainment industry and the younger set are accustomed to all kinds of technical wizardry in their visuals. There is a lot of thinking going on at the moment in all the theatres of the world, but I believe in the product, heart and soul, and we are indeed now seeing signs of a rejuvenation of our audience.

13

CONDUCTING WAGNER

My fear embarking on this chapter is that I might be expected to write a massive tome on the subject at hand. That will have to wait, I'm afraid. What I do want to do is point to some essential markers that have caught my attention during my entanglement with the masterpieces Wagner left us.

I think the number of conductors who don't harbour a desire to get their hands on anything by the great Richard is very small. The idea of reaching the final pages of *Götterdämmerung* or the *Liebestod* from the final pages of *Tristan und Isolde* is one that inevitably provokes curiosity, ambition, and sets the ego on fire. Wagner was a singular personality, at once supremely talented as a musician and as a writer, uncompromisingly ambitious, polemical, shrewd, manipulative and visionary. Even he, however, has a lineage, one that reaches back to Bach and Buxtehude.

The symphonic vigour of his god Beethoven was in Wagner's veins, the keen theatricality and elegance of Weber too. Schubert's unique way with poetry made him a key inspiration. The ever more massive orchestrations of Cherubini and Meyerbeer appealed to his sense of grandeur even if they did not garner his admiration for the latter. He professed to abhor Mendelssohn, but much of Wagner's early music is inspired by works such as the oratorio *Elijah*, full of granitic declamation and movement; and let's not forget Berlioz's outlandish symphonic experiments and Rossini's derring-do, which certainly made Wagner's ears prick up. I have already stated how much Wagner admired Bellini.

Harmonically speaking, Bach and Beethoven (in his late works) had pushed the boat out quite far, and are still today able to stun us with their audacity. Around the time of Beethoven's death in 1827, composers became more and more drawn to chromaticism, enabling them to stretch the harmonic possibilities at their disposal to free them from the corset of the classical period. The chromatic intervals interspersed with the diatonic ones, the scale we know and love, now offered many avenues for colourful detours, beguiling the listener's ears. A master in this burgeoning technique was none other than Frédéric Chopin. The ease with which he slips from one harmonic playground to another is revelatory. Not enough is made of his importance in music history, unfortunately. All this is a prelude to how one might or must approach any score of Wagner's. And they are certainly not all the same. The trajectory of his increasingly complex, beautiful works has provoked book upon book, study upon study.

Though Wagner went on to revolutionise harmony as it was then understood, a continuing preoccupation followed him to the end. Phrase lengths have from time immemorial played a key role in discerning the musical structure of any given work, but with Wagner, the definition of what constitutes a phrase has to be considered in more expansive terms. What I mean is that a single phrase can be an entire act of an opera. Dovetailing each little morsel of a phrase over enormous stretches creates the ever flowing quality that Wagner was aiming for, the harmony reinforcing the text to create an undertow that fascinates, hypnotises and disturbs.

Chromatic harmony especially allowed Wagner the means to musically translate the restlessness inherent in the story of *Tristan und Isolde*. Every tone he uses and that plays a role in any given chord has a double or even triple personality. A note may be a C, but it may also be considered a B sharp or even a D double flat. Each one of these colour personalities, as I call them, will provoke a different destination open to the composer. The element of surprise is now a prominent feature as the composer chooses which path to go down. A new world. Wagner took this concept and allowed himself to roam the musical planet without ever setting foot on firm harmonic ground until the very end of the opera, four and a half hours later. Imagine the amount of study for a conductor approaching this work for the first time, getting to know every stitch of this immense tapestry, hoping to reach a point where they become aware of its place in the context of the greater whole. This takes time. There is no way to blitz-learn this stuff. Wagner demands your lifetime devotion.

His music is constantly described as weighty. Fair enough. The question for me over the years has become: 'Just how much weight can the ear take?' The tints that are most prominent when listening to Wagner's music are dark, darker and darkest. If we go back to Bach and think of his enormous pieces for organ, we certainly remember the thundering bass of the pedals, and the sheer visceral appeal of it. But Bach doesn't use this colour all the time. One of the challenges of conducting Wagner's music is dealing with how to not tire the ear of the listener. Though it is true that the music is often bass-driven (it *is* German music), how constant should the volume of the bass be; how much attention should it seek?

In his *Die Meistersinger von Nürnberg* Wagner gives his own masterclass on texture and transparency. Here, more often than not, the bass instruments are required to play nimbly and with chiselled rhythms in homage to the baroque masters, but still be able to switch on immediately the saturated warmth of the Romantics. This interplay between old and new – the crux of the story – is an important clue to performing all of Wagner's music.

The operas *The Flying Dutchman*, *Tannhäuser* and *Lohengrin* have many passages which benefit from a more Mendelssohnian approach to texture, to make them shine and to better relieve the ear of the listener after more monolithic sections.

The first scene of *Das Rheingold* is a scherzo for orchestra and four singers where the orchestra at first paints a picture of the swirling, playful waters of the River Rhine; but later one of the growing frustrations of Alberich. The accents become more vituperative with each page. The scene must somehow fly in water; the tempo must dance along to the cheeky phrases of the teasing Rhinemaidens. It is a comedy for all intents and purposes – until it is not. When the gold is revealed, the gossamer string textures are such as to have surely made Debussy envious. This lightness that I'm describing has a dramaturgical effect only because it will most certainly be preceded or followed by a scene where the dark end of the colour spectrum is dominant. This was a part of Wagner's genius, emulating the Shakespearean idea of proportion. That he married this to the classical Greek theatre's focus on huge, life-changing dilemmas gave him the ingredients to shape his new concept of music drama and *Gesamtkunstwerk*, the combination of multiple disciplines, forming an overwhelming theatrical experience never before imagined.

The unique and much discussed opening of *Das Rheingold* features the darkest possible aural experience, starting with the lowest E flat and the octave above in the basses, supported by a secret doubling of an organ pedal, menacingly joined in the fifth bar by the bassoons playing the low B flat and the octave above to form a perfect fifth. Twelve bars of unremitting strangeness – and then each of the eight horns, increasingly dovetailed, quietly introduces an embryo of a theme that acts as a genesis. This alluring but knotty web being created is all the more baffling at first for the fact it remains stubbornly over 136 bars in the key of E flat major. Wagner will absolutely not let go, choosing instead to create life by initiating greater rhythmic movement, doubling the speed of the note values not once but twice, while continuing to overlap each entrance of each section of the orchestra. A layer cake of the utmost density. The volume increases naturally, organically, and the introduction of shafts of light and the necessary onward thrust demanded by all this built-up energy create a teeming primordial force hurtling us into the first scene. Any drop in intensity or tempo at the start of Scene 1, where the orchestra suddenly becomes tiny in comparison with what has come just before, would be fatal.

Throughout this book I have devoted a lot of acreage to my preoccupation with details in the process of making music and music drama. An important aside, however, is that whenever I've been given the chance in rehearsal to do a run-through, even if things are still at a rough stage, I've welcomed it. This is particularly important with Wagner because the weight of the details, the weight of the textures, can render the end product musically obese. The context for everything is paramount, the constant forward motion even in slow music essential. A run-through will quickly inform you where the tension is dropping, where more space is necessary, and if the transitions are working.

Perhaps the most elusive aspect of all is the transition. In Wagner's hands it becomes an art form. He rarely passes abruptly from section to section, scene to scene; rather he will wind down or wind up to the next tempo state. On the surface this sounds quite easy, but in reality it is where many conductors come to grief. The organic incremental slowing down or speeding up is very difficult to convey to an orchestra to the degree that each member feels the morphing the way the conductor does. It is so easy to overshoot the amount of slowing down or speeding up, so these moments will need constant attention in rehearsal to make the shifts appear inevitable without ever impeding the overall flow.

Many of the Wagnerian singing roles are demanding in the extreme and with today's more powerful instruments in the orchestra pit the singers need to have something superhuman about them. The expansion of the brass section by Wagner has certainly made the conductor's job much harder. There is no denying that the extra power now in one's hands is awesome, but the degree to which you have to keep an ear on the balance within the orchestra and in concert with the singers becomes a heavy yoke around one's neck. With experience you get used to this and the orchestral musicians know it is a problem, but complacency is *verboten*.

It has often been written that Wagner admired the Italian vocal school, cherishing smooth delivery of the lines, purity of tone and intonation, together with a forward projection of the voice. To achieve this with the singers of today is more and more challenging. Too often singers embark on this repertoire having previously sung far too little Italian repertoire, or even Mozart, and therefore neither the voice nor the musicality is fully or properly formed before the singer launches into the new territory. Wagner's lyrical music is very beautiful and must be sung with a level of tonal purity that gives pleasure to the listener. Today's productions do not make this any easier for certain singers.

The fixation on character requires a singer to dig deep into the psychology of the role and yet keep an almost Olympian idea of singing. The vocal technique must not be thrown overboard to realise a theatrical truth. A struggle, no doubt, but when this is achieved the result can transfix an audience and develop the artistry of the singer. This is what Wagner was aiming for, as Verdi was for that matter. Truth be told, singers in this repertoire will want to sing loud, louder and loudest, afraid that the orchestra will win the day in the decibels sweepstake. This does no favours to the music and certainly shortens the lifespan of a career. Here the conductor as coach must coax the singers into pacing themselves, releasing the power they possess strategically, intelligently.

There are roles that demand a type of declamation of the text that can often come close to natural speech or its inflections and pay scant homage to the bel canto school approach: roles such as Alberich, Mime, Beckmesser. Wagner is scrupulous about the rhythms he writes, particularly for character roles, and this must be the point of departure. He wrote the words and the music, so we have to trust what is on the page. In any language a certain 'tang' on this word or that word will come from one's knowledge of the language. I loved coaching these character roles as there are limitless possibilities for encouraging and calling attention to the often scurrilous, clever machinations of these characters through the brilliant way Wagner has set their words to music. Here consonants lift the words off the page. For the conductor a lack of familiarity with the German

172

language is unthinkable. Wagner's phrasing has all to do with the intrinsic nature of his mother tongue. It is true that even Germans have some trouble deciphering his often convoluted librettos but the rhythms, the accents, the high points of a sentence must be recognised.

In his later works, especially in *Parsifal*, Wagner became preoccupied with a refinement in his orchestrations that would influence every composer who came after him. The principle is the handing over of melodic material using dovetailing. I have discussed dovetailing before but in a somewhat different context. Here the idea is to not be able to hear or, better, define the entrance of the new instrument. That instrument takes over a note that is already being held, blends in with the timbre of the first instrument and takes over the phrase, blossoming while the first instrument drops out of focus or into silence. No big deal, one might think. Oh, but it is. Now acoustically the ear never stops following the material Wagner wants you to focus on; there are no interruptions or bumps, just a seamless beam of continuity in an infinitely varied colour scheme. He does this with chords too, to telling effect. In this way the conductor is perhaps given help in stitching the textures together, but one's ear will always have to make those joins mysterious, especially with blocks of chords. That requires tremendous aural sensibility and imagination. It has been a long time since I conducted *Parsifal* and I miss it terribly. I always felt I could conduct it all over again on the day, such was the illumination I experienced.

I would like to express how fortunate I have been to have these Wagnerian forays that have become a mainstay in my musical life, and what an orchestra I have had at my disposal. One specific factor that always draws me back is how Wagner reinvents himself in every one of his third acts. I was almost in despair when I discovered Act III of *Tristan und Isolde*, the Prelude reducing me to a helpless nothing, such was the profundity, the newness, the emotional intelligence of this next step in ratcheting up the emotional temperature of a work for the opera theatre. Listen to the beginning of Act III of *Die Meistersinger* and see if you feel what I feel. Wagner's almost disconcerting knowledge of what it is to be a human being facing innumerable obstacles to an elusive happiness is something to marvel at, to learn from, and to ponder.

14

SANTA CECILIA

While I was the music director at La Monnaie in Brussels, the management of the Orchestra dell'Accademia Nazionale di Santa Cecilia in Rome came to hear me conduct a concert performance of Dallapiccola's fraught and very beautiful one-act opera *Il prigioniero*. That was in January 2000. On the strength of that event, they invited me to conduct a concert – and it turned out that, for some reason I cannot recall now, I had to cancel. Professor Bruno Cagli, for many years the president of the orchestra and the intendant, never let me forget it. I did finally do a concert with them, in April 2002, and the programme was quite unusual: the second performance of Peter Ruzicka's *Memorial per G. S.* for orchestra, which had been composed as a tribute to the late Giuseppe Sinopoli; Ravel's Piano Concerto in G major and Shostakovich's Tenth Symphony. I remember it as if it were yesterday: at the very first rehearsal while we were rehearsing the Shostakovich there was something in the air; there was a feeling. I could sense it, and the orchestra could too. It all somehow clicked.

The music director at the time, Myung-whun Chung, had stated that he was going to leave, so they were looking for a successor. The concerts went well and, before I knew it, Luciano Berio, who at the time was the orchestra's president, telephoned and offered me the position of music director. This was very much supported by the artistic administrator, Gastón

Fournier-Facio – I think in fact it was he who had convinced Berio that I was the right person for the job. Berio was a very sick man at the time and was not leaving his house, so my only contact with him was over a telephone line. Though I had met him on one occasion at Daniel Barenboim's home in Paris many years previously, we never met in person thereafter.

A symphony orchestra! A dream come true, and in Italy. My mandate started in earnest in 2005, so before that I was appearing with the orchestra from time to time each season. I had no experience whatsoever of how to plan long term with a symphony orchestra. I learned. One of the first thematic projects I planned in advance of my taking up my post was programming three Requiem Masses as a cycle: Brahms's *German Requiem*, Verdi's *Requiem* and Britten's *War Requiem*, three different visions of what the Requiem Mass could be. Although the concept was unusual, it was a personal obsession. All three are massive choral works with soloists. They are highly emotional in different ways, and it was these differences that compelled me to unite them. We did the Brahms just before I took up my position, and the other two came shortly after I had started my tenure. The project cemented my relationship with the wonderful chorus they have in Rome (the Coro dell'Accademia Nazionale di Santa Cecilia), and immediately established my penchant for choosing varying styles of music, often jumping from one to another in the same programme. These choices are not revelatory as such, but in terms of how I could influence the approach and sound of my players and my singers to the vastly different demands of each of these pieces, they helped me to define myself to both the orchestra and the chorus, and to the public. The project won the Franco Abbiati Prize, a most prestigious prize in Italy, so I was definitely buoyed and reassured by this.

176

I soon started to take what were considered some adventurous risks for the Rome audiences: music that was more challenging, by composers such as Maderna (*Aura*), Varèse (*Amériques*) and Boulez (*Notations*). Alongside works of this sort I included several world premieres from a host of mostly Italian contemporary composers: Francesconi, Panfili, Sciarrino, Battistelli, Vacchi, Fedele, D'Amico, Ambrosini, Corrado, Nieder, Sollima.

The non-Italians included the great Hans Werner Henze, who wrote an extraordinary concert opera for me towards the end of his life in 2009. I am ashamed to say it was his first commission from any Italian orchestra, even though he had made Italy his home for over fifty years. The piece was called *Opfergang* (*Immolazione* in Italian). It was scored for a large chamber orchestra including a heckelphone and a Wagner tuba, plus a lot of percussion, two vocal soloists and a male vocal quartet. I not only conducted but also (at Henze's insistence) played the tricky piano part at the same time. The text was based on an unusual story by the Austrian Franz Werfel. The soloists' parts were tailormade for John Tomlinson as Der Fremde (the Outsider, an aggressive villain) and Ian Bostridge as Der kleine Hund (the Small Dog), a beautiful aristocratic dog that abandons its owners to become attached to the villain. A very weird story, which finishes violently for both protagonists, and includes a voice from heaven. The commission was for a piece of approximately twenty minutes in length, a mini-opera. Hans produced a work of fifty minutes' duration.

The second half of the programme was none other than Mahler's *Das Lied von der Erde*; Hans of course knew this. I can still see the mischievous glint in his eye. It was a gargantuan evening, and a very expensive one. But what an event it was. I was beyond proud. I miss Hans very much, as he was so kind to me when I used to visit him in the country and sing his music to him, asking him if I had the right idea or not. I'm not sure he knew what to make of me and my almost-tenor voice.

The Swiss composer Richard Dubugnon wrote a very virtuosic and entertaining *Caprice Romain* for us, and the Chinese-Uyghur Yikeshan Abudushalamu wrote a highly strung but fascinating piece called *Repression*. The number of works receiving their Italian premieres was considerable, including Peter Maxwell Davies's Symphony No. 10 and Jörg Widmann's *Teufel Amor*, two hugely important works, both of which I had already premiered, in London and Vienna respectively. I cannot overstate how having to rehearse in the Italian language affected me, changed me. Of course I would often slip into archaic words from the opera librettos, but by and large my imagery became more poetic and more dramatic.

Every new music director comes with their own repertoire choices, and from early on I think I brought quite a few surprises: not necessarily perhaps what would have been so innovative for some other international orchestras, but for Rome innovative enough. We programmed Ligeti's Violin Concerto; Schoenberg's Violin Concerto, Chamber Symphony, Op. 9, *Friede auf Erden* and *Pelleas und Melisande*; Enescu's *Vox Maris* and Symphony No. 3; Busoni's Piano Concerto; works by Honegger; Szymanowski's opera *Król Roger*; Dallapiccola's *Il prigioniero*; the three Bernstein symphonies and *West Side Story*; Copland's Symphony No. 3; and, in 2013, we put on a memorable concert performance of Britten's *Peter Grimes*, which, like all these works, was completely new for both the orchestra and the chorus.

It goes without saying that Haydn, Mozart, Beethoven, Brahms, Schumann, Tchaikovsky, Mahler, Bruckner, Debussy,

above My parents in 1956, engaged but not yet married.

left With my paternal grandfather, also Antonio Pappano.

below Castelfranco in Miscano.

top My father, the tenor.

bottom Celebrating my brother Patrick's birthday at the *asilo*, Castelfranco.

top left Inga Nielsen, as Violetta (*La Traviata*) in Oslo.

top right The inimitable Romano Gandolfi.

bottom With my wife, Pamela, at the premiere of *Carmen*,
at the Royal Opera House, London, in 2006.

left Susan Chilcott as Ellen Orford in *Peter Grimes* at La Monnaie, Brussels, 1994.

below La Monnaie on tour with *Peter Grimes* in Madrid (me still wearing tails).

top Discussing *Lohengrin* with Daniel Barenboim, Bayreuth, 1999.

bottom In strategic conversation with Keith Warner while rehearsing Wagner's *Ring* at the Royal Opera House in 2012.

top Richard Jones, with me and his then assistant Elaine Kidd, rehearsing
Lady Macbeth of Mtsensk in 2004.

bottom left Christof Loy (with orchestra score) on the set of *Elektra* at the Royal Opera House, 2024.

bottom right John Tomlinson as the unforgettable Minotaur in
Harrison Birtwistle's opera of the same name.

top With Eva-Maria Westbroek, my soprano of choice for many operas at the Royal Opera House.

bottom 'Do you think this could work, Harry?' Talking through the production of *The Minotaur* with Harrison Birtwistle in 2008.

top Conducting the Orchestra and Chorus dell'Accademia Nazionale di Santa Cecilia in Berlioz's *Requiem*, 2019 (count the timpani!).

bottom Taking a bow with the London Symphony Orchestra in 2023, after a performance of *Ein Heldenleben* by Richard Strauss – a very happy moment.

Ravel, Prokofiev, Rachmaninov and Sibelius played starring roles the rest of the time. Bruno Cagli didn't like Bruckner's music but he realised how good it was for my musicians to be exposed to it, so I'm grateful that he let it pass. Sibelius is hardly ever played in Italy except for his Violin Concerto. Now Rome was hearing his symphonies and tone poems. Indeed, we took his Fifth Symphony on tour. Bruckner's Eighth Symphony became an obsession. I realised that the burning Catholicism of this music was naturally congenial to my Romans. When they understood that the trademark opening tremolo was representative of the shimmering flame that is the Holy Spirit, they got it. Together we would build cathedrals of sound.

About three years into my tenure, the orchestra started touring again, which had not been the case in any meaningful way for them for a long time. I had been on tour before but this was something bigger. This was not an opera orchestra; this was a symphony orchestra, my symphony orchestra. Now I could have an orchestra of well over a hundred musicians in full view of the audience. It is very important to be aware that so much of the time with an opera orchestra is spent hushing the players so that the singers are audible. I'm slightly exaggerating the point, but not by much. The conductor in an opera house is working on the internal balance of the orchestra, plus the external balance with the singers. This work can make you crazy in certain pieces such as the big Wagner and Strauss operas.

Not surprisingly, the kind of programming that was desired for an Italian orchestra's touring was almost entirely focused around Italian music: Rossini and Verdi overtures, Puccini's intermezzi plus his *Preludio sinfonico* and *Capriccio sinfonico*, and, not unexpectedly, Respighi's Roman symphonic poems played a big part in our travel plans. We would include a top soloist to round out the programmes so everyone went home happy, even though this meant the orchestra itself felt like something of a bystander. At least this is how the concerts were marketed.

Except for Respighi's *Fountains of Rome* and *Pines of Rome*, none of the other repertoire falls into the accepted canon of symphonic works known to an international public. The Respighi pieces were written for this orchestra in 1916 and 1924 respectively, but they were totally new to me and I revelled in them. Respighi's orchestration is a thing of wonder. Let's not forget he studied with Rimsky-Korsakov in St Petersburg. If I'm honest I have to admit that in the past I had been a bit snobby about this music, but now that I was conducting it for the first time, with this orchestra playing it so idiomatically, I realised just how wrong I had been. Our performances of these works began to make people sit up and listen, and my relationship with these pieces together with this orchestra culminated in a recording of the three Respighi Roman tone poems (*Fountains of Rome*, *Pines of Rome* and *Roman Festival*) and his *Il tramonto* for voice and strings. We took *Fountains* and *Pines* to Carnegie Hall in 2017, the orchestra returning after a forty-eight-year absence!

As we were becoming more successful and our touring engagements increased, I felt that we needed to move on from being pigeonholed with Italian music and show the promoters what else we could do. This took some time, as there was initially some resistance, but we got there, to the point that we played Mahler's First and Sixth Symphonies in the Vienna Musikverein and Konzerthaus, Bruckner's Eighth Symphony in Dresden at the Frauenkirche and again in Vienna, Enescu's Third Symphony at the Enescu Festival in Bucharest, and

Britten's *War Requiem* and Rossini's *Stabat Mater* and *Petite Messe solennelle* in Salzburg. Inevitably the music we were playing on our tours became more central to our programming at home. The pieces needed to be bedded in on home turf before going abroad, so for a time the programming became more conservative than when I had just started with the orchestra.

It is very difficult to convince promoters to agree to 'difficult' repertoire because they have to keep an eye on the ticket sales. Unfortunately, the name Schoenberg on a programme costs you about 20 per cent of your audience in many venues. An unfortunate state of affairs but a reality. The touring, however, has become one of the key components of the orchestra's success in the last fifteen years, bringing an international awareness of its very high quality of playing, and because of this our repertoire possibilities have expanded commensurately. I could not have done any of this without the support and initiative of Mauro Bucarelli, the artistic secretary of the institution, who has been the main liaison with all our artistic partners and a confidant to me, together with Umberto Nicoletti Altimari, whose knowledge of the repertoire is second to none.

Another vital contribution to the orchestra's international reputation in recent years has been the large number of recordings we have made. At the time of writing I have done thirty-five recording projects with them, and they include some multiple CD albums of operas and choral works. A fair number of our discs have been of Italian music – and that might sound surprising when I say now that, when I began my tenure, a vital element that I felt needed revitalising was the orchestra's *italianità*. I must emphasise that they were technically in very good shape – Maestro Chung had done a marvellous job with them on sound, intonation and ensemble – but their Italian character and spirit needed to be emphasised to a greater degree. I'm not talking about the musical equivalent of more tomato sauce, but the authentic Italian way: the singing tone, the theatricality, the flair, the colours – the sensuality of approach that one expects from an Italian orchestra. Those were certainly the qualities that had seduced Leonard Bernstein into becoming a regular guest conductor and the orchestra's honorary president for the last seven years of his life. He died in 1990.

Before taking on the job in Rome I had had very little to do with the music of Gioachino Rossini. Not one of his operas figured in my choices for the opera house in the first few years of my tenure at Covent Garden, or elsewhere. I had convinced myself that Rossini's music was too exposed for a conductor like me; it was perhaps too motoric, harmonically too basic. What a fool I was. The musicians of the Santa Cecilia taught me all about this music through the innate brilliance, virtuosity and humour they brought to every turn of phrase. Bruno Cagli had been one of the founders of the Rossini Opera Foundation, linked closely to the Rossini Opera Festival in Pesaro. Mauro Bucarelli, who was already working alongside him in Pesaro and was an ardent Rossinian himself, was the other half of the one-two punch to get me to programme more of Rossini's music in the symphonic season, and so it turned out.

The *Stabat Mater*, a hugely influential work in the history of Italian music, became one of our calling cards. The combination of the Santa Cecilia Chorus and Orchestra, both of which inherently understood how this music breathed, made this a seminal experience for me. We performed this piece at the Salzburg Festival paired with Haydn's Symphony No. 104 (as a young man Rossini was dubbed *Il Tedeschino* – 'the little German' – because of his affinity with the Austro-German classical style of composition), and later in the afternoon we performed his *Petite Messe solennelle* with my wife Pamela and me playing the two pianos. A great day. Rossini also orchestrated this last work and so we programmed that too. There is nothing at all 'petite' about this piece, especially in this greatly upholstered version. I remember struggling to make the textures work, which forced me to do quite a bit of 'surgery', changing dynamic balances left, right and centre. I don't know if it really worked. The original version for two pianos, harmonium, small chorus and soloists is a jewel. With wonderful soloists I was able to record both the *Stabat Mater* and the orchestrated *Petite Messe solennelle*. I long to add the small version of the *'Petite'*.

Having had no idea of its existence, I was made aware recently of another Rossini choral work, one that is hardly ever performed: *Messa di Gloria*. It became another voyage of discovery as the piece is totally different from the more famous other two compositions. It was written earlier in Rossini's career while he was writing operas for the illustrious Teatro San Carlo in Naples, which meant he had the top singers in the world at his disposal. The theme of the work being the Glory of God allowed him to write a more celebratory piece, glorifying not only God, but also the human voice and its superhuman capabilities. The choral part is relatively unshowy except for an eccentric and difficult fugue that acts as the finale. It is quite clear that Rossini farmed this last movement out to another composer. They did that in those days. Two of the movements include considerable virtuoso obbligatos for the solo clarinet and the cor anglais, played amazingly by the Santa Cecilia Orchestra's Alessandro Carbonare and Maria Irsara. Coming out of the Covid pandemic we were able to commit this to disc from our 'live' performances.

I never in a million years thought that I would be persuaded to consider Rossini's last opera, *Guillaume Tell*. Cagli initially had to twist my arm to perform the original French version in concert. First of all, I didn't really know what it was apart from a couple of excerpts and the overture, which everyone knows (well, only the last part). He opined that it would be as triumphant an inauguration of a new season as could possibly be imagined. He was very persuasive, and he was the boss after all. I can still hear his gravelly voice pointing out all the features of what for him was the crowning glory of the early days of bel canto. The opera is very long indeed and I couldn't see how I was going to make it work in concert, but once I delved into the score a world opened up for me. I couldn't wait to get my teeth into it. The energy of this music is frightening. The overture is just a taster of the fantastic onslaught that is to come. I felt that with every day of study the music got more and more under my skin; even the recitatives are more exciting than anything written before or after. The biggest shock for me, however, was that I finally realised that this was the music that formed Verdi.

As an aside, I have to say that despite the undeniable greatness of Verdi, only Rossini was able to maintain this level of energy throughout his enormous trajectory, keeping the dramaturgical pull and driving the drama forward like a tidal wave. Some might think, 'Mmm, Wagner?' Listen to the finale of this opera and you will hear what was the obvious inspiration for the rainbow music in the finale of *Das Rheingold*. It seems crazy now when I think of it, but the success of this venture was such that we decided to programme *Guillaume Tell* again in another season and make a recording of it. We even brought it to the Proms in London. Gerald Finley was the memorable protagonist on the recording. I decided then and there that I had to do the piece in the opera house at Covent Garden. It was preceded by *Il barbiere di Siviglia* and followed by *Semiramide*. I was hooked on Rossini.

Something that helped me immeasurably to revive the orchestra's intrinsic Italianate identity was the initiation of several projects recording Italian operas. Decades earlier this orchestra had played for many famous opera recordings, and I felt that I had an opportunity to return it to that heritage. We made opera recordings with the starriest of casts: as well as *Guillaume Tell*, we set down *Aida*, *Otello*, *Madama Butterfly*, and most recently *Turandot*. Added to these were several opera recital discs and Verdi's *Requiem*, a life-long dream. The interplay with the singers was for me a crucial tool to enhance the flexibility of the orchestra and to introduce them to what playing for opera is all about. The degree of listening had to become more acute, the timing of placing chords had to become more accurate, and they had to sing on their instruments, all to project the text and the situation clearly and dramatically. Although there are other ways of improving these things, I knew this would be the right way for this orchestra, and there was so much new music to explore: music that is their patrimony.

In symphony after symphony over eighteen years I have immersed myself in what we call symphonic argument or the composer's development of his materials, plus the strategic and structural plotting and planning of how to pace a movement of a symphony and its individual sections. With the orchestra now front and centre, with no singers in sight, my level of focus had to become sharper. The orchestra was the whole show. I studied assiduously during this time to make the often daunting structures seem inevitable and to make them truly mine.

I strongly believe in storytelling but you have to know intimately all the threads in play to convincingly and thoroughly communicate sonata form, where the inevitable conflict of competing themes is on display. I came to realise that it was exactly this kind of focus that needed to be a stronger part of my armoury, so this period was an immense learning curve. I'm a better musician now than I was before because I have had to look inside myself and come up with the answers to questions I had never had to face in the operatic world. The true Italian character of my musicians surprised me. I am a hybrid, Anglo-Italian-American, not the real thing. Their natural ebullience was reassuring and entertaining, but Italians are complex, often betraying a certain melancholy and cynicism. However, their generosity, warmth, empathy and flair are real and I have basked in these characteristics.

What was challenging at the beginning of my tenure was the less than convincing rehearsal etiquette. Federico Fellini made a very funny film about an Italian orchestra – *Orchestra Rehearsal* – and many of the clichés he used are literally true: the constant chattering and bickering, and the appalling lack of concentration and focus. As I grew up in England and America, I was reared with more of an Anglo-Saxon approach to professionalism, so in Rome there were several battles I had to fight in the early days. I was constantly being told, 'Oh, you should have heard what it was like in years gone by.' Well, that did nothing for me, and I worked very hard to get everyone to understand that if we were going to make any steps forward, then we had to be a team with a mission. I certainly used the football team analogy – something the Italians know a lot about. But I found myself becoming more and more schoolmasterish and this made me very unhappy. I kept pressing forward but the rehearsals from time to time became extremely Mediterranean. In the end the music was bigger than both me and my musicians, and eventually we always found a way to be flexible and creative in rehearsals.

If I can identify the one composer that was able to neutralise the discipline issues, it was Johann Sebastian Bach. I was determined to programme his *St John Passion* and *St Matthew Passion*, the Magnificat and the Mass in B minor. These pieces together form a body of work that is stupefying in its importance, and the privilege of being anywhere near them is a gift from God. The rehearsals resembled prayer meetings. There was intense quiet as we forged forward, surrendering our collective talent as a gift to our musical father. The experiences were extraordinary, especially because for me personally I couldn't help thinking that I was being given a chance to collect all those hours playing Bach's music on the piano over many years, and share and translate them somehow for the orchestra and the chorus so they better understood where I was coming from in this seemingly unfamiliar territory. There is no question that as a conductor you reinvent yourself with each composer. You must find something inside yourself that illuminates each composer's world, and guide your players and your audience with authentic conviction. The conductor as salesman is an important concept. Convincing musicians who are sceptical comes up more than you would imagine. Getting past the grumbling or the eye-rolling and forging ahead with total conviction is difficult, but the concert will happen, the show must go on.

Without really knowing I was initiating anything, something called *Caro pubblico* became very important for our audience. If I was conducting something more difficult or unknown, perhaps a premiere or music that is rarely performed in Rome,

I would bring out a microphone and speak about the piece for three to five minutes. Just saying the words 'Caro pubblico, buona sera' ('Dear public, good evening') broke down a barrier between us on the platform and our audience, eliminating the sense of austerity and needless ritual. I felt very strongly from the audience that it was being given the key to how to listen to the unfamiliar and/or provocative. Essential.

When I took up my post in the autumn of 2005, a government edict was in force decreeing that no new players could be engaged on permanent contracts, which was the same for other sectors of society. Only freelancers could be hired as extra musicians for the individual concerts. With most orchestras there is always a need for extra players to fill the gaps, but we were in a bizarre situation of missing as many as thirty fixed-player positions; something completely untenable for the future of the orchestra. Fortunately, after two tense years, this destructive policy was dropped, allowing us over a period of time to audition and appoint more than thirty young players into the orchestra. That injection of young talent – mostly Italian, though not entirely – revitalised the orchestra. It turned Santa Cecilia into an ideally balanced ensemble with veterans, very young players, and people in between, all interconnecting and feeding off each other. A new brilliance came into the playing. Today the orchestra is famous for its beautiful string sound, but the sensational solo principals in all departments – the woodwinds, brass and percussion – are world class. Frustratingly in Italy, a country that is defined by its artistic heritage, the constant struggle with the government to fund the Santa Cecilia Orchestra was not something I could have imagined possible. The powers that be have always finally done so, but the singular lack of a guarantee each and every year was wearying. We were superlative ambassadors for the Italian nation abroad, so it was dispiriting not to have been able to count on this necessary support and security over a long span.

I can't overstate the vital role that the superb Santa Cecilia Chorus plays in our musical life in Rome, and I was very lucky to have had pre-eminent chorus masters such as Norbert Balatsch, Roberto Gabbiani, Ciro Visco and Piero Monti. Honegger's oratorio *Jeanne d'Arc au bûcher* was a defining event for the chorus, another season inauguration. We staged it with Keith Warner directing, sets and costumes by Es Devlin, and the astonishing French actress Romane Bohringer as Joan of Arc. The chorus revelled in the strangeness and the beauty of this score. I'm dying to do it again. This was but one among many titles: I've mentioned the Requiems, Bach, Rossini and the Italian operas, but add to that works as important as Beethoven's *Missa solemnis*, Berlioz's *La Damnation de Faust* and *Grande Messe des morts*, Mendelssohn's *Elijah*, Liszt's *Faust Symphony*, Mahler's Eighth Symphony, Puccini's *Messa di Gloria*, Petrassi's choral works, and, surprisingly, Morricone's symphonic choral works as well as his film music.

Much of my activity in Rome was filmed and broadcast by RAI, Italy's public national broadcaster. Its music documentaries and concerts are often shown at preposterously late hours, but at least they are available. I had to suffer looking at myself on screen. Though not bad most of the time, a certain physical rigidity is evident and my eyes are not always as engaged as they should be. Practise what you preach.

Pamela and I made many friendships during our time in Rome. The entire experience of reconnecting with my Italian roots was deepened each time we were invited to a friend's house, sometimes for the simplest of meals, at other times for a banquet. The Italians know how to do both. Nicola Bulgari, grandson of the founder of the Bulgari luxury-goods brand, became a close personal friend. I don't think there is anyone on the planet who loves music as much as he does, and when he found out that I loved the songs of the American songbook as much as he did, we became fast friends. For him classical music is just part of the story, and I believe that to be true as well. Nicola's generosity to me and Pamela has been nothing short of extraordinary. He always reminds me to live life, to take it all a bit easier, and that it can't always be about the music. Together with his wife Beatrice we have shared unforgettable lunches, dinners, performances, walks and old movies – his passion, along with vintage automobiles.

This reconnection with my roots took on one deeply personal element that I could not possibly have foreseen happening. After my nomination as music director, I conducted a few concerts before beginning my tenure two years later, and in July 2004 I conducted one in Benevento. That is the largest town close to the village of Castelfranco in Miscano where my parents were born. The concert took place in the small Roman amphitheatre and the whole programme was based on the 'Romeo and Juliet' theme: the Overture to Bellini's *I Capuleti e i Montecchi*, Tchaikovsky's *Romeo and Juliet* Overture and Bernstein's *Symphonic Dances from 'West Side Story'*. The orchestra kindly agreed to come down there for almost no money as a favour to me because I was receiving an award called the Golden Gladiator – Il Gladiatore d'Oro. Very kitsch. My parents decided they were going to come over from America to be at the event, and they invited a whole bunch of people from their village to join them. The trip was a big risk for my father as he had been very ill with complications from diabetes – he'd had a triple heart-bypass operation, he'd had a leg amputated, his eyes were bad,

190

and he had to have dialysis three times a week. My mother had been keeping him alive on borrowed time for a decade, and so it was a miracle to see them come to this concert so full of joy and to see my father so delighted to be back in Italy for the first time in over nine years.

After the concert I had to go back to London for just three days and then planned to join them again immediately afterwards. While I was away my parents started looking for a house to buy in Castelfranco. They were staying there for their visit, and my father was happier than he could ever remember, so they decided they would return each year for six months. It was going to transform their lives: they were going to be with people they had grown up with, they would lead the Italian village life again, and they would breathe the mountain air. One morning they were in a car on their way from Castelfranco to Benevento for my father's dialysis, a fifty-kilometre ride, and just as they were reaching the outskirts of the village my mother looked out of the window for a few moments. When she turned round again, my father had gone. He passed suddenly. He had died in the village where he was born. It was a terrible shock, but my father had been so happy: he had left that village when he'd been just twenty-three years old and he knowingly or unknowingly came back to die there at the age of seventy. It was heartbreaking for us and yet so beautiful at the same time.

It was Gastón Fournier-Facio who broke the news to me. He and others had frantically been trying to get through to me over and over again without success – for some reason my phone line had been inaccessible. On my return to Italy I was due to play the piano in a concert in my father's honour. It had been arranged that the concert would take place in the now unused church where my parents had been baptised. I was accompanying singers and also playing some chamber music, but now I was giving this concert in my father's memory. In fact, it was to be the first occurrence of what was to become an annual event. Ever since then, each year I have done a memorial concert for my father, enlarging the event each time.

I have invited members of the Orchestra of the Royal Opera House and the Santa Cecilia Orchestra to take part, and additionally a singing competition was inaugurated in my father's name. This was the idea of my dear colleague Francesco Ivan Ciampa, a Benevento native. Finally, as an off-shoot development, the enterprising mayor of Castelfranco, Antonio Pio Morcone, helped raise money to build a temporary open-air stage, and I started to conduct symphonic concerts there with the Orchestra Filarmonica di Benevento, which is a group whose members were originally members of the Nicola Sala Conservatory of Music in Benevento. They get better and better each year and this gives me enormous satisfaction. The event was put on hold by Covid-19, but otherwise I have been doing concerts with them every August, and 2,500 people from all over the region have attended each time, free of charge. That is a lot of people in a village of 800 inhabitants.

In the years after my father's death I was fortunate that my mother would come over each summer and spend some time in the village and, of course, attend the concert. We could celebrate the memory of my father together, but what gave me the most pleasure was watching her walk down the cobblestone streets as if she owned them, greeting acquaintances left and right, with bags of charisma and her head held high. For that short period of time she became a teenager again. She is now ninety years of age and the trip is all but impossible. But with her you never know. She has reserves of strength I can only dream about. As part of her morning routine back in the United States, to this day she recites the rosary while lifting ten-pound weights in each hand, and then she dances to my recording of the finale of Beethoven's Fifth. This is a sight to behold; she is quite something.

I started this book by writing about my parents. The visits to the south of Italy remind me each time what the essence of my parents is, and therefore what I am. The sweat, the grit, the ambition and the perseverance are all in that little town. I would like to conclude this instalment with a personal picture of the relationship I had with my father in the last years of his life. I frequently telephoned home when I was in Oslo, Brussels and London, and until my father had to stop most of his travelling because of his health, my parents used to visit me from time to time. They adored Vienna and Paris. My father always came whenever he could to what he considered important performances – when I did my first *Otello*, with Giuseppe Giacomini singing the title role, he was there like a shot, and *Manon Lescaut* in Vienna was another unmissable event for him – but over the years he was not somebody with whom I could share my disappointments, the ups and downs that are the normal waves of a career in music. I have been blessed with amazing opportunities, but I still sometimes doubt myself. Whenever he sensed any lack of confidence he would say, 'Why you put yourself down? Why you so negative?' He was always pumping me up: 'You are the best!' That was just his way. When he departed from this world those words were very much missed, as you can imagine.

I often shared the first and second edits of my recordings with him and he would give his opinions and share ideas and feelings, especially about music he had known and loved all his life. He would get so caught up in the tumult of the voices together with the lush sounds of the orchestra – no more so than in Puccini's *Tosca*. There is a film of the two of us listening to it and I keep asking if the tempi are right. He keeps saying, 'Yes, yes, yes', sensing some doubt on my part. He wouldn't have it, but being a part of the process made him very happy and proud.

He could never understand why I was so attracted to all those eternally long Wagner operas. When I was about to do my first *Siegfried* in Vienna in 1993, he asked me, 'How long is it?' I said, 'Five to five and a half hours in the theatre.' 'Ma, pecché?' ('But why?') 'Ma pecché always questi funeral?' (A mix of English and the Benevento dialect for 'Why always these funerals?') 'Why you not conduct something *allegro* – like a *Carmen*?' I have conducted *Carmen* a lot, by the way. He could never get over the length and the stupefying complexity of Wagner, nor could he come to terms with some of my other repertoire, such as *Erwartung* and *Wozzeck*.

After all the suffering he had to endure when I was living at home and listening to Bartók string quartets and Boulez's *Le Marteau sans maître*, I did still baffle him at times. I once said to Pierre Boulez, 'You know you ruined my parents' life at one time because I listened to *Le Marteau sans maître* so many times they didn't know what the hell had got into me.' He said sincerely but tongue in cheek, 'Oh, I'm very sorry . . .'

To this day I keep in close contact with my mother by telephone. It isn't the same as being there with her, and I don't have the responsibility that my brother Patrick does to see that she's OK – but it is crucial for me that I am in touch as much as possible. After all these years on the telephone I am able to read her every mood by the nuances of her voice, so she can't hide anything from me, as older people are wont to do. She tells me everything.

My tenure as music director of the Santa Cecilia Orchestra and Chorus officially came to an end in July 2023 after an eighteen-year collaboration. In April 2023 we played our final Rome concerts. It was a terrific programme that somehow summed up my time there: a world premiere, *Dosàna nóva* by Claudio Ambrosini; the *Four Last Songs* of Richard Strauss with the wondrous Asmik Grigorian and, to come full circle, Shostakovich's Tenth Symphony, with which I began this Roman adventure. The orchestra played its heart out for me and each and every member has my greatest admiration and thanks.

15

MOZARTIAN INTERMEZZO

In 2017 the Victoria and Albert Museum published a book edited by Kate Bailey entitled *Opera: Passion, Power and Politics* and I was asked to write a few lines about Mozart's *Le nozze di Figaro*. Instead of a music history lesson, I decided to plunge straightaway into describing the music. The process gave me such joy that I wanted to include it here as an intermezzo of sorts.

———————

Giving the upbeat to the *Le nozze di Figaro* Overture is the quintessential split-second decision to commit mischief. Tense, eyebrows raised, the whites of the bassoonists' eyes in front of me, with a flick the music flies past. Wait for me, Cherubino, breathless, late perhaps, it's a wedding day. The occasion is announced politely, no, haughtily by oboes and horns (we are in the house of the Count and Countess), the whole band explodes indecorously in celebration. Bursts of instrumental colour, peals of laughter, much showing off, scales, fanfares, a musical party. Ah, but wait, there are clandestine goings on, too. Darting eyes, secrets, the sudden shutting of doors, hiding. Will they be found out? Oh, my God, the preparations – and we're so late!!! Run!

Susanna and Figaro, servants in a fine manor house, are about to get married, and they are both busy. The orchestra tells you exactly what's going on. The second violins' semiquavers

196

give you the prenuptial 'buzz' in the room, while the cellos and double basses pronounce a long 'Mmm!' Figaro is taking measurements in the room for the marriage bed, the first violins metronomically pecking out the centimetres. He is pleased with himself. A vaguely erotic atmosphere pervades. The bassoons join in and concur that Figaro is a genius, such a genius, as they climb higher and higher. Susanna looks to see what the fuss is about (flutes and oboes, inquisitively). He dances a quadrille! Men! The oboe preens, joined by the flute, the fiddles shiver in admiration – what a gorgeous Spanish woman is Susanna. She admires the fit of her new hat, triplets complimenting too. Woodwinds just so.

Figaro and Susanna sing over each other at cross purposes, now together, a fractious Latin couple, and so in love, tumbling into a bawdy embrace. It goes on: in something akin to actual speech rather than song (we call this *recitativo secco*, dry recitation being the rather dull translation – it means no orchestra, just a keyboard) we find out that their room is in close proximity to the Count's rooms. Alarm bells. 'You stupid Figaro, don't you know why he's given us this room?' (This dry recitation can be very spirited and certainly pushes the action forward.) Figaro launches the most delicious little duet, with the orchestra imitating bells: 'Come here, go there' – the life of the servant. Susanna reverts to the minor key (*uh-oh*), the bell imitations become dangerous and plaintive. 'You'll be sent off on an errand (*din din*) and I'll be a sitting duck for the Count's predatory advances (*DON DON*). Do you want to hear the rest?' Musical hesitations everywhere. Figaro becomes dark and vengeful. Now alone, he sings to the invisible Count: 'If you want to dance this dance, then I'll play along' (pathetically he is shadowed by the horns, the traditional theatrical symbols for the cuckold), pretending everything is fine, but then (the music becomes turbo-charged with impossible trills, and impossible Italian), 'I'll turn your world upside down!' Revolution is around the corner . . .

Have I conveyed my love for this piece and its energy with the descriptions I've given above? I hope so. This is how I need the Mozart experience to be for me. Every word, every gesture: pure theatre.

No one comes close to Mozart's awareness of human motivation, nor the knowledge that life is an adventure to be experienced, often dangerous, often painful, but exhilarating and essential at the same time. The only way I know how to engage with his operas, and in particular this one, is by considering every detail (there are a multitude) from every angle and perspective, and through the prism of every character. Let me tell you that every character is, in the end, out for himself or herself. The other name for this opera is *La Folle journée* ('The Crazy Day'). This household is most certainly dysfunctional, and Mozart has truly thought of all the preposterous ins and outs of this impossible wedding day with the help of his rogue-genius librettist Lorenzo Da Ponte (1749–1838). The rascals must have had such fun.

Either sitting alone at the study table or in the midst of the hustle and bustle of rehearsals (there is no opera that is more fun to work on), I'm constantly trying to understand or fathom what the wordless orchestra is trying to say. It has perhaps the loudest voice, but it has in my mind the most secrets to reveal if one listens really carefully.

The mirth of Act I is balanced by its polar opposite, Act II. We meet the Countess for the first time, a showbiz trick of introducing a new character comparatively late on. Four stately chords followed by three tired semiquavers and then a heart-breaking melody (Beethoven stole this musical signature over and over) that truly weeps, then a cry of anguish followed by secret sobs, another cry and 'why me'. All of this before any words have been sung. The Countess languishes (she is married to a serial philanderer). She sings in exquisite pain to love itself, asking for some remedy for her sighing melancholy. There is a feeling of wallowing in her sadness, but how profoundly human that is, and the orchestra sighs for her. She wants to die; she goes to a musical precipice. We stop . . . no, she doesn't do it. She finishes in a whimper, the clarinet and bassoon trying to console her.

The young scamp Cherubino enters and sings a lovely song, the fiddles plucking cheekily, mandolin-like, the accompaniment, the clarinet and the bassoon amorous, the oboe sighing exaggeratedly. The boy is nervous, but he sings well. He steals furtive glances at the Countess – he is in love he thinks. The big surprise of the night is that the Countess is aroused; how could she not be by *that* modulation into A flat major? 'One minute I'm freezing, another my soul is on fire, and then back again.' (The horns bathe this phrase in a warm glow.) Mozart and Cherubino are innocent and sly seducers. The sexual tension is palpable and, honestly, who can blame the Countess for being tempted out of her gloom, despite her languishing aria having been sung only a few moments before? Marriage, infidelity, constancy, first love, class warfare – it's all here.

I could go on forever. See this opera, listen to this opera. It will teach you so much. And you will laugh and cry, and laugh and cry . . .

16

CONDUCTING VERDI'S *REQUIEM*: AN APPRECIATION OF MOVEMENTS 1 AND 2

Movement 1: *Requiem*

When approaching Verdi's *Requiem*, it is extraordinary to realise that this great masterpiece was written by a composer who struggled with the whole notion of the Church as a political force in society. He certainly grew up with the words of the Latin Catholic Mass and the Mass for the Dead, or Requiem. Though he would never define himself a believer, he inherently understood that Italian Catholicism is intertwined with, defined even, by the fear of judgement, the fear of God.

This awe-struck fear is expressed in many different ways in his *Requiem*, a work for large orchestra, chorus and four soloists lasting the best part of ninety minutes, in which the detail of its diversity is so astonishingly inventive in virtually every bar that I am devoting this chapter to a personal analysis of its first half: the *Requiem* and *Dies irae* sections. Before I begin, it must be said as a prelude how strongly Rossini's choral works, in particular his *Stabat Mater*, influenced Verdi. Listening to the first bars of Rossini's marvellous work, one is immediately struck by the colour of the cellos in unison with the bassoon, because this combination would be the template for so many works in Verdi's *oeuvre*, especially *Don Carlos*, *Otello* and the *Requiem*. This mahogany hue seems effortlessly to penetrate the soul of the listener, yet is actually quite rudimentary in orchestration terms.

The *Requiem* begins in A minor – a key that is somehow hermetically sealed in its own darkness. Straightaway a rapt atmosphere is created by the muted strings playing *pianissimo*. The drooping melody in the cellos – falling once and then again, without hope in a mysterious duet with silence, prepares us for an achingly harmonised and expanded version of the falling theme, interrupted by what seems like choral rumblings but which is in reality the word 'Requiem'. It is crucially important that this is performed on the breath, more air than voice. Verdi has specified *sotto voce* (under the voice, or hushed), and the 'R' of 'Requiem' is rolled generously but in a whisper – almost as a shiver, as if the word dare not be expressed. These first vocal fragments are sung separately by the male and female choruses in a very low range, but as the string orchestra begins to open up in a revelatory contrary motion, a two-bar phrase arriving with a *crescendo* at the dominant key, E major, the expectation is created that now the whole chorus must sing in full voice – but instead Verdi writes for them *il più piano possibile* (as quietly as possible) as they sing 'Requiem aeternam' ('Eternal rest'). This is so difficult to get right, but it is the first of many musical *coups de théâtre* (yes, I use that term). As the strings recede, the chorus is magically revealed with breathtaking intensity.

A pleading descending melody in the first violins follows as four lonely sopranos sing 'Dona eis, Domine' ('Grant them, Lord'): the melody moves sequentially, its repetitiveness and displaced accents bound under a single extraordinarily long phrase mark. The orchestra then provokes what might be hope as all of a sudden the dominant seventh chord resolves with a *crescendo* to A major: but again it arrives with a *subito* triple *pianissimo* (suddenly very, very quietly) to prepare for the text 'Et lux perpetua' ('And perpetual light'). The radiance of this moment is palpable, but it is the orchestra that sings out the melody, the chorus acting as spectators murmuring hopefully, then gradually losing hope as the phrasing becomes more and more broken up.

Something very strange is happening: in Italian choral or operatic repertoire, if the orchestra spurs something on, usually you get a response, but here we have the opposite. Again it is as though the chorus almost dare not say the words – out of fear. Already, in Verdi's setting of the *Requiem*'s opening stanza – 'Requiem aeternam dona eis, Domine, et lux perpetua luceat eis' ('Grant them eternal rest, Lord, and let perpetual light shine upon them') – he has created an atmosphere of apprehension through constantly dashing our expectations.

Suddenly another surprise: the disintegration of the chorus's 'luceat eis' culminates not in the nothingness that you are expecting but in an explosive hymn written in a strict fugue. Verdi famously had a chip on his shoulder about fugue writing because one of the reasons he was rejected by the Milan Conservatory of Music in his entrance examination was the professors' allegation that he was useless at writing counterpoint and fugal music. He certainly showed them in the end. Most of his operas have sections of fugal writing, and he was enjoying rubbing their noses in it. The fugue here – 'Te decet hymnus' ('We sing hymns to you') – bursts forth in a quicker tempo now in the brighter key of F major, starting with the basses and moving upwards. The melody itself is quite stolid, more reminiscent of a Protestant hymn, but because it comes after so much soft singing it packs a real punch. Before it reaches *fortissimo* however and after only eight bars, suddenly at 'Deus in Sion' ('God in Zion') Verdi introduces a radical *diminuendo* to triple *pianissimo*, an arresting effect. The voices *crescendo* again – 'et tibi redetur votum in Jerusalem' ('and unto thee shall the vow be performed in Jerusalem') – and the music continues with ever more startling dynamic contrasts.

Unfortunately, there is a tendency in performances of a lot of Verdi's music (and Italian music in general) to ignore many of the details of his dynamic markings. The operas are especially badly served in this regard. Italian music is fragile; it needs care. Because a lot of it is immediately singable or 'easy', the onus is on the performers to respect it, and go beyond the obvious. Verdi is very clear but very concise, relying on the intelligence, good taste and rigour of his performers. Fortunately, the *Requiem* tends to be treated with greater reverence because it is spiritual, but I can tell you one has to fight tooth and nail to achieve what Giuseppe wrote.

There are four soloists still waiting to make their first entries – and they do so after an almost total repeat of the initial intro- ductory music, only this time in the chorus instead of 'luceat eis' almost disappearing, the music opens out again, this time into an A major that is quite different from the perpetual light of before. It's a most compelling lead in, provoking the tenor to sing 'Kyrie eleison' ('Lord, have mercy'). As he begins, the colour in the orchestra underneath changes completely from anything we have so far heard: the cellos, without mutes now, and bassoons in unison have a rhythmic descending scale that quickly makes the music more solid and less ethereal, creating a sense of journeying forward, and while the orchestra moves downwards the tenor aspires upwards towards God as he begs for mercy. He even has the temerity to ask for it almost hero- ically, ending with a flourish. The bass then sings in similar tones though with a longer *crescendo*, until the soprano enters, and this time her phrase ending is really emphatic and marked *largo, pesante* (broadly and with weight). Finally, the mezzo-soprano joins and the soloists overlap with arching phrases.

So, each demand for mercy is very individual. But who are these four people? I tend to think of them in Verdi's *Requiem* as individuals in a greater crowd – the voices of four characters, as Verdi depicts them for us, who have the courage to come out from the crowd and represent the people to God. The mezzo-soprano is in some ways the strongest, most confident personality, and her first entry in this section catalyses the re-entries not only of the other soloists but also of the chorus in a reiteration of the *Kyrie eleison* text, which now sounds resplendent. Verdi soon takes it down from *fortissimo* to *pianissimo*, with a febrile little *staccato* figure in the first violins, soon joined by the second violins and the violas. Meanwhile the first flute, the first bassoon, the third horn and the cellos double the four sections of the chorus as one by one they sing the first snippet of the original *Kyrie eleison* melody. The soloists provide musical embroidery with short phrases containing an unusual displaced accent, like a shudder.

When the key unexpectedly shifts to C sharp major, the text is now sung in seraphic rather than heroic tones by the soloists, becoming impatiently ecstatic at the repeated word 'eleison' – and here the all-important timpani in this work makes its first entrance, hammering the point home. The procedure continues, now going quickly through many complex key changes, and when 'eleison' is repeated, this time emphatically by the chorus as well as by the soloists, Verdi cleverly brings us back to A minor. Here the music is pleading in a demanding way, with the accent on the offbeat of the bar, a stubborn reinforcement from the timpani, and the bass line repeatedly moving downwards, painting a picture of relentless imploring. The music moves modally to a *fortissimo* D minor chord but then immediately *diminuendos* – there is no response from God. Instead, there's a beautiful silence – then, together with the woodwinds, the women soloists and just a few women in the chorus followed by the men soloists and just a few chorus men sing the word 'eleison' triple *pianissimo* and with what we call *portato*: the notes palpitate, almost having tears in them as Verdi briefly introduces minor-key colorations.

Verdi now takes us to the conclusion of this movement, first by generously moving to A major as a brief expression of comfort and hope as the soloists, chorus and orchestra combine with lush expressions of the tenor's original *Kyrie eleison* theme. They are grandly reinforced by the timpani – but soon the music *diminuendos* again and all the singers are marked *morendo* (dying away): it's as if they can't make the strength of their pleading stick . . . they lose hope. Two bars of anxious syncopated throbbing from the violins, and violas, with the cellos and first bassoon uneasily now recalling their descending unison phrase from the beginning of the *Kyrie eleison* – and then out of nowhere a *pianissimo* chord of F major with the word 'Christe' ('Christ'). A change to B flat major for 'Christe' again almost tricks us into believing Verdi will stay in this new harmonic environment. But no, the dominant seventh chord on E that follows brings relief by taking you back to A major, the whole movement travelling from the darkness to the light. This is no better crystallised than by the final upward-reaching gesture of the violins, a reversal, a transformation of the initial descending cello and bassoon phrase underpinning the solo tenor's first entrance. The movement then ends on two resigned hushed chords over a timpani rumble. How glorious it is to be able to perform music like this with such enormous forces. Yes, the loud passages are thrilling, but let me tell you that a true *pianissimo* achieved when everyone is singing and playing is even more so.

Movement 2: *Dies irae*

It's almost frightening to look at the page of the score where Verdi suddenly unleashes the colossal rage of the *Dies irae* with an artillery: four bassoons, bass tuba, timpani, a hugely important bass drum (the bigger the better), four trumpets, four extra trumpets offstage, four trombones, four horns, two flutes, piccolo, two oboes, two clarinets, and a very large string section plus a very large chorus. The Day of Wrath and the Day of Judgement explodes, hammered out by violent accents and with howling and screaming in both the choral voices and the orchestra, as the wild scales of the flutes, clarinets and oboes fly and hurtle against the bassoons in contrary motion. Maniacal trills of F sharp and G in the woodwind, horns and trumpets collide in a huge dissonance with a held G in the first sopranos, altos and tenors of the chorus while the remainder of the chorus roars and hollers, dropping down chromatically, all of them singing 'Dies irae' ('Day of wrath'). It's a terrifying din. The strings have two bars of a furiously cascading downward race of semiquavers that tumble into the depths, provoking a syncopated and almost atomic response from the bass drum playing *fortissimo* offbeat accents – and Verdi has given precise indications as to how the drum head should be tensioned to give the loudest and strongest impact.

It is a battle between one person on the bass drum and a hundred or more others playing against them. It's a fantastic metaphor for the Day of Judgement – we are there as individuals before God, and we can beat our drum as loudly as we want but . . . In performance, with so much intense clamour in the orchestra, the conductor has to maximise the potency of the chorus, and in this opening section it makes a huge difference if you have some brave altos who can go up to a high G and double the second sopranos' part and also if you can have as many sopranos as possible on the long sustained G – additionally it's ideal if you have some baritones that can successfully double the second tenors' part. These are the techniques I learned from Romano Gandolfi and Vittorio Sicuri all those years ago! If you can get all this to work, it creates a tremendous noise.

Just look at the text immediately after the words 'Dies irae': 'dies illa, solvet saeclum in favilla, teste David cum Sibylla' ('this day of wrath shall consume the world in ashes, as fore-told by David and Sibyl') – the fear of the world falling apart. Everything in the music is descriptive of these words: the syn-copations throwing everything off kilter, the headlong semi-quavers repeating almost like gunfire, the woodwinds wailing and swirling, the timpani dislocating everything against the beat as the music momentarily stutters at the words 'solvet saeclum' and then again at 'teste David'. This *Requiem* has been accused of being an opera – well, there's no question it conjures up terrifying images, but Mozart also does that in the *Dies irae* of his *Requiem*, and few have ever accused him of writing an operatic Mass. Verdi goes further though, and his harmonic daring in a very short space of time is dramatically disrupting: from G minor we progress through very unsettling diminished chords to arrive at an improbable E major.

After more chaos with rushing repeated notes topped by screaming woodwinds, we come to a change with an enor-mous sustained set of chords, all impenetrably harmonised: in

207

Nr. 2. Dies iræ

descending but now uninterrupted long lines the chorus repeats the words of the *Dies irae* sung so far, this time doubled by almost the entire orchestra but additionally underpinned by a massive continuous rumble from bass drum and timpani. It is as though the tempest reaches its height and pulverises everyone – but very soon it dies down, and again we reach an extreme level of quietness. This is one of the great challenges for the performers in this work – playing and singing very quietly just seconds after they have been at full throttle is very difficult indeed.

As we are about to reach 'Quantus tremor est futurus, quando judex est venturus, cuncta stricte discussurus!' ('What trembling there will be when the Judge shall come to weigh everything strictly!'), Verdi gives us a very threatening dissonance in the trombones – A flat against B flat – reinforced by a low B flat in the third and fourth bassoons. The violins and cellos have little shuddering figures and there's a nervous kind of off-the-beat plucking, *pianissimo*, in the first and second horns, oboes, flute and piccolo – it's as if they can't catch their breath. Now the chorus sings *pianissimo sotto voce* as though they too can't catch their breath with 'Quantus tremor est futurus!' Verdi brilliantly evokes this by breaking up the words into short gasps: 'Quan–tus tremor – est – futurus –', but then for the arrival of the judge he changes to long notes: 'Quando juuhhdex esst venturus' is how it sounds. And with 'cuncta stricte discussurus!' he puts in accents – all so that this passage is sung in a disquieting tense manner. It ends totally unexpectedly with a shift to C minor – and a sustained triple *pianissimo* chord.

Two trumpets in unison sound an ominous dotted-note fanfare and they are echoed by unison trumpets from afar. Verdi has written 'in the distance, and invisible' for these four echoing trumpets that play in pairs an octave apart, but you can take risks with where you place them so as to best achieve what he wanted. I like to have them in the auditorium but very high up, so that they are coming from somewhere far above, with each pair on opposite sides. This can create difficulties of ensemble so you have to be careful just how far apart you put them. After the unison-note fanfares are played and echoed, they are repeated, now with the interval of a minor third, then again as diminished chords, and finally as major chords. They then move and *crescendo* in chromatic harmonic progressions, and the fanfare rhythm develops into repeated emphatic triplets played simultaneously by the offstage and the orchestral trumpets, becoming louder and louder. It's a tremendous cacophony for the listener, almost becoming too much to take – until the rest of the brass and the timpani crash in. *Tutta forza* – with very greatest force – is Verdi's marking. They reiterate the original fanfare theme, now in A flat minor – the darkest of keys. The fanfare rhythms turn into relentless triplets prompting a thunderous entrance of the bass drum, the men's chorus and the rest of the orchestra in the cataclysm that is 'Tuba mirum spargens sonum, per sepulcra regionem, coget omnes ante thronum' ('The trumpet, scattering its terrifying sound through the tombs of every land, will gather all before the throne').

The conductor will most definitely have to reinforce the chorus basses with the tenors and the altos with the sopranos. It's your only hope. The offstage trumpets re-enter abetted by the orchestra trumpets. The chorus finally breaks into four parts but the mayhem continues until out of nowhere there is a communal blast of A major from which everyone abruptly cuts off. There is a deathly silence. 'Mors stupebit et natura' ('Death and nature shall be stunned').

The strings fearfully initiate a musical tic in triple *pianissimo* answered ominously by the bass drum and the double basses *pizzicato*. The bass soloist intones his first phrase almost demonically, rising with a *crescendo*, which receives a most cruel response from the horns on a forced, muted F sharp. With each repetition of his text, the bass's voice seems to wither into a whisper answered with a surprisingly conciliatory hushed A major.

With quasi-stentorian tones the mezzo-soprano now introduces the *Liber scriptus* ('the written book') on a one-note melody that reinforces the gravity of the moment with each repetition of the A natural. The curling up to the E natural *pianissimo* offers little consolation, and in fact the timpani shudders in response. Verdi continues in a more conventional quasi-operatic vein underpinned by nervous cello figurations. The mezzo-soprano is very grand here – a figure of awe that impels the chorus to mutter repeatedly and almost inaudibly 'dies irae'.

The brass now introduces what at first sounds like a benevolent gesture but then gains in momentum, provoking the mezzo's *fortissimo* 'Judex ergo cum sedebit, quidquid latet apparebit: nil inultum remanebit' ('When the judge takes his seat, all that is hidden shall appear, nothing will remain unavenged'). This section develops into a march-like coda of considerable force, sending the soloist to a startling high A flat. Thereafter the musical terrain becomes more fragmentary, almost disintegrating with each reiteration of the word 'nil'. Verdi sets up a situation of almost unashamed theatricality and the mezzo-soprano doesn't disappoint, delivering a final volley in *fortissimo*.

A beautiful trio ensues: 'Quid sum miser tunc dicturus? Quem patronum rogaturus, cum vix justus sit securus?' ('What shall I, a wretch, say then? To which protector shall I appeal when even the just man is barely safe?'). Once again Verdi sets the atmosphere with repeated notes – this time with two clarinets that just sigh briefly and then disappear. Now comes a most unusual obbligato from the first bassoon: an aching repeating phrase of six *pianissimo* notes, the first note short and *staccato*, the other five *legato*. The notes are of the G minor chord but with a chromatic twist: it's almost serpentine, while the mezzo-soprano sings, 'Quid sum miser tunc dicturus?' She has a melodic line that descends in the minor key – a familiar gesture in this work. Here the mezzo-soprano is no longer the authoritative figure of before – she is now just one of the people, asking, 'Where shall I turn?' Declamation is nowhere to be found. Against her melody the writhing bassoon obbligato continues; then when she reaches 'Quem patronum', the singer has a very unusual octave jump at 'vix Justus'. It's almost as though she is defending herself – and the bassoon answers her benignly for once. There follows a chromatic scale in the cellos, a lament, the bassoon obbligato starts again, and then the tenor enters with the original theme, with the soprano and mezzosoprano soon joining him.

We have in this section a passage where these three soloists repeat the phrase 'Quem patronum rogaturus', singing together and totally unaccompanied, in closely spaced harmony, chromatically moving through expressive passing dissonances. As one of a list of composers of Italian liturgical music that goes back many centuries, Verdi knew his Palestrina, and this is one of a number of places in this work where he writes music that could almost have been composed in the Renaissance.

The orchestra now joins in, with the return of the bassoon obbligato and sighing figures in the other woodwind instruments accompanying the singers. Then the three soloists return to being individuals as one by one they sing alone, each one again asking a separate part of the question, 'Quid sum miser tunc dicturus?' The last voice is the soprano – she drops a whole octave, fading away as she plaintively asks, 'When even the just man is barely safe?'

The answer comes: 'Rex tremendae majestatis, qui salvandos salvas gratis: salva me, fons pietas' ('King of awful majesty, you freely save those worthy of salvation: save me, font of pity'). The chorus basses suddenly cry out in a terrifying outburst, and Verdi creates the awe of God's majesty here with the bassoons, trombones, tuba, double basses and cellos all in unison playing a double-dotted and thus powerfully rhythmic figure that drops right down over one and a half octaves, hurtling towards the abyss, all reinforced by a *fortissimo* timpani roll. As the figure drops down, its volume is subdued and the key of C minor changes unexpectedly to A flat major as the tenors, supported by the horns, very softly now repeat, 'Rex tremendae majestatis'.

This procedure is repeated but with the tenors this time singing 'qui salvandos salvas gratis', and then one by one the four soloists enter as individuals with 'salva me, fons pietas'. They sing as individuals because the text here could not be more personal: 'save *me*, font of pity'. There's a great warmth in their melody, with the soprano singing in more urgent terms – and as they repeat the words many times Verdi takes us on an extraordinary harmonic journey expressing these same four words in many varied ways. The chorus joins presently with a mix of 'Rex tremendae majestatis' and 'salva me'. This is now the people pleading 'save me', and they become more insistently demanding of God's attention as their notes, reinforced now by the soloists, become shorter and more emphatic. The solo soprano finally takes hold of everyone, stopping them in their tracks by pleading just on her own on a very long note, sustained with a *crescendo* and *diminuendo*, and with this she brings the music back to the soloists as individuals in, incredibly, the key of F sharp major after we had started this section in C minor. The way Verdi travels from key to key with a sense of unexpected discovery is an important innovation in his creative output.

The soprano and mezzo-soprano alternate 'salva me' in expressive curved lines while the chorus almost whispers 'salva me'. The tenor soloist now intones something different: followed by the bass, he rises up in a scale, more beseechingly trying to get through to God, and this unleashes a mighty reaction from the orchestra and the chorus, who volley back and forth with the soloists. The music picks up pace and becomes more and more animated to the point where everything almost runs away with itself, the solo soprano flying all the way up to a high C as everyone desperately demands salvation. It culminates in a unanimous C major *fortissimo* 'salva me'.

But . . . they are greeted by silence. Still there is no response from God. Timidly now in *pianissimo*, marked *dolce*, the bass soloist offers 'salva me' in a fragment of the soloists' previous melody – and Verdi takes this cell and now builds a fragile edifice of music rising up from it brick by brick, as it were, in the chorus, orchestra and then soloists, from *pianissimo* to *mezzoforte*, pictorially suggesting voices rising to heaven. It finishes grandly, but very humanly, and the strings answer with a consoling phrase almost as though God is now saying, 'Let me reflect.'

For salvation, the mezzo-soprano and soprano as individuals sing an extended duet: 'Recordare, Iesu pie, Quod sum causa tuae viae: Ne me perdas illa die. Quaerens me, sedisti lassus:

Redemisti crucem passus: Tantus labor non sit cassus. Iuste iudex ultionis, Donum fac remissionis, Ante diem rationis' ('Remember, gentle Jesus, that I am the reason for your time on Earth: do not cast me out on that day. Seeking me, you sank down wearily; you saved me by enduring the cross: such travail must not be in vain. Just judge of punishment: give me the gift of redemption before the day of reckoning'). First individually, and then together, they sing a beautiful but simple melody. Verdi takes the words 'gentle Jesus' as his cue for this benign episode. An oboe, a clarinet and two flutes insistently but very quietly cite the 'salva me' theme from before, creating a satisfying unity of structure or dramaturgy at this point. The writing becomes more and more emotional and in the best bel canto tradition the female soloists intertwine their voices in an unusual cadenza without accompaniment, both covering an impressive range. They end quietly.

Without a link the tenor sings a solo aria: 'Ingemisco tamquam reus, culpa rubet vultus meus; supplicant parce, Deus. Qui Mariam absolvisti, et latronem exaudisti, mihi quoque spem dedisti. Preces meae non sunt dignae; sed tu bonus, fac benigne, ne perenni cremer igne. Inter oves locum praesta, et ab haedis me sequestra, statuens in parte dextra' ('I groan as a guilty one, and my face blushes with guilt; spare the supplicant, O God. You, who absolved Mary Magdalen, and heard the prayer of the thief, have given me hope as well. My prayers are not worthy, but show mercy, O benevolent one, lest I burn forever in fire. Give me a place among the sheep, and separate me from the goats, placing me on your right hand'). This is the most pictorial of the solo arias with its gentle bucolic descriptions of nature. The character of the tenor's music is filled with guilt: perhaps he is a criminal; he longs for freedom and forgiveness in nature. The redemptive pastoral element is so very beautifully captured by Verdi here.

Harmonically the aria is ambiguous at the start and wanders around without a proper tonal centre, as though the tenor, this character, is lost as he sings, 'I groan as a guilty one, and my face blushes with guilt; spare the supplicant, O God.' Then, as he sings to God how He who has forgiven Mary Magdalen has given him hope, the warm key of E flat major is firmly established and he breaks into melody, but in the pulsating accompaniment of the strings there are unusually placed accents. The orchestra then imitates his ravishing melisma on 'absolvisti' and the tenor moves up to a high B flat that Verdi has marked *dolcissimo*. As we have heard before, the music as it rises up in pitch suggests reaching up to heaven: 'mihi quoque spem dedisti' – God has given this guilty one hope. We start to hear instrumental gestures that foreshadow the allusions to nature and the sheep about which he will soon sing: little pastoral suggestions of shepherds on the bassoon and oboe, and the first and second horns playing rustic open fifths. It's all quite unexpected in a Requiem, but it humanises the text so intimately – somehow this is the atmosphere of Aida's 'O patria mia': the landscape, the terrain, loneliness, homesickness . . . the sounds and songs of your country, no more beautifully expressed than when the oboe plays solo – an unmistakable image of a shepherd playing his pipe. The tenor quite suddenly becomes more majestic as he moves to the end of his aria with a plea to God to place him on his right hand. Just as in the preceding duet, dramaturgically speaking there has been a loss of musical composure in this aria, and this fits in with the general atmosphere of the Requiem.

But now, all of a sudden the orchestra cooks up a ministorm to introduce the bass soloist: 'Confutatis maledictis flammis acribus addictis, voca me cum benedictis. Oro supplex et acclinis, cor contritum quasi cinis: gere curam mei finis' ('When the damned are silenced, and given to the fierce flames, call me among the blessed ones. I pray, suppliant and kneeling, with a heart contrite as ashes: take my ending into your care'). Verdi ferociously and succinctly conjures up the image of the damned souls being thrown into the flames as the bass, marked *con forza* (forcefully), plunges an octave down. The timpani, clarinet and violins all shudder onto a disturbing diminished chord joined by bassoons, horns, violas and cellos. The image is repeated; everything halts to a pause. The bass sings a brief plea in a sweetly voiced tone. The key here is A major – and now Verdi shifts to one of the darkest of all keys, C sharp minor, for the bass to sing the wonderful images in the text: 'I pray, suppliant and kneeling, with a heart contrite as ashes: take my ending into your care.' He has a soothing *cantabile* melody, but in the accompaniment Verdi ingeniously inserts an occasional dropping octave figure in the double basses and first bassoon that recall his 'maledictus' octave jump at his entrance before, reminding us that there is always the warning for the damned: it's subtle business, but it's there. As he repeats 'with a heart contrite as ashes', the bass sings a descending phrase going down and down step by step: almost as though his head is drooping before God, not aspiring – it is the guilt and weight of a transgressor's contrition.

The bass sings his text in its entirety, but Verdi won't let it go just like that – he has to recreate the warning of the Day of Judgement and the damned. This time as the bass again sings 'Confutatis maledictis, flammis acribus addictis', the orchestration is far more intense: the timpani hammer out *fortissimo* semiquavers; the basses and cellos and the violins fly against each chromatically; the flutes and piccolo wail up to the top of their ranges – vivid images of flames burning the damned. Again a sudden shift in the music to potential peace with 'voca me cum benedictis', although the bass returns to a more forceful pleading tone. The orchestra answers with syncopations as though it hasn't heard the words, and it takes us back to the C sharp minor of before as the bass with orchestra repeats the opening material.

As the aria moves towards its end, the oboes have a rising figure that portents the bass's final repeat of 'I pray, suppliant and kneeling, with a heart contrite as ashes', which he now sings more apprehensively. As he reaches his final words, 'take my ending into your care', he suddenly sings them with a fierce urgency. Verdi shows us again and again how skilled he is at finding ever new colours when the text repeats.

The bass's final phrase triggers a horrendous repetition of the *Dies irae* opening. Each time it has recurred there has been a variation, and this time while it vents its fury Verdi suddenly changes key from G minor to E flat minor. The violins trill and then career up with a soaring plaintive melody that immediately dies down, preparing us, as calm is restored, for the *Lacrymosa*, in B flat minor: 'Lacrymosa dies illa, qua resurget ex favilla, judicandus homo reus. Huic ergo parce, Deus. Pie Jesu Domine: dona eis requiem. Amen' ('That day is one of weeping, on which shall rise from the ashes the guilty man, to be judged. Therefore, spare this one, O God. Merciful Lord Jesus: grant them peace. Amen'). Verdi had originally used a version of this melody in the first, French-language version of *Don Carlos*, but here it is much more simply orchestrated: he marks the chords in the strings 'long and lamenting' – and if they are played correctly as he indicates, they weep.

The dark colour of the mezzo-soprano then enters, and Verdi indicates 'with much expression' as she sings the opening phrase. The music rises in pitch sequentially before dropping down again – her attempts to get close to God through prayer are futile at first. The bass then joins and sings the same music while the mezzo-soprano, marked *piangente* (weeping), laments on the offbeats, her gestures seconded by the woodwinds.

Verdi abandons this colour as the soprano soloist with the chorus sopranos and altos, followed immediately by the mezzo-soprano, enter *dolcissimo* (very sweetly) with the words 'Huic ergo parce, Deus' ('Therefore, spare this one, O God'). They are accompanied by shimmering strings, flutes, piccolo and bassoon. It's a momentary vision of light, though, because Verdi quickly reintroduces the *Lacrymosa*, sung now by all four soloists and the chorus, and this time it is enriched with a raft of additional forms of weeping: there is dissonance on the offbeat, syncopation after a crotchet rest, a lamenting counter-melody – a festival of tears. Being an Italian, Verdi never lost sight of the origins of the funereal band, and he introduces its *oompapa* here in the low brass accompanied by the timpani and bass drum: we don't quite hear it clearly but it's there. Then the soprano breaks free from the crowd and rises up chromatically with the violins to a high B flat – it's as though something has been pierced and we are back into the world of potential hope for peace as we come to the radiant key of F major. The chorus responds by dovetailing one by one in each section with 'Huic ergo parce, Deus', and this builds to a full-throated plea for salvation from all the singers, reinforced by the full orchestra.

The soloists continue unaccompanied, singing, 'Pie Jesu Domine: dona eis requiem' ('Merciful Lord Jesus: grant them peace'). As with the passage in the *Quid sum miser* section earlier, the music and its aura harks back to the Renaissance and Palestrina, but this time the writing is even more harmonically intricate – and it is very difficult indeed to sing and to stay in tune. The music captures the words here with the utmost purity – the marking again is *dolcissimo* and Verdi puts in little sighing accents that delicately humanise the expression. With the reappearance of the chorus and the orchestra, we come back partially to the atmosphere and melody of the *Lacrymosa*, but with the words of the 'Pie Jesu' – a beautiful stroke, as it transforms a dark idea into light. The chorus, doubled by strings, bassoons and clarinets, breaks out briefly into a fearful plea again with an emphatic downward-moving 'dona eis requiem', quickly disappearing into a soft *tremolando* from the violins and violas – and although we sense that this very long *Dies irae* movement is coming to its end, we just don't know how Verdi will close it. Will it end in the major key with hope, or the minor key with fear?

We are kept in the dark as the chorus and soloists reiterate the combination of the *Lacrymosa* melodic cell with the 'Pie Jesu' text, this time though with very quiet bass-drum strokes portentously added to the orchestral accompaniment. A few subdued wisps of the *Lacrymosa* cell from the strings, all the singers intone 'Requiem' twice, a *tremolo* from the strings alone keeps us in suspense – and then finally the bass soloist takes a positive lead with 'dona eis requiem', which induces all the soloists, the chorus and the orchestra to reach the key of B flat major peacefully. We are home – *but!* – out of nowhere 'Amen' from all the singers with the entire orchestra floats in and swells up on a chord of G major! Why? How? Another complete surprise, with one of these third-interval-related chords with which Verdi creates magic. It is like a huge sigh of relief.

The *Dies irae* section now closes with three bars of consoling *pianissimo* B flat major chords from the whole orchestra, richly textured as only Verdi can make them.

17

INVESTING IN THE YOUNG

I have had the great pleasure in the last few years of doing quite a number of masterclasses with young singers. This has given me the opportunity to be a 'maestro' in the real sense of the word – that is, a teacher. While that word has always been fundamental to my understanding of what my job as a conductor should be, I don't think that its true meaning or the reality of its situation is always understood. Especially at the start of my career as a conductor, I found it almost embarrassing if someone in an orchestra called me 'maestro'; they knew ten times more than I did most of the time, and they were certainly aware of it.

If you are fortunate enough to survive the beginning of your career constantly confronting new scores and often scary, seasoned orchestral players, and then work hard enough and become sufficiently experienced to deserve the name 'maestro', well, OK – but how do you learn once you are a conductor? Do you take lessons again? Not really.

In actual fact, it is when you are with younger people teaching them, when you do whatever it takes to get the message across, describe the music's needs, not hesitating to use visual or poetic imagery, that is most important of all to me. This is a situation where you are watching what the effects of all you are saying may be on the people you are teaching: that is the only way a conductor can really learn. By seeing what kind of a reaction you can elicit, only then do you learn about conducting. Sometimes you can plant a seed and all of a sudden a flower will blossom very quickly; sometimes you plant a seed and you aren't sure if it has generated any effect, but then maybe two or three years later you find out that there has been a late blooming. It is an enormous satisfaction, but it's also the elixir for nourishing oneself and going forward – because it doesn't matter how many times you might be called a 'maestro', you yourself will need to continue to develop.

You cannot always be explaining to people what you think they should do. You too need to be nurtured, and whereas some people may do this by having a conversation with another conductor and others may do it by watching video recordings of conductors, I believe a conductor is best sustained by teaching. Through sharing your knowledge and absorbing the responses to what you are imparting, you learn afresh. I have touched on the masterclasses I have been giving with singers who are members of the Royal Opera House's Jette Parker Artists Programme.

I work with two singers in a session, each doing two arias, usually chosen by them, and I furnish the audience with descriptions of who the characters in the arias are and the general plot outline. Taking each aria in turn, I first let the singers go all the way through from start to finish. They usually do very well – these young singers are very, very talented, and usually they are quite impressive at this first run-through. From early on in the session I spend a lot of time on how the singer *looks* when they are singing. It is surprising how singers can sing well, yet with eyes that are not engaged, eyes that are not communicating the thought or the idea behind what the music and text are meant to be conveying. I am insistent that the eyes of the singer are a feature of their presentation, because a theatre audience will be some distance away from the performer. If the eyes are not engaged, the face is closed to all intents and purposes and you have something akin to a manikin up there – characterless. Believe me, even if there is a musical communication, if there is no real communication of character, of thought, of all the different components, the performance will ultimately be dull.

Breathing is another issue that is more critical in the context of the singer's communication to the audience than is sometimes realised. Sometimes when singers take a breath, they momentarily check out from their character, although they may be singing and phrasing beautifully. That split second's hiatus really does stultify the connection between them and the audience and, of course, the dramatic situation. I have mentioned how I learned such a great lesson from Joan Sutherland when I saw the continuation of the thought through the eyes all the while that she was singing, so that the audience was never aware of her diaphragm being released and engaged when she breathed. It is surprising how many singers take their breaths too soon in an aria. Sometimes, when there is an introduction in the orchestra, they will begin to breathe three or four seconds before they have to sing their first note. What then happens is that the air has no place to go but upwards, and inevitably the body and facial expression stiffen. Unless the singer has a particularly challenging phrase, they should take their starting breath in the rhythm and character of the music as the conductor gives the upbeat for their entry. So many singers make this mistake: they are overly tanked up with air, so their chest is too high and they can't join it up with the diaphragm that gives the support to the voice and holds up the sound by keeping the air moving through the vocal cords.

I try to instil in young singers the importance of being flexible – not being rigidly dominated by habits of the muscles. Muscle memory can be positive for locking something down in the position of the voice, but if the singer cannot change and discover new ways of using their voice, there won't be progress. There can be an element of fear of this in the singer (the devil you know . . .) so sometimes you have to tease them into trying new approaches: 'Nah, come on, you did that better before, I know you can do it . . . Ah . . . you see!' In these classes they never stop having to perform, no matter how many times I ask them to repeat something, because there is an audience. I'll turn to the audience and say, 'Did you see how she connected with the word there? Did you see the star quality that came out?' So the audience learns in these sessions too: with aural and visual proof – and that's very important for the kinds of masterclasses I like to do.

All of this is in the overall pursuit of communicating the character and their situation convincingly. The singer is an actor – through the words, through the colours, through the dynamics. Why does the composer put in a dynamic marking? If the marking is to sing softly, why is it there? It isn't enough just to say, 'I'll sing it softly because the score says so.' The singer has to go to the heart of the matter and get under the skin of the music. The accompaniment will hold clues: in its character, its harmonies, its shape, its dynamics, its orchestration. These are pointers for the singer to colour the voice in a certain way, to move the tempo a certain way, to bite on the words in a certain way . . .

Recently I have started doing masterclasses at the Royal Opera House with groups of young singers and no audience, so that the participants are observing other singers working with

225

me as well as working with me themselves. As they are voice savvy, this way they learn more quickly: they pick up pointers and maybe they see themselves in the mirror for certain elements, including interpretation, musicality, pronunciation, facial expression, and so on. If this might give the impression of a schoolmaster lecturing his pupils, I promise you that is not what it's about. These young singers are remarkable and a hundred per cent engaged, and part of the reason is because I try to keep the energy of the music and the action flowing all through the sessions, allowing no pause for my comments, just flow and energy and information, and they never get tired. It's similar to the technique I use in the recording studio: never let the momentum of the session falter, never let it deflate. It's marvellous how much energy these singers can find and how they can discover their capabilities. My reason for writing about all this here is not to toot my own horn but, returning to what I was mentioning before about learning as one teaches, to say that I think I have learned over the years how to be of service and be a *consigliere* – and for me this whole process of investing in young talent is profoundly rewarding. I discover the skills of these greatly gifted artists of our future, and I can't wait to share the world of opera with them.

A few years ago, I decided I wanted to extend my work with young people into the domain of young orchestras. As with the vocal masterclasses, it was my desire to share information I have picked up in my life that impelled me to do this – and what better way than to share it with a hundred people all in one go? So, I began in 2017 by reconnecting with the Verbier Festival, where I had conducted the Jeunesses Musicales World Orchestra and the Curtis Symphony Orchestra in the festival's second and third seasons in 1995 and 1996 (this was before the festival created its own orchestra of young musicians in 2000). The nineteen-year absence was a very big gap of time that I wanted to make up, and I am very happy that in doing so it led me to a new association with the festival – but once again Covid had other ideas.

For the 2017 concert I conducted Brahms's Second Piano Concerto with Yefim Bronfman, and Richard Strauss's *Ein Heldenleben*: a very ambitious undertaking for a young orchestra.

The young musicians of the Verbier Festival Orchestra are the crème de la crème: they have been auditioned and trained by superior masters. Nevertheless, *Ein Heldenleben* – literally, 'A Hero's Life' – is a great obstacle course for any orchestra. As is the case with a lot of Strauss's symphonic tone poems, it is autobiographical in its story line, in fact more directly so than all but one of the others. It is very densely scored and detailed in its depiction of a life lived: a life of work, of love, of marriage, of detractors and opponents, of critics, of doing battle against all the forces that have been against the hero at one time or another – and then, after conquering all these real or imagined foes, of taking stock of his life and looking back. In doing so Strauss quotes many works of his younger days, some of which weren't successful. It is a moving experience, as he interweaves these extracts retrospectively, progressing to the resigned acceptance that life has to come to an end. However, even at the end of his life, he is still haunted by the energy of his youth and the battles he fought. We hear sudden disturbing, screaming outbursts just as the music feels as though it is calmly ebbing to its close. Finally, he recovers and expresses his acceptance at the very end: the acceptance that he has lived life, and now he can let go.

A key element in *Ein Heldenleben* is Strauss's marriage. It was a very interesting marriage. His wife Paulina was a real character – she was capricious, headstrong, and could be very unreasonable – but they loved each other devotedly. He needed her and somehow they made the marriage work. Strauss portrays Paulina in the orchestra's extended solo violin part, which is played by the leader. The capriciousness, the tears and lamentations, the fits of pique are all there. She is married to a man who is basically married to his work (this sounds terribly familiar . . .). The music describes it all: the very definition of a tone poem. But what is also there is Strauss's reaction to her. At first he is so patient, and you can just see him sitting there in his armchair listening to her babble on: 'Yes, my dear . . . oh yes, my dear . . . oh yes, of course, my dear.' But then Strauss marks a certain phrase *mit Sehnsucht* ('with desire'). So, there is an erotic component. She calms down and the two sing a love duet. You can't believe the thrill of conducting this section, this mini opera scene.

The reason I am going into such detail is because I think *Ein Heldenleben* is a marvellous work for teaching. Firstly, like all Strauss's music, it makes virtuosic demands on the musicians – the string writing is greatly challenging; the violin solo is a tour de force; and the woodwinds are challenged beyond belief, made not only to sing, but to cackle, having to play very short and ugly sounds pointedly in the cacophony that depicts the critics. And secondly, because it is about a life lived. How beautiful it is to be able to teach this music and at the same time inform these young people about the realities of life – about the life that they are just embarking on. If one or two out of a hundred in the orchestra are already married, that's a lot – so to have the opportunity to discuss how marriages work (or don't work?) . . . Well, I am no psychiatrist, but through this music the relationship of man to woman is imparted with tremendous insight – and flair and theatricality. You must talk about the details of how Strauss has depicted this unusual but remarkably steadfast relationship, so that the players will know just how to paint this complex psychological duet, and maybe glean something for their own future relationships.

Doing battle against enemies real or imagined is such an important theme because most artists carry a raft of insecurities on which others might prey. The development of a young mind is a journey full of traps, false starts, wrong paths taken, but also opportunities, wondrous discoveries and potential achievements. Ingenuity and tenacity in the face of challenge are key. In a rehearsal or a masterclass I am there to challenge. Together we find solutions to what might at first seem insurmountable obstacles. Although Strauss was by all accounts a very confident man, I am sure he had to do battle with his inner demons, and he has put it all on display in this work. How differently he does this from Mahler; there is rarely anything tawdry in Strauss's depiction of the hero. He never reveals too much about himself. About others, yes. To be able to speak about these issues using music as the conduit is an amazing outlet for me, giving me the ability to make concrete my passions and my thoughts, but we aren't sitting around a campfire, we are working very hard on Strauss's extremely demanding musical and technical details to produce something that lives.

Two years later, in 2019, I conducted an even younger orchestra when I worked on two symphonies with the National Youth Orchestra of the United States of America for their European tour in 2019: Prokofiev's Symphony No. 5 and again a work by Strauss, this time his *Alpine Symphony* – and I discovered what a fantastic teaching piece the *Alpine Symphony* is too! First of all, for all the players it makes even greater demands than *Ein Heldenleben*, most especially in the brass and woodwind writing, and particularly in the protracted ending of the work. Strauss demands the utmost beauty of tone and perfect intonation when the players are exhausted after a very long and very difficult haul. And then there's the subject of this wonderful work. Simply put, it is about climbing a mountain – starting at the bottom, reaching the top, and coming back down again: but this is all a metaphor for, once again, a life lived. This time there is a very strong pantheistic element. As you climb the mountain you see magical scenery but you also encounter vicissitudes and obstacles of every kind – the thorny thickets on the wrong route, the glacier, the deadly precipice – and you are constantly reminded of your mortality. There is a downward whistling dive from the woodwind every now and again, perfectly describing looking over your shoulder to see how far you have climbed and seeing how at any moment you could plunge to your death. When you reach the top of the mountain after all these potential disasters, the air becomes very thin. Instead of the blaze of glory in the full orchestra, now hardly anything is happening. After a very brief brass fanfare announcing the actual arrival, there remains a ghostly tune on the oboe with a very soft *tremolo* on high strings floating underneath. It is as though, whether you are a believer or not, at that moment you see God – whatever God means to you. This moment is unique, frightening and beautiful.

Conductors are not supposed to preach at rehearsals, but I admit I often do, especially with youth orchestras. I want my musicians to know the why of everything that we are aiming for. This takes explanation. But are you interesting enough, are you engaging the musicians, or are you wasting their time?

Returning to the summit: we must now come back down the mountain, which is often harder than going up. Rumblings prepare you for a storm that is, to say the least, biblical: imagine Verdi's *Dies irae* times ten and that will give you an idea of what you are about to face with the lashing of the strings, the howling of the woodwind and the crashing of the brass and timpani and percussion – the possibility of death just around the corner. The din, the complexity and the excitement of this section have to be heard to be believed. Like any storm, if you survive it, you will have seen something that changes your life forever – and so it is in Strauss's *Alpine Symphony*. I certainly felt changed.

Although the *Alpine Symphony* does not deal with the day-to-day issues of relationships of *Ein Heldenleben*, it does deal with how we as humans observe nature as a metaphor or mirror of human existence. We are indeed secondary to nature – but our relationship to it here is living a life: a life of reaching out to get to the top of the mountain, followed by returning home, and releasing. It is a very long and protracted finale: Strauss just can't let go of it. Here I had the challenge of trying to instil in young people the energy, the brain space, to ruminate about life in a way they can't possibly be expected to fully understand because they are at the beginning of their lives – but then it's precisely this that makes this work, like *Ein Heldenleben*, such a wonderful teaching piece. As young musicians they are faced both with the technical challenges of playing the tone poem and the psychological challenge of understanding what the music is saying, and that's a seminal experience for them. You don't wait until you are an old man before you conduct Bruckner's Eighth Symphony. You will probably conduct it better when you are seventy than you will when you are thirty, but you experience it when you are young. You may not understand a thing, but you throw yourself into it, and that is of very great importance as you plant the first seeds for what will grow and grow as time goes by. And this is why the more substantial and important the music is, the more valuable it is for young students. You don't give them music to play that is conveniently comfortable for young people; you subject them to the most difficult and challenging works, musically and psychologically and for deeper understanding, because it's not only about the music: it's about growing up too, and through the music they can grow up with a wealth of connections, memories, feelings. In my mind there is no better school.

18

AT THE PIANO

I don't have anything near as much time as I would like for playing the piano, and this frustrates me – but even if I spend just five minutes at the instrument, I am able to commune with a part of me that allows space for me not only to solve musical problems I have been obsessing about, but also to return to that joyous place that made me choose music as my life's vocation.

When I am touching the keys and making the music myself, while carrying the baggage I have in my ears and head and heart from all the conducting I do with all the sounds I have heard, I am able to think completely afresh through the piano about how music actually works, how sound works. In a way I am experimenting with myself and this has been fundamentally important. Any good pianist should be thinking orchestrally, creating a kaleidoscope of colours, and in my aural memory I have a huge library!

I am not cut out to be a soloist (though secretly I wish I was), but I have been blessed to play the piano in the song repertoire with artists such as Ian Bostridge, Joyce DiDonato, Diana Damrau, Waltraud Meier, Matthias Goerne, Thomas Hampson, Rockwell Blake and the late and sorely missed Dmitri Hvorostovsky. This world, where inspired words join melody and harmony to conjure up little stories, miniature operas in themselves, is a haven for me. I thrive in this environment, to which I must bring all my fascination for text, colour and drama and create a supporting foundation for these superlative artists who must share with their audiences every facet of the human condition. To give of their best they must have a partner who is interested in the details of each story they are telling, someone who is there at every moment to underline what is being expressed. For me these partnerships are worth their weight in gold.

My first important foray was a Rossinian adventure. The inimitable tenor and Rossini specialist Rockwell Blake and I recorded a disc of Rossini's songs, of which there are many. Most of them are in Italian, but an important group are in French, finding Gioachino at his most inspired. The piano parts are sometimes quite flashy and sometimes quite simple, but always piquant, full of humour, and easy on the ear. Sadly this record is no longer available.

The two composers to whom I have been particularly close are Franz Schubert and Hugo Wolf. From a purely pianistic point of view the two cannot be more different. Playing Schubert's songs is the ultimate challenge, but not for the reasons you might imagine. The writing is often deceptively simple, using very few notes in many of the songs, and chordal writing is predominant. Yet you have to weigh and balance each chord, finding just the right note to single out to maintain a logical thread for the listener, fitting a sequence of these chords in a context that is always fluid, always drawing the listener forward. You wouldn't believe the awkward hand positions one has to adopt to get the right sounds, even though on the page the music frequently looks as though it's been written for a beginner. Oh, but how refined the pedalling must be; a constant dance between the sustaining pedal and the soft pedal. To this last point I would add that for a lot of Schubert's piano accompaniments the less pedal the better, even none at times, but maintaining a singing tone on the piano is essential. The unabashed sweetness of the tone must be a point of departure so that Schubert can then surprise us with his trademark acid tones and accents that will underpin the misfortunes of many of his narrators.

Each song demands an often radically different approach to piano playing. You must paint each poem differently with your hands and your ears, and on top of it you have to be ready to play like a virtuoso. This is especially difficult because you might have played three slow songs in a row, and then suddenly there are fireworks. Your contorted chord-fingers have to be ready to fly. Schubert wrote over five hundred songs, but the three cycles, *Die schöne Müllerin*, *Winterreise* and *Schwanengesang*, are the pinnacles. The first has eluded me up to this point, but the second and third I have performed quite a few times.

Winterreise is an Everest of sorts for the pianist as well as the singer, and I won't ever forget the first time I played it. Matthias Goerne came to sing it at La Monnaie in 2002, just a couple of months after I had taken up my post at the Royal Opera House. In fact he jumped in at the very last minute as another singer cancelled due to illness on the morning of the scheduled performance, so we only had time for a forty-five-minute rehearsal onstage. *Winterreise* happens to be a bit longer than forty-five minutes! There's the best part of seventy minutes of music, so at the rehearsal we were able to touch on only certain parts of the cycle – quite a lot of the music we didn't have time to go through at all. Later, just as we were about to go on stage for the performance, Matthias asked me, 'You've played this a lot, yes?' When I said, 'No, this is the first time', he howled with laughter and walked onto the stage – with me haplessly

235

following right behind. Well, I did get through it and perhaps a bit more, but it was harrowing, as you can imagine.

Just recently I have had the opportunity to perform the cycle several times with Ian Bostridge, culminating in three concerts in Berlin, Munich and Hamburg. To perform in front of an audience that can instantly understand every word, share in every nuance chosen by the performers, was a life-changing experience. The level of concentration of the audience listening to and watching Ian's amazing, highly personal interpretation was awesome. The two of us felt so free in this setting, trudging through this remarkable winter masterpiece, arriving at the shockingly stark ending exhausted, empty but fulfilled. Ian has written a marvellous book about this cycle, but I would need to write another one to say all I have thought about this experience.

I have performed *Schwanengesang* with Ian on a few occasions, though quite a few years ago now, and we were also able to record it. I remember the hours I spent at home trying to get the rippling effect in the first song convincingly, the military drum effects in other songs, and the ever awkward *staccato* quavers in 'Ständchen'. I also remember revelling in the pitch-black sounds of 'Der Doppelgänger' and the quasi-orchestral piano part of 'Der Atlas'. When I play this music, I am brought by this great genius to a place that is solitary, infinitely sad, but I feel I don't want to be anywhere else.

Ian and I made a recording of a selection of Wolf's songs that captured my imagination like little else. The piano parts are glorious, though often very tricky. They are rarely minimalist in the same way Schubert's songs often are, but rather more obviously romantic and descriptive in a more florid style. What he shares with Schubert is the notion that the song composer must capture the psychological complexity of the poetry. Wolf pushes this further. It is the era of Sigmund Freud; it is music of the modern era, the era of Mahler, Strauss and even Schoenberg. The harmonic palate he is using is richer, but always individual. Along with Mahler, Strauss and Schoenberg, Wolf was an ardent Wagnerite, so his music comes from there, but I must confess that for me he is able to conjure up more convincingly than the others that which is spiritual in nature. Many of his songs have religious titles and spirituality as the focus. The way his rapt creations draw you in is unique; the stillness total. I have also to admit that I love to let my fingers fly in the more extroverted songs. One can dream of being a virtuoso, no?

My dear friend Dmitry Sitkovetsky, the violinist, conductor and arranger, asked me to record some Mozart sonatas for violin and piano, the idea being that we would record the whole cycle over time. This music is eternally youthful, and every section is like an operatic scene. My world. You can hear the machinations of the various characters in each turn of phrase, each gorgeous melody. Yet there are no words. I think I played relatively well in these sessions, spurred on by Dmitry's elegance, but I was extremely nervous. The music is very exposed, any blemish immediately noticed, so fear sometimes got the better of me. I remember shaking during some of the solo passages, playing softer and softer and softer, almost losing contact with the instrument. This made me desperate, as I love the music so much. We weren't recording live, so naturally I could repeat things and make them better, but I was somehow shaken by the experience.

To my great regret I decided not to continue the project after this first CD. I have tried to get to the bottom of this fear. I think it has something to do with my breathing becoming blocked or rigid, which renders me not free. That impacts on everything.

My bursts of practising before such a project are very intense, but I probably needed more time for the material to sink in. I have recently been listening to the recording again and I am really sad I didn't continue and finish the project because I am obviously very connected to this music and I admire Dmitry so much.

I have made some improvement with time, thought and practice, and in the domain of chamber music, the music of Johannes Brahms has been my focus in recent years: the cello sonatas, the clarinet sonatas, the Clarinet Trio, the violin sonatas, the Op. 8 Piano Trio, and the Piano Quintet in F minor. Though the piano parts in these pieces are by no means easy, I am more at home playing this music, which is orchestrally conceived for the piano. Together with Luigi Piovano, one of the two principal cellists of my orchestra in Rome, I have done many recitals throughout Italy and elsewhere. Though we have played the sonatas of Beethoven, Debussy, Prokofiev and Shostakovich, it is the sonatas of Brahms that we keep coming back to. These two sonatas, so different from each other yet so rich in meaning, have taught us about listening, about balance, about tone quality and colour. We have recorded these two works, and also included two small pieces by Giuseppe Martucci ('the Italian Brahms'). I was fortunate to have a Steinway from the late 1870s for these sessions and I remember this being a very happy and intense experience.

We have introduced the Rachmaninov Cello Sonata to our repertoire – which means I have learned a much more demanding piece to play on the piano. It has been good for me to up my game technically. I have the spirit of the music very much within me, but my fingers are sometimes lazy. This is such a different musical world from that of Brahms. Rachmaninov unleashes the sonata form in a way that allows the performers greater freedom to interpret, to shape the music with unabashed romanticism with its horizontal phrasing and its spontaneous emotionalism. There's the sheer exhilaration of its virtuosity – if you can manage it – and the wonderful expressive warmth of the third movement, which is so vocal in its phrases, is a gift. The scherzo has the devil in it as much of Rachmaninov's music does, and the finale soars. Luigi has been a tenacious and ever searching partner and I owe him a lot. He has also become an accomplished conductor.

Another artist I had the pleasure of accompanying is the violinist Janine Jansen. She is such a striking musician, full of life and with such a lyrical soul. I recently took part in a most unusual DVD documentary and CD recording with her. She was playing on twelve different Stradivari violins brought from all over the world – at great insurance expense, I might add! We recorded a selection of highly varied repertoire, mostly encore pieces: Schumann, Brahms, Clara Schumann, Vieux-temps, Heuberger, Tchaikovsky, Rachmaninov, Suk, Falla, Ravel, Elgar, Szymanowski, Kreisler, Kern. Hearing Janine playing Kreisler's music on two different Stradivari violins that he himself played and recorded on was so moving, as it also was to hear her play the stormy lines of Vieuxtemps's *Désespoir* on his violin. We even recorded the slow movement of Rachman-inov's Cello Sonata arranged for violin. Just imagine how I felt listening to all those different instruments, including the Alard, the most famous of all the Stradivari violins, and reacting to all those different colours as I accompanied Janine! I truly felt the spirits of the greats from the past were in the room with us. We made the DVD documentary in Cadogan Hall in London in the midst of the Covid-19 pandemic, and in fact Janine came down with Covid badly, so after the two preparatory rehearsals we had to wait three weeks before she had the strength to play again. How I didn't get the virus then was anybody's guess. Getting the recordings finally made was a tour de force for her because she had become very weakened indeed. It was a marvel to see her triumph over her illness and play so miraculously. It was all a magical experience for me, getting to know repertoire that was mostly new to me, and inspiring to be made aware of the world of another instrument to such an illuminating degree. So many different voices . . .

Sometimes one has to have dumb courage. After performing Camille Saint-Saëns's Organ Symphony with my Santa Cecilia Orchestra in concert and recording it live, it was decided we needed something special as a filler for the CD release. More special than this you can't get: Saint-Saëns's *Carnival of the Animals* for two pianos and chamber ensemble with the legendary pianist Martha Argerich. Can you imagine me playing two pianos with Martha Argerich? I am alive to be able to say I survived it. By that I mean that she is known for her breathtaking speed at the keyboard, but I managed to stay with her. At least most of the time. To be making music on that level was an opportunity sent from heaven.

I need chamber music in my life. All the musicians are in a situation where they are able to share their ideas. Even when I am conducting, I do encourage dialogue with the performers as much as practically possible – but in chamber music the conversation is much more fluid, as we are all equal partners. I am stimulated by comments from the players, and for me it is interesting when someone might have a completely different viewpoint from mine – the more viewpoints there are, the more there is to share. And this is a reason why you need to approach chamber music with patience and time in rehearsal. The road of exploration and discovery is fundamental in this genre. You just cannot rush it; the interpretation needs to grow organically, gradually finding that unified approach. This means playing over the music many times, taking risks and trying different things, thereby establishing a feeling that whether there are two, three or six musicians, everyone is conversing freely and confidently with the music. It is when this happens that the experience of chamber music becomes so intensely human.

In 2018 I experienced this voyage of discovery in an especially inspiring way when I played Elgar's Piano Quintet for the very first time, in Berlin. It was part of a chamber music programme given by the Boulez Ensemble at the Boulez Saal, in which I was both playing and conducting, having been invited by Daniel Barenboim. I conducted Britten's Sinfonietta for chamber orchestra – his opus 1, a wonderful piece – and also Birtwistle's 5 *Lessons in a Frame*, and then I played in the Elgar Piano Quintet. I had set aside the time to learn it thoroughly, but I got to learn it on a totally different level while I was rehearsing it with the musicians. Each rehearsal added more and more layers of understanding of the structure, the strategy for delivering the performance, and the poetry and fire that lies in this piece. It is a beautiful thing to be part of the mechanism of making music in this way, and for me it is especially rewarding to be responsible for producing the sound on the piano myself. Instead of my day job telling everyone else what they should be doing, here it is I who have to play the music and, my goodness, does it remind me how difficult that is to do and how demanding music is on the instrumentalists who have to convey it as naturally as a singer would. When I am playing, I try to make that maxim my goal – to have a total feeling of naturalness. It takes a lot of time – and I wish I had more of that time available.

19

AS ONE ERA ENDS
A NEW ONE STARTS

As I approach the end of this book, I am understandably preoccupied with the goodbyes I have already said and will have to say in the near future. After eighteen years at the helm of the Santa Cecilia Orchestra and Chorus in Rome I look back with pride, a certain amount of exhaustion, and the hope that the institution's future trajectory points towards great music-making and continued success. As Conductor Emeritus I will return to Rome each season, and at Easter 2024 I will bring the orchestra and chorus to the Salzburg Easter Festival to perform Ponchielli's *La Gioconda*, an opera dear to my heart. This is a first for Santa Cecilia and it is seen as a marvellous opportunity for all involved. Our performances will include symphonic and choral concerts as well, celebrating Italian music. But as I very much look forward to these exciting plans, I do also feel a sense of loss, of separation. Breathing the alluring air of Italy will be a much rarer occurrence now, sharing the Italian humour with my musicians will now be fleeting, and making the type of music they can deliver will fall to someone else. Daniel Harding has been named as my successor; I am more than pleased for Santa Cecilia.

In the middle of this inner turmoil, I am also coming to grips with having been chosen as Sir Simon Rattle's successor to lead the London Symphony Orchestra. I am not just happy; I am thrilled. This is huge. I have conducted the orchestra since 1996 in many concerts and recordings. In fact, I met them for the first time in Abbey Road Studios for a recording of Puccini's *La rondine*, one of the first in a Puccini cycle that EMI Classics instigated, and a novelty for both me and the orchestra. The LSO had just come off a particularly thorny week of contemporary music, so when they discovered *La rondine*, they felt as if they had died and gone to heaven, such was the charisma of the music. I will never forget giving the first downbeat and the orchestra exploding with energy and drive – a Ferrari in all but name. I have never stopped collaborating with them since I went through my limited symphonic repertoire in those early years. Imagine conducting Elgar's First and Second Symphonies for the first time with them. Walton's First. Unforgettable experiences.

The whirlwind that was my first four weeks as chief conductor designate showed me just how lucky I was to be chosen to lead their fabulous group, and we have already been touring. The chemistry seems very natural . . .

In September 2022 we were all taken by surprise by the death of Queen Elizabeth II, which heralded the end of an era that started before many of us were born. The then Prince of Wales became King Charles III and plans were set in motion for his Coronation. To my immense surprise and delight, I was asked to conduct the music during the service in Westminster Abbey. No one would have predicted I would be doing that when I was living just around the corner in Old Pye Street.

On 6 May 2023, players from eight leading British and Canadian orchestras formed the crackerjack forty-strong ensemble, somehow squashed into the organ loft overlooking the congregation. King Charles chose a richly varied programme of British music through the ages from Orlando Gibbons to Patrick Doyle, commissioning twelve contemporary composers for the celebration. Before the actual Coronation itself, I conducted a concert of a lively mix of orchestral music (among the composers were Holst, Vaughan Williams, Elgar of course, plus a host of new works) and vocal music featuring the soprano soloist Pretty Yende.

The challenge of this great honour, however, was to achieve what needed to be achieved for the service of the Coronation itself. Andrew Nethsingha, the newly installed choirmaster of the Abbey, conducted the enlarged choir (including girls' voices) from below. The several big choral numbers required orchestral accompaniment, bolstered by the organ and a brass-fanfare choir. My job, with the help of a TV monitor on Andrew, was to coordinate his choir with my orchestra. An opera conductor has to deal with this scenario quite often when a band plays offstage at the same time as a pit orchestra. This past experience certainly helped me navigate this treacherous musical task, but the preliminary rehearsals at the beginning of the week were not easy in any way. To achieve good coordination, it is not simply a matter of 'being together'. There is an infinite amount of give and take between the distant parties. The trick is to figure out who gives and who takes, and when. At first it seemed impossible. Slowly over the next couple of days it started to gel as Andrew and I came to understand each other and the peculiarities of the Abbey acoustic. Throughout, the orchestra was patient and fervent in their musical expression and the choir sang superbly.

On the day, we were ready for it, and I have rarely come across such a strong desire from all involved to get it right. It was a proud moment for all of us that we did. The bonus for me personally was that I got to know so many new and extraordinary musicians as well as so much new music.

A lovely birthday present was the New Year's announcement that the King had bestowed on me another honour, Commander of the Royal Victorian Order. My mother was very pleased.

London is a cultural Mecca; it always has been and it always will be. However, there is no question that the arts and their institutions have been through a period of unprecedented financial stress. The Covid period was a well-documented disaster for the entertainment sector, many people losing their jobs forever, many going hungry, others painfully reinventing their lives. The economic difficulties in 2023 were devastating, but it is during challenging times that the government through the Arts Council of England (ACE) must show that it has a plan to keep the arts alive, reward continuing quality, and create a stimulating and hopeful environment for talent up and down the country. The opera sector is still seen as some kind of playground for the elite, and I have recently even heard that the Arts Council believes there is no growth prospect for the art form. Rubbish.

If it is deemed important that more people should come to the opera house, then help us lower the prices so we can get more people in. This is the way it is done in Germany, France and Italy, to mention only three countries. There the arts are considered a bulwark of society. How is it that with all the talent we have in Great Britain, both in theatre and in music, the government can't see that this amazing group of artists is a crown jewel that, by the way, brings a lot of money to many city centres? The laziness that brings about kneejerk cuts to arts funding is tragic and infuriating.

The English National Opera was humiliated early in 2023, with no logical plan coming from the Arts Council for an achievable future for the company. The ENO is an internationally recognised institution with a tremendous history of excellence. If it is experiencing difficulties, you don't crush it, you help it. The plan now is that the ENO will be relocated up north to Manchester by 2029. We'll see . . . The BBC Singers, a fantastic group of expert singers, was axed. There was such an outcry at this that they have been reinstated, but who knows for how long? As I write it seems that the Welsh National Opera is also under enormous pressure. This company is an iconic institution that must be kept thriving at all costs. What it brings to its region is invaluable. To the powers that be, 'Come on, do something!'

The most traumatic wrench for me has undoubtedly been the thought of leaving the Royal Opera House in July 2024. It has been my artistic home for twenty-two years. I have written in depth about the place and the people in it, and I feel that I am just getting started. However, it is my choice to leave. The opera house needs new blood and I am delighted that Jakub Hrůša is taking over from me. This will surely be an important new era for Covent Garden.

I must mention the sequence of operas I led in May–June of 2023. On paper it looked more than ambitious, I would say almost greedy. I have never said I wasn't greedy. However, this experience, though back-breaking in its demands, has made me focus as at no other time. The trio of operas was Berg's *Wozzeck* (after a hiatus of twenty-one years), Verdi's *Il trovatore* (my first time in the theatre) and my fourth go at Massenet's *Werther* (an obsession). Together with Puccini's *Turandot* in March–April, the stylistic variety shows that I am doing just what I set out to do. I am not content to stay put in one corner of the repertoire, and the position of music director has given me the licence to explore far and wide.

Pamela and I will be staying in London for the foreseeable future, embarking on the new adventure with the LSO, but also maintaining an ongoing relationship with the Royal Opera House. In September 2023 I began a new *Ring* cycle, starting with *Das Rheingold*, together with the renowned stage director Barrie Kosky, and I will complete the cycle over the next three years. Wagner keeps pulling me back in . . .

Fans of classical music will have noticed how much more content there is online. Is this a good thing? I think classical music has to come to terms with the technological advances in the distribution of music and how it reaches its public. I am a staunch believer that live music is the 'true' experience and there is no amount of technology that can replace it. But I am also aware that the diffusion of something that is strong, compelling, beautiful and informative will always be for the good. Every year the equipment gets better and better, and offers far superior quality to that of even a few years ago. The educational side of this phenomenon is paramount if we want to grow our audience. However, the pitching of the message must never stoop to dumbing down. Classical music can be explained or elucidated, even confronting the obstacles of terminology and technique, in a joyous, inviting manner.

All of us with the opportunities to do so have a responsibility to preach the gospel of music and art in general. It has been proved over and over again that music ignites a positive stimulation and development of the brain. Everything else, including maths, science and social interaction, falls better into place. This is not my opinion; it is a fact. Therefore it follows that music is a fundamental right for every human being, in particular for our young. Why do we keep having to shout this to the authorities and be met with stone-cold apathy?

There will always be visionary individuals or groups creating small pockets where what I'm raving on about does take place, but it needs to become an accepted symbol of our national pride, and that must surely come from the top. Brexit has happened, but let's show the world what kind of society we want. We should be a beacon.

I wrote that a conductor must survive the beginning of their career, usually against difficult odds. I have survived the beginning of my career and a lot more, but I am now beginning a new chapter in my life that will ask a lot of questions of me, pose a lot of challenges, and – I hope – open exciting new vistas. The London Symphony Orchestra is a gift from heaven and I am impatient to explore where this relationship can go.

I am truly blessed to have this life.

ACKNOWLEDGEMENTS

My sincere thanks go to my good friend Jon Tolansky, whose idea this book was and who guided me through its planning stages and beyond. Ros Edwards, my literary agent, was also invaluable in helping me express my thoughts and supported me throughout. Grateful thanks too to Belinda Matthews, who took a leap of faith and agreed to publish my book before we both knew how it would turn out. I am also indebted to her colleagues at Faber – Anne Owen, Hannah Knowles, Kate Burton, Jill Burrows and Kate Hopkins.

Over my twenty-two years at Covent Garden, I was blessed to have had two indispensable PAs, Rosemary Lowther over the first two-thirds of my tenure and Lottie Johnson for the last third, both of whom with infinite patience enabled me to achieve what I needed to in the meagre twenty-four hours of each day.

Winfried and Kerstin Roch of CCM International were Santa Cecilia's touring promoters and believed in us from the beginning. It is impossible to imagine how we could have succeeded so well without them. I must also thank Nicola and Paolo Bulgari for their immense generosity towards the Orchestra dell' Academia Nazionale; it was a lifeline. Thanks also to Loreto Santamaria, my indefatigable PA, a Spanish fireball.

Peter Alward and Alain Lanceron of EMI/Warner Classics recognised what I could accomplish in the recording studio and kept the opportunities coming in a splendidly varied repertoire, together with fabulous soloists.

Appreciative thanks too to Nick Mathias and Thomas Walton at IMG Artists, who continue to do an outstanding job.

My thanks and admiration to the people of Castelfranco in Miscano.

Lastly, I want to commend anyone who has the courage and determination to choose a life in music. There is nothing better.

Sir Antonio Pappano

DISCOGRAPHY

Much of the information for this discography was originally compiled by Brian Godfrey, who died in 2016.

Works are presented in alphabetical order under composer within the following genres: opera, choral and orchestral music, chamber music, songs and song-cycles. Extracts from some complete opera recordings may be collected on other recordings. Unless otherwise indicated, recordings are CDs.

The following abbreviations are used:

AP – Antonio Pappano; *c* – conducted by.

HUGO ALFVÉN
'The Forest Sleeps', Op. 28 No. 6
'So Take My Heart'
Barbara Bonney *soprano*, AP *piano*
(Decca, 1999)

ANON.
'When that I was and a little tiny boy'
Ian Bostridge *tenor*, AP *piano*
(Warner, 2016)

HAROLD ARLEN
'Over the Rainbow'
Joyce DiDonato *mezzo-soprano*, AP *piano*
(Erato, 2014)

BÉLA BARTÓK
Violin Concerto No. 1 (Sz. 36)
Janine Jansen *violin*, London Symphony Orchestra *c* AP
(Decca, 2014)

LUDWIG VAN BEETHOVEN
Fidelio
(DVD/Blu-ray)
Lise Davidsen *Leonore*, David Butt Philip *Florestan*, Georg Zeppenfeld
Rocco, Simon Neal *Don Pizarro*, Amanda Forsythe *Marzelline*, Robin
Tritschler *Jaquino*, Egils Siliņš *Don Fernando*, Filipe Manu *First Prisoner*,
Timothy Dawkins *Second Prisoner*, Orchestra and Chorus of the Royal
Opera House, Covent Garden *c* AP
(Opus Arte, 2020)

Symphony No. 5 in C minor, Op. 67
Orchestra dell'Accademia Nazionale di Santa Cecilia *c* AP
(Santa Cecilia Orchestra, 2005)

An die ferne Geliebte
and individual songs and folk songs
Ian Bostridge *tenor*, Vilde Frang *violin*, Nicolas Altstaedt *cello*, AP *piano*
(Warner, 2019)

VINCENZO BELLINI
Norma
(DVD/Blu-ray)
Sonya Yoncheva *Norma*, Sonia Ganassi *Adalgisa*, Joseph Calleja *Pollione*,
Brindley Sherratt *Oroveso*, Vlada Borovko *Clotilde*, David Junghoon
Kim *Flavio*, Orchestra and Chorus of the Royal Opera House, Covent
Garden *c* AP
(Opus Arte, 2016)

ALBAN BERG
Lulu
(DVD/Blu-ray)
Agneta Eichenholz *Lulu*, Michael Volle *Dr Schön/Jack the Ripper*, Klaus
Florian Vogt *Alwa*, Jennifer Larmore *Countess Geschwitz*, Gwynne
Howell *Schigolch*, Philip Langridge *Prince/Manservant/Marquis*, Heather
Shipp *Dresser/Schoolboy/Groom*, Peter Rose *Animal Trainer/Athlete*, Will
Hartmann *Painter/Policeman/Negro*, Jeremy White *Banker/Professor*,
Orchestra of the Royal Opera House, Covent Garden *c* AP
(Opus Arte, 2009)

IRVING BERLIN
'I Love a Piano'
Joyce DiDonato *mezzo-soprano*, AP *piano*
(Erato, 2014)

HECTOR BERLIOZ
Les Troyens
(DVD/Blu-ray)
Bryan Hymel *Énée*, Eva-Maria Westbroek *Didon*, Anna Caterina
Antonacci *Cassandre*, Fabio Capitanucci *Chorèbe*, Hanna Hipp *Anna*,
Brindley Sherratt *Narbal*, Ashley Holland *Panthée*, Pamela Helen
Stephen *Hécube*, Robert Lloyd *Priam*, Ed Lyon *Hylas*, Ji-Min Park *Iopas*,
Barbara Senator *Ascagne*, Ji Hyun Kim *Helenus*, Jihoon Kim *Ghost
of Hector*, Orchestra and Chorus of the Royal Opera House, Covent
Garden *c* AP
(Opus Arte, 2012)

Grande Messe des morts
Javier Camarena *tenor*, Santa Cecilia Academy Chorus,
Royal Concertgebouw Orchestra *c* AP
(RCO Live, 2019)

'Une puce gentille' (*La Damnation de Faust*)
José van Dam *bass-baritone*, Orchestra of the Théâtre de la Monnaie
c AP
(Cypres, 2002)

LEONARD BERNSTEIN
Prelude, Fugue and Riffs
Symphony No. 1 ('Jeremiah')
Symphony No. 2 ('The Age of Anxiety')
Symphony No. 3 ('Kaddish')
Nadine Sierra *soprano*, Marie-Nicole Lemieux *mezzo-soprano*, Josephine
Barstow *speaker*, Alessandro Carbonare *clarinet*, Beatrice Rana *piano*,
Orchestra e Coro dell'Accademia Nazionale di Santa Cecilia *c* AP
(Warner, 2018)

HARRISON BIRTWISTLE
The Minotaur
(DVD/Blu-ray)
John Tomlinson *The Minotaur*, Johan Reuter *Theseus*, Christine Rice
Ariadne, Andrew Watts *Snake Priestess*, Philip Langridge *Hiereus*,
Orchestra and Chorus of the Royal Opera House, Covent Garden *c* AP
(Opus Arte, 2008)

GEORGES BIZET
Carmen
(DVD/Blu-ray)
Anna Caterina Antonacci *Carmen*, Jonas Kaufmann *Don José*,
Ildebrando D'Arcangelo *Escamillo*, Norah Amsellem *Micaëla*, Elena
Xanthoudakis *Frasquita*, Viktoria Vizin *Mercédès*, Jean-Sébastien Bou *Le
Dancaïre*, Jean-Paul Fouchécourt *Le Remendado*, Matthew Rose *Zuniga*,
Jacques Imbrailo *Moralès*, Orchestra and Chorus of the Royal Opera
House, Covent Garden *c* AP
(Decca, 2007)

PHILIPPE BOESMANS
Wintermärchen
Dale Duesing *Leontes*, Susan Chilcott *Hermione*, Arthur Debski
Mamillius, Cornelia Kallisch *Paulina*, Juha Kotilainen *Antigonus*, Franz-
Josef Selig *Camillo*, *Voice of the Oracle*, Anthony Rolfe Johnson *Polixenes*,
Kris Dane *Florizel*, Heinz Zednik *Green*, Chorus and Orchestra of the
Théâtre de la Monnaie *c* AP
(Deutsche Grammophon, 1999)

ARRIGO BOITO
Mefistofele
'Dai campi, dai prati'
'Giunto sul passo estremo'
Jonas Kaufmann *tenor*, Orchestra e Coro dell'Accademia Nazionale
di Santa Cecilia *c* AP
(Decca, 2010)

'L'altra notte'
Anna Netrebko *soprano*, Orchestra e Coro dell'Accademia Nazionale
di Santa Cecilia *c* AP
(Deutsche Grammophon, 2015)

WILLIAM BOLCOM
'Amor' (*Cabaret Songs*)
Joyce DiDonato *mezzo-soprano*, AP *piano*
(Erato, 2014)

JOHANNES BRAHMS
Symphony No. 4 in E minor, Op. 98
New York Philharmonic Orchestra *c* AP
(New York Philharmonic Orchestra, 2010)

Violin Concerto in D, Op. 77
Janine Jansen *violin*, Orchestra dell'Accademia Nazionale
di Santa Cecilia *c* AP
(Decca, 2015)

Cello Sonata No. 1 in E minor, Op. 39
Cello Sonata No. 2 in F major, Op. 99
Luigi Piovano *cello*, AP *piano*
(Arcana, 2019)

BENJAMIN BRITTEN
Peter Grimes, Op. 33
Embroidery Aria
'The truth . . . the pity . . . and the truth'
Sea Interlude: Dawn
Susan Chilcott *soprano*, William Cochran *tenor*, Orchestra of the Théâtre
de la Monnaie *c* AP
(Cypres, 1997)

The Turn of the Screw, Op. 54
Anthony Rolfe Johnson *Prologue/Peter Quint*, Susan Chilcott *Governess*,
Anne Bolstad *Miss Jessel*, Leo van Cleynenbreugel *Miles*, Lyndy Simons
Flora, Anne Evans *Mrs Grose*, Orchestra of the Théâtre de la Monnaie
c AP
(Accord, 1998)

War Requiem, Op. 66
Anna Netrebko *soprano*, Ian Bostridge *tenor*, Thomas Hampson *baritone*,
Orchestra e Coro dell'Accademia Nazionale di Santa Cecilia *c* AP
(Warner, 2013)

Seven Sonnets of Michelangelo, Op. 22
Six Hölderlin Fragments, Op. 61
Who Are These Children?, Op. 84 (Nos. 3, 6, 9, 11)
Winter Words, Op. 52
Ian Bostridge *tenor*, AP *piano*
(EMI, 2013)

Fancie
Ian Bostridge *tenor*, AP *piano*
(Warner, 2016)

GEORGE BUTTERWORTH
A Shropshire Lad
Ian Bostridge *tenor*, AP *piano*
(Warner, 2018)

WILLIAM BYRD
Caleno custure me
Ian Bostridge *tenor*, AP *piano*
(Warner, 2016)

PABLO CASALS
El cant dels ocells
Han-Na Chang *cello*, Orchestra dell'Accademia Nazionale
di Santa Cecilia *c* AP
(EMI, 2005)

ALFREDO CATALANI
'Ebben? . . . Ne andrò lontana' (*La Wally*)
Anna Netrebko *soprano*, Orchestra dell'Accademia Nazionale
di Santa Cecilia *c* AP
(Deutsche Grammophon, 2015)

FRANCESCO CILEA
Adriana Lecouvreur
'L'anima ho stanca'
'La dolcissima effigie'
Jonas Kaufmann *tenor*, Orchestra dell'Accademia Nazionale
di Santa Cecilia *c* AP
(Decca, 2010)

'Io son l'umile ancella'
Anna Netrebko *soprano*, Orchestra dell'Accademia Nazionale
di Santa Cecilia *c* AP
(Deutsche Grammophon, 2015)

L'Arlesiana
'È la solita storia'
Jonas Kaufmann *tenor*, Orchestra dell'Accademia Nazionale
di Santa Cecilia *c* AP
(Decca, 2010)

MUSIC FOR THE CORONATION OF THEIR MAJESTIES
KING CHARLES III AND QUEEN CAMILLA
Coronation Orchestra *c* AP
(Decca, 2023)

ERNESTO DE CURTIS
'Non ti scordar di me'
Joyce DiDonato *mezzo-soprano*, AP *piano*
(Erato, 2014)

GAETANO DONIZETTI
Anna Bolena (extracts)
Maria Stuarda (extracts)
Roberto Devereux (extracts)
Diana Damrau *soprano*, Sara Rocchi, Irida Dragoti *mezzo-sopranos*,
Saverio Fiore, Domenico Pellicola *tenors*, Andrii Ganchuk *baritone*,
Fabrizio Beggi *bass*, Orchestra dell'Accademia Nazionale
di Santa Cecilia *c* AP
(Warner, 2019)

CELIUS DOUGHERTY
'Love in the Dictionary'
Joyce DiDonato *mezzo-soprano*, AP *piano*
(Erato, 2014)

ANTONÍN DVOŘÁK
Cello Concerto in B minor, Op. 104
Mario Brunello *cello*, Orchestra dell'Accademia Nazionale
di Santa Cecilia *c* AP
(EMI, 2011)

Rondo in G minor for Cello and Orchestra, Op. 94
Han-Na Chang *cello*, Orchestra dell'Accademia Nazionale
di Santa Cecilia *c* AP
(EMI, 2005)

Symphony No. 9 in E minor, Op. 95 ('From the New World')
Orchestra dell'Accademia Nazionale di Santa Cecilia *c* AP
(EMI, 2011)

EDWARD ELGAR
In the South, Op. 50
Orchestra dell'Accademia Nazionale di Santa Cecilia *c* AP
(ICA, 2012)

Symphony No. 1 in A flat, Op. 55
Orchestra dell'Accademia Nazionale di Santa Cecilia *c* AP
(ICA, 2012)

Sospiri, Op. 70
Janine Jansen *violin*, AP *piano*
(Decca, 2020)

PÉTER EÖTVÖS
Alle vittime senza nome
Orchestra dell'Accademia Nazionale di Santa Cecilia *c* AP
(Wergo, 2017)

MANUEL DE FALLA
Danse espagnole
Janine Jansen *violin*, AP *piano*
(Decca, 2020)

GERALD FINZI
Let Us Garlands Bring, Op. 18
Ian Bostridge *tenor*, AP *piano*
(Warner, 2016)

STEPHEN FOSTER
'Beautiful Dreamer'
Joyce DiDonato *mezzo-soprano*, AP *piano*
(Erato, 2014)

UMBERTO GIORDANO
Andrea Chénier
(DVD/Blu-ray)
Jonas Kaufmann *Andrea Chénier*, Eva-Maria Westbroek *Maddalena de Coigny*, Zeljko Lučić *Carlo Gérard*, Denyce Graves *Bersi*, Elena Zilio *Madelon*, Rosalind Plowright *Contessa de Coigny*, Roland Wood *Roucher*, Peter Coleman-Wright *Fléville*, Eddie Wade *Fouquier-Tinville*, Adrian Clarke *Mathieu*, Carlo Bosi *Incredibile*, Peter Hoare *Abbé*, Jeremy White *Schmidt*, John Cunningham *Major-Domo*, Yuriy Yurchuk *Dumas*, Orchestra and Chorus of the Royal Opera House, Covent Garden *c* AP
(Warner, 2015)

'Come un bel dì di maggio'
'Un dì, all'azzurro spazio'
'Vicino a te'
Eva-Maria Westbroek *soprano*, Jonas Kaufmann *tenor*,
Orchestra dell'Accademia Nazionale di Santa Cecilia *c* AP
(Decca, 2010)

'La mamma morta'
Anna Netrebko *soprano*, Orchestra dell'Accademia Nazionale
di Santa Cecilia *c* AP
(Deutsche Grammophon, 2015)

Fedora
'Amor ti vieta'
Jonas Kaufmann *tenor*, Orchestra dell'Accademia Nazionale
di Santa Cecilia *c* AP
(Decca, 2010)

ALEXANDER GLAZUNOV
Mélodie, Op. 20 No. 1
Han-Na Chang *cello*, Orchestra dell'Accademia Nazionale
di Santa Cecilia *c* AP
(EMI, 2005)

CHARLES GOUNOD
Faust
Roberto Alagna *Faust*, Bryn Terfel *Méphistophélès*, Angela Gheorghiu
Marguerite, Simon Keenlyside *Valentin*, Sophie Koch *Siébel*, Della Jones
Marthe Schwertlein, Matthew Rose *Wagner*, Orchestra and Chorus of the
Royal Opera House, Covent Garden *c* AP
(EMI, 2004)

EDVARD GRIEG
Six Songs, Op. 48
'From Monte Pincio', Op. 39 No. 1
'Last Spring', Op. 33 No. 2
'I Love But Thee', Op. 5 No. 3
'The Princess'
'Solveig's Song' (*Peer Gynt*)
'A Swan', Op. 25 No. 2
'With a Water-lily', Op. 25 No. 4
Barbara Bonney *soprano*, AP *piano*
(Decca, 1999)

IVOR GURNEY
'Under the Greenwood Tree'
Ian Bostridge *tenor*, AP *piano*
(Warner, 2016)

GEORGE FRIDERIC HANDEL
Giulio Cesare
'Da tempeste il legno infranto'
'Se pietà di me non senti'
Inga Nielsen *soprano*, Helsingborg Symphony Orchestra *c* AP
(Danacord, 1985)

JOSEPH HAYDN
Arianna a Naxos (Hob. xxvɪb/2)
Joyce DiDonato *mezzo-soprano*, AP *piano*
(Erato, 2014)

'She never told her love'
Ian Bostridge *tenor*, AP *piano*
(Warner, 2016)

RICHARD HEUBERGER (arr. Fritz Kreisler)
Midnight Bells (*Der Opernball*)
Janine Jansen *violin*, AP *piano*
(Decca, 2020)

ROBERT JOHNSON
'Full fathom five'
'Where the bee sucks'
Ian Bostridge *tenor*, AP *piano*
(Warner, 2016)

JEROME KERN
'Yesterdays' (*Roberta*)
Janine Jansen *violin*, AP *piano*
(Decca, 2020)

'Can't Help Lovin' Dat Man' (*Show Boat*)
'The Siren's Song' (*Leave It to Jane*)
'Life upon the Wicked Stage' (*Show Boat*)
'Go Little Boat' (*Oh, My Dear!*)
'All the Things You Are' (*Very Warm for May*)
Joyce DiDonato *mezzo-soprano*, AP *piano*
(Erato, 2014)

ERICH WOLFGANG KORNGOLD
'Adieu, good man devil', Op. 29 No. 3
'Come away, death', Op. 29 No. 1
'Desdemona's song', Op. 31 No. 1
Ian Bostridge *tenor*, AP *piano*
(Warner, 2016)

FRITZ KREISLER
Liebesleid
Syncopation
Janine Jansen *violin*, AP *piano*
(Decca, 2020)

ÉDOUARD LALO
Cello Concerto in D minor
Han-Na Chang *cello*, Orchestra dell'Accademia Nazionale
di Santa Cecilia *c* AP
(EMI, 2005)

Symphonie espagnole in D minor, Op. 21
Maxim Vengerov *violin*, Philharmonia Orchestra *c* AP
(EMI, 2003)

RUGGERO LEONCAVALLO
'Testa adorata' (*La bohème*)
Jonas Kaufmann *tenor*, Orchestra dell'Accademia Nazionale
di Santa Cecilia *c* AP
(Decca, 2010)

Pagliacci
(DVD/Blu-ray)
Aleksandrs Antonenko *Canio*, Carmen Giannattasio *Nedda*, Dimitri
Platanias *Tonio*, Benjamin Hulett *Beppe*, Dionysios Sourbis *Silvio*,
Orchestra and Chorus of the Royal Opera House, Covent Garden *c* AP
(Opus Arte, 2015)

'Qual fiamma – Stridono lassù'
Anna Netrebko *soprano*, Orchestra dell'Accademia Nazionale
di Santa Cecilia *c* AP
(Deutsche Grammophon, 2015)

'Vesti la giubba'
Jonas Kaufmann *tenor*, Orchestra dell'Accademia Nazionale
di Santa Cecilia *c* AP
(Decca, 2010)

FRANZ LISZT
'Comment, disaient-ils' (S276)
'Der du von dem Himmel bist' (S279)
'Enfant, si j'étais roi' (S283)
'Der Fischerknabe' (S292a No. 1)
'Freudvoll und leidvoll' (S280)
'Im Rhein, im schönen Strome' (S272)
'Die Loreley' (S273)
'Mignons Lied' (S275)
'O komm im Traum' (S282)
'Oh! quand je dors' (S282)
'S'il est un charmant gazon' (S284)
'Über allen Gipfeln ist Ruh' (S306)
Barbara Bonney *soprano*, AP *piano*
(Decca, 2001)

ANATOLY LYADOV
The Enchanted Lake
Orchestra dell'Accademia Nazionale di Santa Cecilia *c* AP
(EMI, 2009)

GUSTAV MAHLER
Symphony No. 6 in A minor
Orchestra dell'Accademia Nazionale di Santa Cecilia *c* AP
(EMI, 2011)

'Im Lenz'
'Maitanz im Grünen'
'Winterlied'
Ian Bostridge *tenor*, AP *piano*
(EMI, 2010)

Des Knaben Wunderhorn: Three Songs
Ian Bostridge *tenor*, AP *piano*
(Warner, 2018)

GIUSEPPE MARTUCCI
Romances
Luigi Piovano *cello*, AP *piano*
(Arcana, 2019)

PIETRO MASCAGNI
Cavalleria rusticana
(DVD/Blu-ray)
Eva-Maria Westbroek *Santuzza*, Aleksandrs Antonenko *Turiddu*,
Elena Zilio *Mamma Lucia*, Dimitri Platanias *Alfio*, Martina Belli *Lola*,
Orchestra and Chorus of the Royal Opera House, Covent Garden *c* AP
(Opus Arte, 2015)

'Mamma, quel vino è generoso'
'Viva il vino spumeggiante'
Jonas Kaufmann *tenor*, Rosa Feola *mezzo-soprano*, Cristina Reale *soprano*,
Orchestra dell'Accademia Nazionale di Santa Cecilia *c* AP
(Decca, 2010)

Iris
'Apri la tua finestra'
Jonas Kaufmann *tenor*, Orchestra dell'Accademia Nazionale
di Santa Cecilia *c* AP
(Decca, 2010)

JULES MASSENET
Manon
Angela Gheorghiu *Manon*, Roberto Alagna *Des Grieux*, Earle Patriarco
Lescaut, José van Dam *Comte des Grieux*, Gilles Ragon *Guillot de
Morfontaine*, Nicolas Revenq *De Brétigny*, Anna Maria Panzarella
Poussette, Sophie Koch *Javotte*, Susanne Schimmack *Rosette*, Nicolas
Cavallier *Innkeeper,* Chorus and Orchestra of the Théâtre de la Monnaie
c AP
(EMI, 1999)

'Adieu, notre petite table'
'Je marche sur tous les chemins'
Inga Nielsen *soprano*, Helsingborg Symphony Orchestra *c* AP
(Danacord, 1985)

Werther
Roberto Alagna *Werther*, Angela Gheorghiu *Charlotte*, Thomas
Hampson *Albert*, Patricia Petibon *Sophie*, Jean-Philippe Courtis *Le Bailli*,
Jean-Paul Fouchécourt *Schmidt*, Jean-Marie Frémeau *Johann*, Pierre
Dupont *Brühlmann*, Sophie Boulanger *Käthchen*, Tiffin Children's Choir,
London Symphony Orchestra *c* AP
(EMI, 1998)

Rolando Villazón *Werther*, Sophie Koch *Charlotte*, Audun Iversen *Albert*,
Eri Nakamura *Sophie*, Alain Vernhes *Le Bailli*, Stuart Patterson *Schmidt*,
Darren Jeffery *Johann*, ZhengZhong *Brühlmann*, Anna Devin *Käthchen*,
Orchestra of the Royal Opera House, Covent Garden *c* AP
(Deutsche Grammophon, 2011)

PETER MAXWELL DAVIES
Symphony No. 10 ('Alla ricerca di Borromini')
Markus Butter *baritone*, London Symphony Chorus and Orchestra *c* AP
(LSO Live, 2014)

FELIX MENDELSSOHN
Elijah
Carolyn James *soprano*, Nancy Maultsby *mezzo-soprano*, Keith Lewis
tenor, José van Dam *bass-baritone*, Chorus and Orchestra of the Théâtre
de la Monnaie *c* AP
(Forlane, 1994)

THOMAS MORLEY
'It was a lover and his lass'
'O mistress mine'
Ian Bostridge *tenor*, AP *piano*
(Warner, 2016)

JEROME MOROSS
'A Lazy Afternoon'
Joyce DiDonato *mezzo-soprano*, AP *piano*
(Erato, 2014)

WOLFGANG AMADEUS MOZART
Don Giovanni (K527)
'Ah, fuggi il traditor'
'In quali eccessi . . . Mi tradì'
Inga Nielsen *soprano*, Helsingborg Symphony Orchestra *c* AP
(Danacord, 1985)

'Fin ch'han dal vino'
Knut Skram *baritone*, Oslo Philharmonic Orchestra *c* AP
(Simax, 1990)

Le nozze di Figaro (K492)
(DVD)
Erwin Schrott *Figaro*, Miah Persson *Susanna*, Gerald Finley *Count
Almaviva*, Dorothea Röschmann *Countess Almaviva*, Rinat Shaham
Cherubino, Jonathan Veira *Bartolo*, Philip Langridge *Don Basilio*,
Graciela Araya *Marcellina*, Jeremy White *Antonio*, Francis Egerton
Don Curzio, Ana James *Barbarina*, Orchestra and Chorus of the Royal
Opera House, Covent Garden *c* AP
(Opus Arte, 2006)

(DVD)

Riccardo Fassi *Figaro*, Giulia Semenzato *Susanna*, Germán E. Alcántara *Count Almaviva*, Federica Lombardi *Countess Almaviva*, Hanna Hipp *Cherubino*, Gianluca Buratto *Bartolo*, Gregory Bonfatti *Don Basilio*, Monica Bacelli *Marcellina*, Jeremy White *Antonio*, Alasdair Elliott *Don Curzio*, Alexandra Lowe *Barbarina*, Orchestra and Chorus of the Royal Opera House, Covent Garden *c* AP
(Opus Arte, 2022)

'Der Vogelfänger bin ich ja' (*Die Zauberflöte* (K620))
Knut Skram *baritone*, Oslo Philharmonic Orchestra *c* AP
(Simax, 1990)

'Ch'io mi scordi di te' (K505)
Inga Nielsen *soprano*, Danish National Symphony Orchestra *c* AP *piano*
(Chandos, 1987)

'Non più! Tutto ascoltai' (K490)
Aleksandra Kurzak *soprano*, Lisa Batiashvili *violin*, London Symphony Orchestra *c* AP
(Deutsche Grammophon, 2012)

'Clarice cara mia sposa' (K256)
'Con ossequio, con rispetto' (K210)
'Dove mai trovar quel ciglio?' (*Lo sposo deluso* (K430))
'Misero! O sogno' (K431)
'Müsst ich auch durch tausend Drachen' (K435)
'Or che il dover' (K36)
'Per pietà, non ricercate' (K420)
'Se al labbro mio non credi' (K295)
'Si mostra la sorte' (K209)
'Va, dal furor portata' (K21)
Rolando Villazón *tenor*, London Symphony Orchestra *c* AP
(Deutsche Grammophon, 2012)

Symphony No. 31 in D ('Paris') (K297)
New York Philharmonic Orchestra *c* AP
(New York Philharmonic Orchestra, 2010)

Violin Sonata in E minor (K304)
Violin Sonata in A (K305)
Violin Sonata in E flat (K380)
Violin Sonata in B flat (K454)
Dmitry Sitkovetsky *violin*, AP *piano*
(Hänssler, 2006)

MODEST MUSSORGSKY
Boris Godunov
(DVD/Blu-ray)
Bryn Terfel *Boris Godunov*, John Graham-Hall *Prince Shuisky*, Ain
Anger *Pimen*, David Butt Philip *Grigory*, John Tomlinson *Varlaam*,
Harry Nicoll *Missail*, Kostas Smoriginas *Shchelkalov*, Andrew Tortise
Yurodivy (*Holy Fool*), Vlada Borovko *Xenia*, Sarah Pring *Xenia's Nurse*,
Rebecca de Pont Davies *Hostess at the Inn*, Jeremy White *Nikitich*,
Adrian Clarke *Mityukha*, Ben Knight *Fyodor*, James Platt *Frontier Guard*,
Nicholas Sales *Boyar-in-Waiting*, Orchestra and Chorus of the Royal
Opera House, Covent Garden *c* AP
(Opus Arte, 2016)

Night on Bald Mountain
Dream of the Peasant Gritzko (*Sorochintsy Fair*)
Orchestra e Coro dell'Accademia Nazionale di Santa Cecilia *c* AP
(<?>, 2024)

HAVELOCK NELSON
'Lovely Jimmie'
Joyce DiDonato *mezzo-soprano*, AP *piano*
(Erato, 2014)

JACQUES OFFENBACH
Les Larmes de Jacqueline, Op. 76 No. 2
Han-Na Chang *cello*, Orchestra dell'Accademia Nazionale
di Santa Cecilia *c* AP
(EMI, 2005)

ANDRZEJ PANUFNIK
Symphony No. 10
London Symphony Orchestra *c* AP
(LSO Live, 2014)

GIOVANNI BATTISTA PERGOLESI
La conversion e morte di San Guglielmo: *Sinfonia*
Nel chiuso centro
Questo è il piano, questo è il rio
Stabat Mater
Anna Netrebko *soprano*, Marianna Pizzolato *mezzo-soprano*,
Orchestra dell'Accademia Nazionale di Santa Cecilia *c* AP
(Deutsche Grammophon, 2010)

AMILCARE PONCHIELLI
La Gioconda
'Cielo a mar!'
Jonas Kaufmann *tenor*, Orchestra dell'Accademia Nazionale
di Santa Cecilia *c* AP
(Decca, 2010)

'Suicidio!'
Anna Netrebko *soprano*, Orchestra dell'Accademia Nazionale
di Santa Cecilia *c* AP
(Deutsche Grammophon, 2015)

Duets
Jonas Kaufmann *tenor*, Ludovic Tézier *baritone*, Orchestra
dell'Accademia Nazionale di Santa Cecilia *c* AP
(Sony, 2021)

I Lituani
'Sì questa estrema grazia'
Jonas Kaufmann *tenor*, Orchestra dell'Accademia Nazionale
di Santa Cecilia *c* AP
(Decca, 2010)

FRANCIS POULENC
'Fancy'
Ian Bostridge *tenor*, AP *piano*
(Warner, 2016)

SERGEY PROKOFIEV
Piano Concerto No. 2 in G minor, Op. 16
Beatrice Rana *piano*, Orchestra dell'Accademia Nazionale
di Santa Cecilia *c* AP
(Warner, 2015)

Sinfonia concertante in E minor, Op. 125
Han-Na Chang *cello*, London Symphony Orchestra *c* AP
(EMI, 2002)

Cello Sonata in C, Op. 119
Han-Na Chang *cello*, AP *piano*
(EMI, 2002)

GIACOMO PUCCINI
La bohème
Leontina Vaduva *Mimì*, Roberto Alagna *Rodolfo*, Ruth Ann Swenson
Musetta, Thomas Hampson *Marcello*, Simon Keenlyside *Schaunard*,
Samuel Ramey *Colline*, Enrico Fissore *Benoît, Alcindoro*, Philip Sheffield
Parpignol, Jeffrey Carl *Sergeant*, Paul Parfitt *Customs Officer*, London
Oratory Boys' Choir, London Voices, Philharmonia Orchestra *c* AP
(EMI, 1995)

(DVD/Blu-ray)
Nicole Car *Mimì*, Michael Fabiano *Rodolfo*, Mariusz Kwiecień *Marcello*,
Simona Mihai *Musetta*, Florian Sempey *Schaunard*, Luca Tittoto *Colline*,
Jeremy White *Benoît*, Wyn Pencarreg *Alcindoro*, Orchestra and Chorus
of the Royal Opera House, Covent Garden *c* AP
(Opus Arte, 2017)

'O soave fanciulla'
Kristine Opolais *soprano*, Jonas Kaufmann *tenor*, Orchestra
dell'Accademia Nazionale di Santa Cecilia *c* AP
(Sony, 2014)

Duets
Jonas Kaufmann *tenor*, Ludovic Tézier *baritone*, Orchestra
dell'Accademia Nazionale di Santa Cecilia *c* AP
(Sony, 2021)

Edgar
'Orgia, chimera dall'occhio vitreo'
Jonas Kaufmann *tenor*, Orchestra dell'Accademia Nazionale
di Santa Cecilia *c* AP
(Sony, 2014)

La fanciulla del West
'Ch'ella mi creda libero'
'Or son sei mesi'
Jonas Kaufmann *tenor*, Orchestra dell'Accademia Nazionale
di Santa Cecilia *c* AP
(Sony, 2014)

Gianni Schicchi
José van Dam *Gianni Schicchi*, Angela Gheorghiu *Lauretta*, Roberto
Alagna *Rinuccio*, Felicity Palmer *Zita*, Paolo Barbacini *Gherardo*, Patrizia
Ciofi *Nella*, James Savage-Hanford *Gherardino*, Carlos Chausson *Betto di
Signa*, Luigi Roni *Simone*, Roberto Scaltriti *Marco*, Elena Zilio *La Ciesca*,
Enrico Fissore *Maestro Spinelloccio*, *Ser Amantio di Nicolao*, London
Symphony Orchestra *c* AP
(EMI, 1997)

(DVD/Blu-ray)
Lucio Gallo *Gianni Schicchi*, Ekaterina Siurina *Lauretta*, Francesco
Demuro *Rinuccio*, Elena Zilio *Zita*, Alan Oke *Gherardo*, Rebecca Evans
Nella, Filippo Turkheimer *Gherardino*, Jeremy White *Betto di Signa*,
Gwynne Howell *Simone*, Robert Poulton *Marco*, Marie McLaughlin
La Ciesca, Henry Waddington *Maestro Spinelloccio*, Enrico Fissore
Ser Amantio di Nicolao, Daniel Grice *Pinellino*, John Molloy *Guccio*,
Orchestra of the Royal Opera House, Covent Garden *c* AP
(Opus Arte, 2011)

'Firenze è come un albero fiorito'
Jonas Kaufmann *tenor*, Orchestra dell'Accademia Nazionale
di Santa Cecilia *c* AP
(Sony, 2014)

'O mio babbino caro'
Inga Nielsen *soprano*, Helsingborg Symphony Orchestra *c* AP
(Danacord, 1985)

Madama Butterfly
Angela Gheorghiu *Cio-Cio-San*, Jonas Kaufmann *Pinkerton*, Fabio
Capitanucci *Sharpless*, Enkelejda Shkosa *Suzuki*, Gregory Bonfatti *Goro*,
Raymond Aceto *Bonze*, Cristina Reale *Kate Pinkerton*, Roberto Valentini
Prince Yamadori, Massimo Simeoli *Imperial Commissioner*, Fabrizio di
Bernardo *Official Registrar*, Orchestra e Coro dell'Accademia Nazionale
di Santa Cecilia *c* AP
(EMI, 2008)

(DVD/Blu-ray)
Ermonela Jaho *Cio-Cio-San*, Marcelo Puente *Pinkerton*, Scott Hendricks *Sharpless*, Elizabeth DeShong *Suzuki*, Carlo Bosi *Goro*, Jeremy White *Bonze*, Emily Edmonds *Kate Pinkerton*, Yuriy Yurchuk *Prince Yamadori*, Gyula Nagy *Imperial Commissioner*, Orchestra and Chorus of the Royal Opera House, Covent Garden *c* AP
(Opus Arte, 2017)

'Addio, fiorito asil'
Jonas Kaufmann *tenor*, Orchestra dell'Accademia Nazionale di Santa Cecilia *c* AP
(Sony, 2014)

'Un bel dì vedremo'
Anna Netrebko *soprano*, Orchestra dell'Accademia Nazionale di Santa Cecilia *c* AP
(Deutsche Grammophon, 2015)

Manon Lescaut
(DVD/Blu-ray)
Kristine Opolais *Manon Lescaut*, Jonas Kaufmann *Chevalier Des Grieux*, Christopher Maltman *Lescaut*, Benjamin Hulett *Edmondo*, Maurizio Muraro *Geronte de Ravoir*, Nigel Cliffe *Innkeeper*, Robert Burt *Dancing Master*, Jihoon Kim *Sergeant*, Nadezhda Karyazina *Musician*, Luis Gomes *Lamplighter*, Jeremy White *Naval Captain*, Orchestra and Chorus of the Royal Opera House, Covent Garden *c* AP
(Sony, 2014)

'Ah! Manon mi tradisce'
'Donna non vidi mai'
'Ah! Non avvicinate!'
'Tu, tu, amore'
Kristine Opolais *soprano*, Jonas Kaufmann *tenor*, Orchestra dell'Accademia Nazionale di Santa Cecilia *c* AP
(Sony, 2014)

'In quelle trine morbide'
Act IV complete
Anna Netrebko *soprano*, Yusif Eyvasov *tenor*, Orchestra dell'Accademia Nazionale di Santa Cecilia *c* AP
(Deutsche Grammophon, 2015)

La rondine
Angela Gheorghiu *Magda*, Roberto Alagna *Ruggero*, William Matteuzzi
Prunier, *Un uomo che fischia*, Inva Mula *Lisette*, Alberto Rinaldi
Rambaldo, Patrizia Biccirè *Yvette*, *Georgette*, *Un voce interno*, Patrizia
Ciofi *Bianca*, *Gabriella*, Monica Bacelli *Suzy*, *Lolette*, Toby Spence
Gobin, Riccardo Simonetti *Périchaud*, Enrico Fissore *Crébillon*, *Rabonier*,
Maggiodomo, London Voices, London Symphony Orchestra *c* AP
(EMI, 1996)

'Parigi! È la città dei desideri'
Jonas Kaufmann *tenor*, Santa Cecilia Academy Orchestra *c* AP
(Sony, 2014)

Suor Angelica
Cristina Gallardo-Domâs *Suor Angelica*, Bernadette Manca di Nissa
Princess, Felicity Palmer *Abbess*, Elena Zilio *Monitoress*, Sara Fulgoni
Mistress of the Novices, Dorothea Röschmann *Suor Genovieffa*, Judith Rees
Suor Osmina, Rachele Stanisci *Suor Dolcina*, Francesca Pedaci *Nursing
Sister*, Anna Maria Panzarella *First Almoner Sister*, *First Lay Sister*, Susan
Mackenzie-Park *Second Almoner Sister*, Deborah Miles-Johnson *Second
Lay Sister*, Rosalind Waters *Novice*, Tiffin School Boys' Choir, London
Voices, Philharmonia Orchestra *c* AP
(EMI, 1997)

(DVD/Blu-ray)
Ermonela Jaho *Suor Angelica*, Anna Larsson *Princess*, Irina Mishura
Abbess, Elena Zilio *Monitoress*, Elizabeth Sikora *Mistress of the Novices*,
Anna Devin *Suor Genovieffa*, Eryl Royle *Suor Osmina*, Elizabeth Key
Suor Dolcina, Elizabeth Woollett *Nursing Sister*, Katy Batho *Novice*,
Gillian Webster, Kathleen Wilder *Almoner Sisters*, Orchestra and Chorus
of the Royal Opera House, Covent Garden *c* AP
(Opus Arte, 2011)

Il tabarro
Carlo Guelfi *Michele*, Neil Shicoff *Luigi*, Maria Guleghina *Giorgetta*,
Riccardo Cassinelli *Il Tinca*, Enrico Fissore *Il Talpa*, Elena Zilio *La
Frugola*, Barry Banks *Un Venditore*, Angela Gheorghiu, Roberto Alagna
Due amanti, London Voices, London Symphony Orchestra *c* AP
(EMI, 1997)

(DVD/Blu-ray)
Lucio Gallo *Michele*, Aleksandrs Antonenko *Luigi*, Eva-Maria
Westbroek *Giorgetta*, Alan Oke *Il Tinca*, Jeremy White *Il Talpa*, Irina
Mishura *La Frugola*, Ji-Min Park *Un Venditore*, Anna Devin, Robert
Anthony Gardiner *Due amanti*, Orchestra and Chorus of the Royal
Opera House, Covent Garden *c* AP
(Opus Arte, 2011)

'Hai ben ragione'
Jonas Kaufmann *tenor*, Santa Cecilia Academy Orchestra *c* AP
(Sony, 2014)

Tosca
Angela Gheorghiu *Tosca*, Roberto Alagna *Cavaradossi*, Ruggero
Raimondi *Scarpia*, Maurizio Muraro *Angelotti*, David Cangelosi *Spoletta*,
Enrico Fissore *Sacristan*, Sorin Coliban *Sciarrone*, Gwynne Howell
Gaoler, James Savage-Hanford *Shepherd Boy*, Tiffin Children's Choir,
Chorus and Orchestra of the Royal Opera House, Covent Garden *c* AP
(EMI, 2000)

(DVD/Blu-ray)
Angela Gheorghiu *Tosca*, Jonas Kaufmann *Cavaradossi*, Bryn Terfel
Scarpia, Lukas Jakobski *Angelotti*, Hubert Francis *Spoletta*, Jeremy White
Sacristan, ZhengZhong *Sciarrone*, John Morrissey *Gaoler*, William Payne
Shepherd Boy, Orchestra and Chorus of the Royal Opera House, Covent
Garden *c* AP
(EMI, 2011)

'Recondita armonia'
Jonas Kaufmann *tenor*, Orchestra dell'Accademia Nazionale
di Santa Cecilia *c* AP
(Sony, 2014)

'Vissi d'arte'
Anna Netrebko *soprano*, Orchestra dell'Accademia Nazionale
di Santa Cecilia *c* AP
(Deutsche Grammophon, 2015)

Turandot
Sondra Radvanovsky *Turandot*, Jonas Kaufmann *Calaf*, Ermonela Jaho
Liù, Michele Pertusi *Timur*, Mattia Olivieri *Ping*, Gregory Bonfatti
Pang, Siyabonga Maqungo *Pong*, Francesco Toma *Prince of Persia*,
Michael Spyres *Altoum*, Michael Mofidian *Mandarin*, Orchestra e Coro
dell'Accademia Nazionale di Santa Cecilia *c* AP
(Warner, 2022)

'Nessun dorma'
'Non piangere, Liù'
Jonas Kaufmann *tenor*, Orchestra e Coro dell'Accademia Nazionale
di Santa Cecilia *c* AP
(Sony, 2014)

'In questa reggia'
'Signore, ascolta!'
Anna Netrebko *soprano*, Orchestra e Coro dell'Accademia Nazionale
di Santa Cecilia *c* AP
(Deutsche Grammophon, 2015)

Le villi
excerpts
London Symphony Orchestra *c* AP
(EMI, 1996)

'Torna ai felice dì'
Jonas Kaufmann *tenor*, Orchestra e Coro dell'Accademia Nazionale
di Santa Cecilia
c AP
(Sony, 2014)

Messa di Gloria
Roberto Alagna *tenor*, Thomas Hampson *baritone*
London Symphony Chorus and Orchestra *c* AP
(EMI, 2000)

Capriccio sinfonico
(Download)
London Symphony Orchestra *c* AP
(LSO Live, 2022)

Crisantemi
Preludio sinfonico
London Symphony Orchestra *c* AP
(EMI, 2000)

'Morire?'
Roberto Alagna *tenor*, AP *piano*
(EMI, 1996)

ROGER QUILTER
'Come away, death', Op. 6 No. 1
Ian Bostridge *tenor*, AP *piano*
(Warner, 2016)

SERGEY RACHMANINOV
Piano Concerto No. 1 in F sharp minor, Op. 1
Piano Concerto No. 2 in C minor, Op. 18
Leif Ove Andsnes *piano*, Berlin Philharmonic Orchestra *c* AP
(EMI, 2005)

Piano Concerto No. 3 in D minor, Op. 30
Leif Ove Andsnes *piano*, London Symphony Orchestra *c* AP
(EMI, 2009)

Piano Concerto No. 4 in G minor, Op. 40
Leif Ove Andsnes *piano*, London Symphony Orchestra *c* AP
(EMI, 2010)

Symphony No. 2 in E minor, Op. 27
Santa Cecilia Academy Orchestra *c* AP
(EMI, 2009)

Symphony No. 2 in E minor, Op. 27
(DVD)
Staatskapelle, Dresden *c* AP
(Euroarts, 2018)

Andante (from Sonata for cello and piano, Op. 19)
Janine Jansen *violin*, AP *piano*
(Decca, 2020)

MAURICE RAVEL
Tzigane
Maxim Vengerov *violin*, Philharmonia Orchestra *c* AP
(EMI, 2003)

Pièce en forme de habanera
Janine Jansen *violin*, AP *piano*
(Decca, 2020)

LICINIO REFICE
'Ombra di nube'
Jonas Kaufmann *tenor*, Orchestra dell'Accademia Nazionale
di Santa Cecilia *c* AP
(Decca, 2010)

MAX REGER
'Waldeinsamkeit'
Inga Nielsen *soprano*, AP *piano*
(Chandos, 1984)

OTTORINO RESPIGHI
Il tramonto
Christine Rice *mezzo-soprano*
Orchestra dell'Accademia Nazionale di Santa Cecilia *c* AP
(EMI, 2007)

Feste romane
Fontane di Roma
Pini di Roma
Orchestra dell'Accademia Nazionale di Santa Cecilia *c* AP
(EMI, 2007)

NIKOLAI RIMSKY-KORSAKOV
Scheherazade, Op. 35
Orchestra dell'Accademia Nazionale di Santa Cecilia *c* AP
(?, 2024)

RICHARD RODGERS
'My Funny Valentine'
Joyce DiDonato *mezzo-soprano*, AP *piano*
(Erato, 2014)

GIOACHINO ROSSINI
Il barbiere di Siviglia
(DVD/Blu-ray)
Pietro Spagnoli *Figaro*, Joyce DiDonato *Rosina*, Juan Diego Flórez *Count
Almaviva*, Alessandro Corbelli *Doctor Bartolo*, Ferruccio Furlanetto *Don
Basilio*, Changhan Lim *Fiorello*, Jennifer Rhys-Davies *Berta*, Bryan
Secombe *Ambrogio*, Orchestra and Chorus of the Royal Opera House,
Covent Garden *c* AP
(Virgin, 2009)

Guillaume Tell
Gerald Finley *Guillaume Tell*, Malin Byström *Mathilde*, John Osborn
Arnold Melchtal, Matthew Rose *Walter Furst*, Frédéric Caton *Melchtal*,
Elena Xanthoudakis *Jemmy*, Marie-Nicole Lemieux *Hedwige*, Carlo
Cigni *Gessler*, Carlo Bosi *Rodolphe*, Celso Albelo *Ruodi*, Dawid Kimberg
Leuthold, Davide Malvestio *Huntsman*, Orchestra e Coro dell'Accademia
Nazionale di Santa Cecilia *c* AP
(EMI, 2010)

(DVD/Blu-ray)
Gerald Finley *Guillaume Tell*, Malin Byström *Mathilde*, John Osborn
Arnold Melchtal, Alexander Vinogradov *Walter Furst*, Eric Halfvarson
Melchtal, Sofia Fomina *Jemmy*, Enkelejda Shkosa *Hedwige*, Nicolas
Courjal *Gessler*, Michael Colvin *Rodolphe*, Enea Scala *Ruodi*, Samuel
Dale Johnson *Leuthold*, Orchestra and Chorus of the Royal Opera
House, Covent Garden *c* AP
(Opus Arte, 2015)

Stabat Mater
Anna Netrebko *soprano*, Joyce DiDonato *mezzo-soprano*, Lawrence
Brownlee *tenor*, Ildebrando D'Arcangelo *bass-baritone*, Orchestra e Coro
dell'Accademia Nazionale di Santa Cecilia *c* AP
(EMI, 2010)

Messa di Gloria
Eleonora Buratto *soprano*, Teresa Iervolino *mezzo-soprano*, Lawrence
Brownlee, Michael Spyres *tenors*, Carlo Lepore *bass*, Orchestra e Coro
dell'Accademia Nazionale di Santa Cecilia *c* AP
(Warner, 2022)

Petite Messe solennelle
Marina Rebeka *soprano*, Sara Mingardo *mezzo-soprano*, Francesco Meli
tenor, Alex Esposito *bass*, Orchestra e Coro dell'Accademia Nazionale
di Santa Cecilia *c* AP
(EMI, 2012)

Andante e tema con variazioni
Overture: *Il barbiere di Siviglia*
Overture: *La Cenerentola*
Overture: *Il Signor Bruschino*
Overture: *Semiramide*
Overture: *William Tell*
Overture: *La scala di seta*
Overture: *Le siège de Corinthe*
Orchestra dell'Accademia Nazionale di Santa Cecilia *c* AP
(Warner, 2014)

'La dichiarzione'
'Mi lagnerò tacendo'
'Nizza'
Péchés de vieillesse
Soirées musicales
'Sorzico'
Rockwell Blake *tenor*, AP *piano*
(EMI, 1995)

'Duetto buffo di due gatti'
Gérard Lesne *countertenor*, Rockwell Blake *tenor*, AP *piano*
(EMI, 1995)

'Beltà crudele'
'La danza'
Joyce DiDonato *mezzo-soprano*, AP *piano*
(Erato, 2014)

CAMILLE SAINT-SAËNS
Samson et Dalila
(DVD/Blu-ray)
SeokJong Baek *Samson*, Elīna Garanča *Dalila*, Łukasz Goliński *High Priest of Dagon*, Blaise Malaba *Abimelech*, Alan Pingarrón *First Philistine*, Chuma Sijeqa *Second Philistine*, Thando Mjandana *Philistine Messenger*, Goderdzi Janelidze *Old Hebrew*, Orchestra and Chorus of the Royal Opera House, Covent Garden *c* AP
(Opus Arte, 2022)

Allegro appassionato in B minor, Op. 43
Han-Na Chang *cello*, Orchestra dell'Accademia Nazionale di Santa Cecilia *c* AP
(EMI, 2005)

Carnaval des Animaux
Organ Symphony No. 3 in C minor, Op. 78
Martha Argerich *piano*, Daniele Rossi *organ*, Orchestra dell'Accademia Nazionale di Santa Ceciliaa *c* AP
(Warner, 2016)

Violin Concerto No. 3 in B minor, Op. 61
Maxim Vengerov *violin*, Philharmonia Orchestra *c* AP
(EMI, 2003)

FRANCESCO SANTOLIQUIDO
I canti della sera
Joyce DiDonato *mezzo-soprano*, AP *piano*
(Erato, 2014)

FRANZ SCHUBERT
'Abschied' (D475)
'An Schwager Kronos' (D369)
'Geheimnis' (D941)
Schwanengesang (D957)
'Widerschein' (D949)
Ian Bostridge *tenor*, AP *piano*
(EMI, 2008)

'An Silvia' (D891)
Ian Bostridge *tenor*, AP *piano*
(Warner, 2016)

CLARA SCHUMANN
Andante molto, Op. 22 No. 1
Janine Jansen *violin*, AP *piano*
(Decca, 2020)

ROBERT SCHUMANN
Introduction and Allegro appassionato, Op. 92
Introduction and Concerto Allegro, Op. 134
Piano Concerto in A minor, Op. 54
Jan Lisiecki *piano*, Orchestra dell'Accademia Nazionale
di Santa Cecilia *c* AP
(Deutsche Grammophon, 2015)

Symphony No. 2 in C, Op. 61
Orchestra dell'Accademia Nazionale di Santa Cecilia *c* AP
(ICA, 2012)

Symphony No. 4 in D minor, Op. 120
Orchestra dell'Accademia Nazionale di Santa Cecilia *c* AP
(ICA, 2010)

Zart und mit Ausdruck, Op. 73 No. 1
Janine Jansen *violin*, AP *piano*
(Decca, 2020)

Dichterliebe, Op. 48
Barbara Bonney *soprano*, AP *piano*
(Decca, 2001)

DMITRI SHOSTAKOVICH
Cello Concerto No. 1 in E flat, Op. 107
Han-Na Chang *cello*, London Symphony Orchestra *c* AP
(EMI, 2005)

Cello Sonata in D minor, Op. 40
Han-Na Chang *cello*, AP *piano*
(EMI, 2005)

JEAN SIBELIUS
'Astray', Op. 17 No. 4
'The Diamond on the March Snow', Op. 36 No. 6
'The Maiden's Tryst', Op. 37 No. 5
'Sigh, Sedges, Sigh', Op. 36 No. 4
'Was It a Dream?', Op. 37 No. 4
Barbara Bonney *soprano*, AP *piano*
(Decca, 1999)

CARL LEOPOLD SJØBERG
'Tonerna'
Barbara Bonney *soprano*, AP *piano*
(Decca, 1999)

WILHELM STENHAMMAR
'Adagio', Op. 20 No. 5
'Fylgia', Op. 16 No. 4
'The Girl Came Home from Her Tryst', Op. 4b No. 1
'I skogen'
'Sverige', Op. 22 No. 2
Barbara Bonney *soprano*, AP *piano*
(Decca, 1999)

RUDI STEPHAN
'Ich will dir singen ein Hohelied'
Ian Bostridge *tenor*, AP *piano*
(Warner, 2018)

RICHARD STRAUSS
Arabella
'Aber der Richtige'
Felicity Lott *soprano*, Orchestra of the Royal House, Covent Garden
c AP
(Virgin, 2004)

Ariadne auf Naxos
'Sein wir wieder gut!'
'Wer ist dieses entzückende Mädchen?'
Susan Chilcott *soprano*, Dale Duesing *baritone*, Orchestra of the Théâtre
de la Monnaie *c* AP
(Cypres, 1997)

'An Ihre Plätze, meine Damen und Herren'
'Grossmächtige Prinzessin'
'Kindskopf! Merkt auf'
Natalie Dessay *soprano*, Felicity Lott *soprano*, Sophie Koch *mezzo-soprano*, Thomas Allen *baritone*, Orchestra of the Royal Opera House, Covent Garden *c* AP
(Virgin, 2004)

Capriccio
Interlude: Moonlight Music
'Morgen mittag um elf!'
Nina Stemme *soprano*, Jeremy White *bass*, Orchestra of the Royal Opera House, Covent Garden *c* AP
(EMI, 2006)

Der Rosenkavalier
'Ist ein Traum'
'Marie Theres', wie gut Sie ist'
'Presentation of the Rose'
Natalie Dessay *soprano*, Felicity Lott *soprano*, Angelika Kirchschlager *mezzo-soprano*, Thomas Allen *baritone*, Orchestra of the Royal House, Covent Garden *c* AP
(Virgin, 2004)

Salome
'Wo ist er, dessen Sündenbecher'
Catherine Malfitano *soprano*, Scot Weir *tenor*, José van Dam *bass-baritone*, Orchestra of the Théâtre de la Monnaie *c* AP
(Cypres, 1992)

'Ach, du wolltest mich nicht deinen Mund küssen lassen'
Nina Stemme *soprano*, Liora Grodnikaite *mezzo-soprano*, Gerhard Siegel *tenor*, Orchestra of the Royal Opera House, Covent Garden *c* AP
(EMI, 2006)

Brentano Lieder, Op. 68 (Nos. 2–5)
Natalie Dessay *soprano*, Orchestra of the Royal House, Covent Garden *c* AP
(Virgin, 2004)

Vier letzte Lieder
Nina Stemme *soprano*
Orchestra of the Royal Opera House, Covent Garden *c* AP
(EMI, 2006)

Burlesque
Bertrand Chamayou *piano*, Orchestra dell'Accademia Nazionale
di Santa Cecilia *c* AP
(Warner, 2020)

Ein Heldenleben
Orchestra dell'Accademia Nazionale di Santa Cecilia *c* AP
(Warner, 2018)

IGOR STRAVINSKY
Three Songs from William Shakespeare
Ian Bostridge *tenor*, AP *piano*
(Warner, 2016)

JOSEF SUK
Píseň Lásky, Op. 7 No. 1
Janine Jansen *violin*, AP *piano*
(Decca, 2020)

KAROL SZYMANOWSKI
King Roger (Król Roger)
(DVD/Blu-ray)
Mariusz Kwiecień *Roger II*, Georgia Jarman *Roxana*, Saimir Pirgu
Shepherd, Kim Begley *Edrisi*, Alan Ewing *Archbishop*, Agnes Zwierko
Deaconess, Orchestra and Chorus of the Royal Opera House, Covent
Garden *c* AP
(Opus Arte, 2015)

La Fontaine d'Aréthuse, Op. 30 No. 1
Janine Jansen *violin*, AP *piano*
(Decca, 2020)

PYOTR ILYICH TCHAIKOVSKY
Waltz and Polonaise (*Eugene Onegin*)
Orchestra dell'Accademia Nazionale di Santa Cecilia *c* AP
(EMI, 2005)

Piano Concerto No. 1 in B flat minor, Op. 23
Beatrice Rana *piano*, Orchestra dell'Accademia Nazionale
di Santa Cecilia *c* AP
(Warner, 2015)

1812 Overture
Andante cantabile, Op. 11
Fantasy Overture: *Romeo and Juliet*
Francesca da Rimini, Op. 32
Symphony No. 4 in F minor, Op. 36
Symphony No. 5 in E minor, Op. 64
Symphony No. 6 in B minor, Op. 74 ('*Pathétique*')
Han-Na Chang *cello*, Orchestra dell'Accademia Nazionale
di Santa Cecilia *c* AP
(EMI, 2005)

Lensky's Aria (*Eugene Onegin*)
Souvenir d'un lieu cher, Op. 42 No. 3
Janine Jansen *violin*, AP *piano*
(Decca, 2020)

ALEXANDRE THARAUD
Arrangements of film music
Alexandre Tharaud *piano*, Orchestra dell'Accademia Nazionale
di Santa Cecilia *c* AP
(Warner, 2022)

MICHAEL TIPPETT
Songs for Ariel
Ian Bostridge *tenor*, AP *piano*
(Warner, 2016)

MARK-ANTHONY TURNAGE
Anna Nicole
(DVD/Blu-ray)
Eva-Maria Westbroek *Anna Nicole*, Susan Bickley *Virgie*, Loré Lixenberg
Shelley, Rebecca de Pont Davies *Aunt Kay*, Allison Cook *Blossom*, Alan
Oke *J. Howard Marshall II*, Gerald Finley *Stern*, Peter Hoare *Larry
King*, Andrew Rees *Doctor Yes*, Jeffrey Lloyd-Roberts *Trucker*, Dominic
Rowntree *Daniel*, Grant Doyle *Billy*, Jeremy White *Daddy Hogan*,
Orchestra and Chorus of the Royal Opera House, Covent Garden *c* AP
(Opus Arte, 2011)

RALPH VAUGHAN WILLIAMS
Fantasia on a Theme by Thomas Tallis
London Symphony Orchestra *c* AP
(LSO Live, 2020)

Symphony No. 4 in F minor
London Symphony Orchestra *c* AP
(LSO Live, 2019)

Symphony No. 6 in E minor
London Symphony Orchestra *c* AP
(LSO Live, 2020)

GIUSEPPE VERDI
Aida
Anja Harteros *Aida*, Jonas Kaufmann *Radames*, Ekaterina Semenchuk
Amneris, Ludovic Tézier *Amonasro*, Erwin Schrott *Ramfis*, Marco Spotti
King, Paolo Fanale *Messenger*, Eleonora Buratto *High Priestess*, Santa
Cecilia Academy Chorus and Orchestra *c* AP
(Warner, 2015)

Don Carlo/Don Carlos
Roberto Alagna *Don Carlos*, Karita Mattila *Elisabeth de Valois*, Waltraud
Meier *Eboli*, Thomas Hampson *Rodrigue*, José van Dam *Philippe II*, Eric
Halfvarson *Grand Inquisitor*, Csaba Airizer *Monk*, Anat Efraty *Thibault*,
Scot Weir *Comte de Lerme, Herald*, Donna Brown *Voice from Heaven*,
Chorus of the Théâtre du Chatelet, Orchestre de Paris *c* AP
(EMI, 1996)

(DVD)
Rolando Villazón *Don Carlo*, Marina Poplavskaya *Elizabeth of Valois*,
Sonia Ganassi *Eboli*, Simon Keenlyside *Rodrigo, Marquis of Posa*,
Ferruccio Furlanetto *Philip II*, Eric Halfvarson *Grand Inquisitor*, Pumeza
Matshikiza *Tebaldo*, Nikola Matišić *Count of Lerma*, Robert Lloyd *Monk*,
Anita Watson *Voice from Heaven*, Orchestra and Chorus of the Royal
Opera House, Covent Garden *c* AP
(EMI, 2008)

(DVD/Blu-ray)
Jonas Kaufmann *Don Carlo*, Anja Harteros *Elisabetta*, Ekaterina
Semenchuk *Eboli*, Thomas Hampson *Rodrigo*, Matti Salminen *Filippo II*,
Eric Halfvarson *Grand Inquisitor*, Maria Celeng *Tebaldo*, Robert Lloyd
Monk, Kiandra Howarth *Voice from Heaven*, Benjamin Bernheim
Count of Lerma, *Herald*, Vienna State Opera Chorus and Philharmonic
Orchestra *c* AP
(Sony, 2013)

Duets
Jonas Kaufmann *tenor*, Ludovic Tézier *baritone*, Orchestra
dell'Accademia Nazionale di Santa Cecilia *c* AP
(Sony, 2021)

I due Foscari
(DVD/Blu-ray)
Plácido Domingo *Francesco Foscari*, Francesco Meli *Jacopo Foscari*, Maria
Agresta *Lucrezia Contarini*, Maurizio Muraro *Loredano*, Samuel Sakker
Barbarigo, Rachel Kelly *Pisana*, Orchestra and Chorus of the Royal
Opera House, Covent Garden *c* AP
(Opus Arte, 2014)

La forza del destino
Duets
Jonas Kaufmann *tenor*, Ludovic Tézier *baritone*, Orchestra
dell'Accademia Nazionale di Santa Cecilia *c* AP
(Sony, 2021)

Macbeth
(DVD/Blu-ray)
Simon Keenlyside *Macbeth*, Liudmyla Monastyrska *Lady Macbeth*,
Raymond Aceto *Banquo*, Dimitri Pittas *Macduff*, Steven Ebel *Malcolm*,
Lukas Jakobski *Doctor*, Nigel Cliffe *Servant*, Jonathan Coad *Herald*, Olle
Zetterström *Assassin*, Elisabeth Meister *Lady-in-Waiting*, Orchestra and
Chorus of the Royal Opera House, Covent Garden *c* AP
(Opus Arte, 2011)

Otello
(DVD/Blu-ray)
Jonas Kaufmann *Otello*, Maria Agresta *Desdemona*, Marco Vratogna *Iago*, Frédéric Antoun *Cassio*, Thomas Atkins *Roderigo*, Kai Rüütel *Emilia*, Simon Shibambu *Montano*, In Sung Sim *Lodovico*, Thomas Barnard *Herald*, Orchestra and Chorus of the Royal Opera House, Covent Garden *c* AP
(Sony, 2017)

Jonas Kaufmann *Otello*, Federica Lombardi *Desdemona*, Carlos Álvarez *Iago*, Orchestra e Coro dell'Accademia Nazionale di Santa Cecilia *c* AP
(Sony, 2019)

'Già nella notte'
'A terra! . . . Sì . . . nel livido fango'
'Willow Song' and 'Ave Maria'
Susan Chilcott *soprano*, Claire Powell *mezzo-soprano*, Vladimir Galouzine, Marten Smeding, Kurt Streit *tenors*, Tom Fox *bass-baritone*, John Cheek *bass*, Chorus and Orchestra of the Théâtre de la Monnaie *c* AP
(Cypres, 1994)

Duets
Jonas Kaufmann *tenor*, Ludovic Tézier *baritone*, Orchestra dell'Accademia Nazionale di Santa Cecilia *c* AP
(Sony, 2021)

Rigoletto
(DVD/Blu-ray)
Carlos Álvarez *Rigoletto*, Liparit Avetisyan *Duke of Mantua*, Lisette Oropesa *Gilda*, Brindley Sherratt *Sparafucile*, Ramona Zaharia *Maddalena*, Eric Greene *Count Monterone*, Dominic Sedgwick *Marullo*, Egor Zhuravskii *Matteo Borsa*, Blaise Malaba *Count Ceprano*, Amanda Baldwin *Countess Ceprano*, Kseniia Nikolaieva *Giovanna*, Louise Armit *Page*, Orchestra and Chorus of the Royal Opera House, Covent Garden *c* AP
(Opus Arte, 2021)

'Cortigiani'
Knut Skram *baritone*, Oslo Philharmonic Orchestra *c* AP
(Simax, 1990)

Simon Boccanegra
(DVD)
Plácido Domingo *Simon Boccanegra*, Marina Poplavskaya *Amelia Grimaldi*, Joseph Calleja *Gabriele Adorno*, Ferruccio Furlanetto *Jacopo Fiesco*, Jonathan Summers *Paolo Albiani*, Lukas Jakobski *Pietro*, Lee Hickenbottom *Captain*, Louise Armit *Maid*, Orchestra and Chorus of the Royal Opera House, Covent Garden *c* AP
(EMI, 2010)

La traviata
(DVD)
Renée Fleming *Violetta Valéry*, Joseph Calleja *Alfredo Germont*, Thomas Hampson *Giorgio Germont*, Monika-Evelin Liiv *Flora Bervoix*, Sarah Pring *Annina*, Haoyin Xue *Gastone de Letorières*, Richard Wiegold *Doctor Grenvil*, Eddie Wade *Baron Douphol*, Kostas Smoriginas *Marquis D'Obigny*, Neil Gillespie *Giuseppe*, Charbel Mattar *Messenger*, Jonathan Coad *Flora's servant*, Orchestra and Chorus of the Royal Opera House, Covent Garden *c* AP
(Opus Arte, 2009)

'Addio del passato'
'È strano . . . Sempre libera'
Inga Nielsen *soprano*, Helsingborg Symphony Orchestra *c* AP
(Danacord, 1985)

'Deh non mutate in triboli'
Inga Nielsen *soprano*, Oslo Philharmonic Orchestra *c* AP
(Simax, 1990)

Il trovatore
Roberto Alagna *Manrico*, Angela Gheorghiu *Leonora*, Larissa Diadkova *Azucena*, Thomas Hampson *Conte di Luna*, Ildebrando D'Arcangelo *Ferrando*, Federica Proietti *Ines*, Enrico Facini *Ruiz*, London Voices, London Symphony Orchestra *c* AP
(EMI, 2001)

Les Vêpres siciliennes
(DVD/Blu-ray)
Lianna Haroutounian *Hélène*, Bryan Hymel *Henri*, Erwin Schrott *Jean Procida*, Michael Volle *Guy de Montfort*, Michelle Daly *Ninetta*, Neal Cooper *Thibault*, Nico Darmanin *Daniéli*, Jung Soo Yun *Mainfroid*, Jihoon Kim *Robert*, Jean Teitgen *Sire de Béthune*, Jeremy White *Comte de Vaudemont*, Orchestra and Chorus of the Royal Opera House, Covent Garden *c* AP
(Warner, 2013)

Duets
Jonas Kaufmann *tenor*, Ludovic Tézier *baritone*, Santa Cecilia Academy Orchestra *c* AP
(Sony, 2021)

Ave Maria (1880)
Libera me (*Messa per Rossini*)
Maria Agresta *soprano*, Santa Cecilia Academy Chorus and Orchestra *c* AP
(Warner, 2013)

Messa da Requiem
Anja Harteros *soprano*, Sonia Ganassi *mezzo-soprano*, Rolando Villazón *tenor*, René Pape *bass*, Santa Cecilia Academy Chorus and Orchestra *c* AP
(EMI, 2009)

Quattro pezzi sacri
Donika Mataj *soprano*, Santa Cecilia Academy Chorus and Orchestra *c* AP
(EMI, 2012)

HENRI VIEUXTEMPS
Désespoir, Op. 7 No. 2
Janine Jansen *violin*, AP *piano*
(Decca, 2020)

HEITOR VILLA-LOBOS
'Food for Thought' (*Magdalena*)
Joyce DiDonato *mezzo-soprano*, AP *piano*
(Erato, 2014)

RICHARD WAGNER
Parsifal
(DVD/Blu-ray)
Simon O'Neill *Parsifal*, René Pape *Gurnemanz*, Gerald Finley *Amfortas*,
Angela Denoke *Kundry*, Willard White *Klingsor*, Robert Lloyd *Titurel*,
Orchestra and Chorus of the Royal Opera House, Covent Garden *c* AP
(Opus Arte, 2013)

Der Ring des Nibelungen

Die Walküre
(DVD/Blu-ray)
Stuart Skelton *Siegmund*, Emily Magee *Sieglinde*, John Lundgren *Wotan*,
Nina Stemme *Brünnhilde*, Sarah Connolly *Fricka*, Ain Anger *Hunding*,
Alwyn Mellor *Gerhilde*, Lise Davidsen *Ortlinde*, Kai Rüütel *Waltraute*,
Claudia Huckle *Schwertleite*, Maida Hundeling *Helmwige*, Catherine
Carby *Siegrune*, Monika-Evelin Liiv *Grimgerde*, Emma Carrington
Rossweisse, Orchestra and Chorus of the Royal Opera House, Covent
Garden *c* AP
(Opus Arte, 2018)

'Winterstürme wichen dem Wonnemond'
(DVD)
Plácido Domingo *tenor*, Vienna State Opera Orchestra *c* AP
(Deutsche Grammophon, 2010)

Siegfried
Act III scene 3
Deborah Voigt *Brünnhilde*, Plácido Domingo *Siegfried*, Orchestra of the
Royal Opera House, Covent Garden *c* AP
(EMI, 1999)

'Da lieg auch du, dunkler Wurm'
'Forest murmurs'
'Forging Song'
'Nothung! Neidliches Schwert!'
'Nun sing! Ich lausche dem Gesang'
Plácido Domingo *Siegfried*, David Cangelosi *Mime*, Natalie Dessay
Woodbird, Orchestra of the Royal Opera House, Covent Garden *c* AP
(EMI, 2001)

Götterdämmerung
'Brünnhilde, heilige Braut!'
'Dawn'
'Siegfried's Rhine Journey'
'Siegfried's Funeral Music'
'Zu neuen Taten'
Plácido Domingo *Siegfried*, Violeta Urmana *Brünnhilde*, Orchestra of the
Royal Opera House, Covent Garden *c* AP
(EMI, 2001)

Tristan und Isolde
Plácido Domingo *Tristan*, Nina Stemme *Isolde*, Mihoko Fujimura
Brangäne, René Pape *King Marke*, Olaf Bär *Kurwenal*, Jared Holt *Melot*,
Ian Bostridge *Shepherd*, Rolando Villazón *Young Sailor*, Matthew Rose
Steersman, Orchestra and Chorus of the Royal Opera House, Covent
Garden *c* AP
(EMI, 2004)

Act II scene 2
Plácido Domingo *Tristan*, Deborah Voigt *Isolde*, Violeta Urmana
Brangäne, Orchestra of the Royal Opera House, Covent Garden *c* AP
(EMI, 2000)

'Mild und leise'
(DVD)
Waltraud Meier *Isolde*, Vienna State Opera Orchestra *c* AP
(Deutsche Grammophon, 2010)

PETER WARLOCK
'Pretty Ring Time'
'Sweet and Twenty'
Ian Bostridge *tenor*, AP *piano*
(Warner, 2016)

KURT WEILL
Four Walt Whitman Songs
Ian Bostridge *tenor*, AP *piano*
(Warner, 2018)

JOHN WILSON
'Take, O take those lips away'
Ian Bostridge *tenor*, AP *piano*
(Warner, 2016)

HUGO WOLF
Eichendorff Lieder (5)
Goethe Lieder (2)
Mörike Lieder (18)
Ian Bostridge *tenor*, AP *piano*
(EMI, 2005)

RICCARDO ZANDONAI
'Giulietta, son io' (*Giulietta e Romeo*)
Jonas Kaufmann *tenor*, Orchestra e Coro dell'Accademia Nazionale
di Santa Cecilia
c AP
(Decca, 2010)

The Complete Symphonic, Concertante and Sacred Music Recordings
Orchestra e Coro dell'Accademia Nazionale di Santa Cecilia *c* AP
(Warner, 27-CD box set, 2024)

A documentary, *Il Maestro Pappano*, is available on DVD (Cypres, 2002).

INDEX

Abbey Road recording studios, London, 92, 243
Abudushalamu, Yikeshan, 178; *Repression*, 178
Aka Moon, 79
Alagna, Roberto, 83, 92, 145, 147
Allen, Jonathan, 153
Altimari, Umberto Nicoletti, 181
Alward, Peter, 145
Ambrosini, Claudio, 177; *Dosàna nóva*, 195
American songbook, 16, 190
Amner, Richard, 44
Argerich, Martha, 82, 240
Arts Council of England, 130, 245
Associated Board of the Royal Schools of Music, 7–8
Auderghem, Belgium, 89
Austria, 101, 132

Bach, Johann Sebastian, 15–16, 166–8, 187, 189; *The Art of Fugue*, 16; Chromatic Fantasia and Fugue, 15; English Suite, 15; French Suite, 15; inventions, 15; Italian Concerto, 15; Magnificat, 187; Mass in B minor, 187; partitas, 111; preludes and fugues, 15; *St John Passion*, 187; *St Matthew Passion*, 187; sinfonias, 15
Bailey, Kate: *Opera: Passion, Power and Politics*, 196
Baker, Janet, 164
Balatsch, Norbert, 189
Balsadonna, Renato, 119, 132
Banda musicale della Polizia di Stato, Rome, 152
Baratta, Paolo, 4
Barbirolli, John, 154, 156
Barcelona, 34–5, 37
Barenboim, Daniel, *plate*, ix, 43–6, 49–52, 86, 176, 241
Bartók, Béla: *Mikrokosmos*, 15; string quartets, 194
Bartoletti, Bruno, 41–2
Battistelli, Giorgio, 177
Bavarian State Opera, 68
Bayreuth Festival, *plate*, ix, 43–4, 46, 49, 51, 60, 76, 79, 86–7
BBC Singers, 246
BBC Television, x, 162–3
Beard, Alex, 129–30
Beeson, John, 26–7
Beethoven, Ludwig van, 15–16, 47, 97, 166–7, 178, 199; cello sonatas, 238; *Fidelio*, 97; *Missa solemnis*, 189; Romance in G, 7, 11; sonatas, 15; symphonies, 15;

295